Using

SOCIAL MEDIA

in the classroom

Education at SAGE

SAGE is a leading international publisher of journals, books, and electronic media for academic, educational, and professional markets.

Our education publishing includes:

- accessible and comprehensive texts for aspiring education professionals and practitioners looking to further their careers through continuing professional development

- inspirational advice and guidance for the classroom

- authoritative state of the art reference from the leading authors in the field

Find out more at: **www.sagepub.co.uk/education**

Using

SOCIAL MEDIA

in the classroom

a best practice guide

Megan Poore

Los Angeles | London | New Delhi
Singapore | Washington DC

Los Angeles | London | New Delhi
Singapore | Washington DC

SAGE Publications Ltd
1 Oliver's Yard
55 City Road
London EC1Y 1SP

SAGE Publications Inc.
2455 Teller Road
Thousand Oaks, California 91320

SAGE Publications India Pvt Ltd
B 1/I 1 Mohan Cooperative Industrial Area
Mathura Road
New Delhi 110 044

SAGE Publications Asia-Pacific Pte Ltd
3 Church Street
#10-04 Samsung Hub
Singapore 049483

Editor: James Clark
Assistant Editor: Monira Begum
Project Manager: Jeanette Graham
Assistant Production Editor: Nicola Marshall
Copyeditor: Carol Lucas
Proofreader: Isabel Kirkwood
Marketing Manager: Catherine Slinn
Cover Design: Jennifer Crisp
Typeset by: C&M Digitals, (P) Ltd, India
Printed by: Replika Press

Library of Congress Control Number: 2011943674

British Library Cataloguing in Publication data

A catalogue record for this book is available from the British Library

ISBN 978-1-4462-0280-7
ISBN 978-1-4462-0281-4 (pbk)

To Alice, Rachel, Ella, Archie, and Will.

CONTENTS

LIST OF FIGURES

LIST OF TABLES

ABOUT THE AUTHOR

Megan Poore is an Assistant Professor in Teacher Education at the University of Canberra where she works closely with pre-service teachers in preparing them for teaching and learning in digital environments. She is known for her best practice approaches to integrating digital technologies into both university and school settings, and this includes developing strong digital pedagogies as well as sound approaches to risk management. She has also worked as an academic skills adviser and an educational designer at the Australian National University, giving her a unique understanding of the issues that confront students and teachers in the integration of digital technologies into their everyday study and work practices. Megan holds a PhD in Social Anthropology from the Australian National University.

ACKNOWLEDGEMENTS

Author's acknowledgements

Over the past few years I have worked with many students and colleagues who have trialled and tested the use of social media in their classrooms at my urging – and often despite their own better judgement. Without their bringing me problems, questions, triumphs, and observations I would not have been able to compile the understanding I have managed here.

The book owes most to Jake Francis, whose attention to detail and precise mind were essential in helping me build an understanding of legal and policy issues as they relate to Terms of Service.

Thank you also to Gail Craswell, who gave me a start on the book-writing process by inviting me to be co-author on the second edition of her excellent *Writing for Academic Success*, also published by Sage.

Thank you to James Clark and Monira Begum at Sage for editorial input and assistance.

Finally, thank you to my Strike Team colleagues, Kerrie Heath, Phil Roberts, and Steve Shann for the best teaching experience I've ever had, and thank you to Matthew Thomas for reading and commenting on parts of the text.

Publisher's acknowledgements

Sage gratefully acknowledges the contributions of the following reviewers who read the proposal and draft chapters along the way:

Ian Addison, Primary ICT Coordinator
St John the Baptist Primary School, Waltham Chase, Hampshire, UK

Andy Connell, Senior Lecturer, Faculty of Humanities and Social Sciences
Keele University, UK

Margaret Meredith, Senior Lecturer Primary Education
York St John University, UK

Nicole Mockler, Senior Lecturer, School of Education
The University of Newcastle, Australia

Sarah Prestridge, Lecturer, School of Education and Professional Studies
Griffith University, Australia

PREFACE

This book is intended to bring together the information you need to safely, knowledgeably, and creatively integrate social media into your classroom. It aims to provide novices with a place to start, those who are unsure with some confidence, and the already adept with, potentially, a more nuanced and in-depth understanding of all that makes up successful social media use in education.

Using Social Media in the Classroom is not meant to be definitive (such a treatment would require a much longer text) but it *is* comprehensive: it covers everything from theory and pedagogy, to everyday practice; it describes the 'big stuff' of blogs, wikis, social networks, and podcasting – and how those things can support longer-term classroom projects – and it details the 'small stuff' that can give you quick classroom wins, such as instant messaging, clippings, Twitter, mindmapping, and document sharing. But, just as importantly, an entire set of chapters is devoted to discussing the sociocultural contexts of social media: digital literacy, 'digital natives', digital participation, and the 'digital divide' are all explored in relation to you and your students. Finally, matters relating to online risk and in-class practicalities are presented, as a way of helping you through the intricate ground of copyright, privacy and confidentiality, Terms of Service, content distribution, bandwidth quotas, backups, data control and security, and more.

The book eschews the step-by-step 'how-to' approach in the belief that this model of help – and the instruction manual itself – is obsolete in the context of social media. Rather, social media tools are designed with 'how-tos' as part of their very structure, and, as small, often unnoticeable improvements are continually made to social media services, instruction manuals quickly become outdated whenever web developers update their software. Instead, the book describes general principles of functionality so that you can jump in and start exploring on your own. Further to this, however, *Using Social Media in the Classroom* provides advice on matters that require special consideration as regards the use of various social media tools and services in the classroom. So, for example, when using a social network with your students the question of whether or not to 'friend' your students on Facebook is addressed; the potential for 'edit wars' on wikis is dealt with, as are podcasting legal issues; and whether or not your class blog should be public or private is examined, amongst other things.

To further help you navigate these areas, additional material is provided on a companion website for the book. Handouts, planning forms, checklists, and additional links can all be found at http://www.sagepub.co.uk/poore. I strongly encourage you to visit the site, to make the most of the materials hosted there, to contribute your own resources and ideas, and to take part in discussions. I will be monitoring the site and will be available periodically to offer advice and feedback on the forums.

Before we move on, though, here are some points to bear in mind about the text itself. Throughout the text I use the terms 'class' and 'classroom' to refer to anything to do with your actual teaching practice; so, a 'classroom' is not limited to the face-to-face time you spend with your students, but also filters through to the tasks they might do at home, or the activities they undertake in more 'mobile' environments.

Finally, it is important to note that although cyberbullying is covered explicitly in a single chapter, cyber*safety*, on the other hand, is not. This is because the entire text is about cybersafety at its varying levels. Instead of simply concentrating on preventative measures or on early interventions that educate children and young people to the harmful effects of cyberbullying, this text adopts a rather broader approach to cybersafety. In having an understanding of the internet that encompasses educational theory, pedagogy, and practice, and in understanding the dynamic social, legal, and policy contexts that concomitantly govern our use of social media, we gain a much deeper and richer appreciation of how digital technology influences our lives.

COMPANION WEBSITE

The website

Most chapters have website material which extends the chapter content. This may include additional material which space limitations prevented including in the book, references to further reading or to related web links, or further activities for exploring questions raised in the chapter. The companion website for the book can be found at www.sagepub.co.uk/poore

PART 1

GETTING STARTED: THE ESSENTIALS

This part lays the groundwork for your use of social media in the classroom. We discuss rationales for, and benefits of, using social media with your students, as well as how social media can support constructivist approaches to teaching and learning (Chapter 1). Educational design principles, general service considerations (Chapter 2), and functional commonalities (Chapter 3) are also covered.

CHAPTER 1

SOCIAL MEDIA AND EDUCATION

Overview

This chapter prepares the social, theoretical, and pedagogical ground for your social media explorations. It situates new technologies in the current media landscape before providing more specific detail on where social media are positioned in the contemporary educational context. In particular, we examine various constructivist-based approaches to learning because it is through these approaches that learning in digital environments proves most successful.

The recent media landscape

The internet has not always been 'social' – that is, it hasn't always given us the ability to interact in real time with our friends, family, colleagues, and strangers as we do on Facebook or via Skype. In fact, the first 'version' of the web ('Web 1.0' as it is now retrospectively referred to) was a 'read-only' web for most of us: if we didn't have access to special knowledge, such as how to write html code, or special technology, such as servers, then we could only read the content that other people had written and published on their websites. But around 2005 there was something of an evolution of the internet and the next generation of the web, 'Web 2.0', was born.

Web 2.0

Today, we don't need access to special knowledge or special technology in order to have a website or a web presence. Instead, we can publish our own material on the internet by using services that make it easy for us to do so, and this is why 'Web 2.0' is also known as the 'read-write web': we can write it as well as read it.

> ### Key point. What is Web 2.0?
>
> 'Web 2.0' simply describes a 'second generation' of the internet; it is not a software package, even though it has a name that makes it sound like one.

Although 'Web 2.0' has been a useful phrase for 'tech-types' in describing this 'read-write web', the term can be a little confusing. Instead, this book prefers the term 'social media' to describe the tools, services and applications that this 'next gen internet' and other digital technologies provide us with.

> ### Key point. Is there a difference between the web and the internet?
>
> Yes, there is. The internet is the underlying architecture that allows the digital transfer of information. The web, on the other hand, is simply a platform that sits on top of the net and uses it to deliver content. Thinking of it this way, you can see how the apps on your smartphone or tablet device aren't websites, but they nevertheless use the internet to transfer data.

Social media, then, include everything from blogs, wikis, and podcasts to Facebook, Twitter, YouTube, and Google. In fact, the digital tools and services that you probably already use in your everyday work, study, and social lives can be described as 'social media'. For example, Facebook is a service that helps you communicate with your friends and find out what they are up to; blogs are a way of expressing your opinion on a topic; and YouTube allows you to upload and comment on videos. All are social media. And, in recent years, social media have changed the way in which information circulates in our cultures.

Traditional versus social media

Up until the advent of Web 2.0, the flow of information through our broadcast, 'one-to-many' media – newspapers, television, books, magazines, and the like – typically went only the one way: from producer to consumer. Some of these traditional media formats supported response mechanisms (such as the letters columns of newspapers) but the feedback was slow to turn around and often out of date by the time it was published. Social media, however, challenge this paradigm because they are formed around the idea of 'networked' media and allow for instantaneous and simultaneous commentary on, and reaction to, material posted on the internet in a process of many-to-many communication. If we were to identify the qualities that characterise social media we could say that they are all about:

- Participation
- Collaboration
- Interactivity
- Communication
- Community-building
- Sharing
- Networking
- Creativity
- Distribution
- Flexibility
- Customisation.

As you make your way through this text, you will notice these qualities underpin the ways in which social media can be used in education.

Why social media in education?

Because of its 'read-only' nature, the early web, Web 1.0, largely supported transmission-style educational practices: material was posted, usually via a learning management system (LMS) such as Moodle, WebCT, or MyClasses, and students were able to view it or download it, but that's about as far as things went. These 'industrial' practices (characterised by mass production and economies of scale) tended to replicate old-fashioned educational routines based around the notion of the monolithic learner; that is, material was 'pushed' to a student who then absorbed it as a single individual, often with-out interacting with peers (Attwell, 2007). This, of course, is to simplify things for the sake of analysis, and it would be fair to say that most classrooms in contemporary schools do not operate in such an anachronistic manner – but early web technologies did. In other words, even though practices in schools moved on some time ago to embrace more social forms of learning, Web 1.0 technologies simply weren't capable of supporting anything other than already outmoded, largely didactic pedagogies.

Indeed, there is much criticism in the literature of this industrial model of education, and much confidence in the potential of social media to free us from the constraints of transmission teaching (Attwell, 2007; Conole, 2008; Fitzgerald and Steele, 2008). As Conole points out, '[t]here has never been a closer alignment between the current practices of Web 2.0 technologies and what is put forward as good pedagogy' (2008, online). And, as Fitzgerald and Steele assert:

> Social software and Web 2.0 services open a channel for exploring the value of social and collaborative production, including peer learning, and a variety of practices that support formative assessment models. (Fitzgerald and Steele, 2008, p. 30)

Social media are ideal for educators because they are nimble, flexible, easy to use, and often very powerful: they focus on doing one thing only (for example, photosharing or animation) and on doing that thing well. Social media are also continually in development: they are said to be in 'perpetual beta' mode, meaning that improvements to the software are always being made and that students are always working with the latest version of the product. Moreover, with social media, students can participate easily in the creation of content, websites, and their own learning spaces, meaning that these tools can be stu-dent and class focused rather than teacher driven. John Dewey recognised the importance of such approaches almost a century ago when he stated that there should be 'more opportunity for conjoint activities in which those instructed take part, so that they may acquire a social sense of their own pow-ers and of the materials and appliances used' (2004 [1916], p. 39, emphasis removed). We can now readily create such opportunities for students because social media platforms put education – not the teacher – at the centre and thus allow students to take part more actively and creatively in their own learning.

Benefits of using social media in education

If used correctly, social media can have many benefits in the educational set-ting, depending on the task and the type of media employed. For example, they provide excellent tools for socialising students into the online world and for teaching them about appropriate online communication practices. They can also be highly motivational for students. Having said this, however, it should be emphasised that social media are not a panacea for all educational dilemmas. There is growing evidence that, because of their hyperlinked architecture, social media can prove more distracting than focusing (Carr, 2010). The trick is to design teaching and learning tasks that demand deep, considered engagement with a topic, as opposed to surface occupation with a technology or tool. To this end, tasks that require not just comprehension but higher-order cognitive activity (such as creativity, synthesis, and evaluation) should be developed if you want to intelligently integrate social media into your classroom.

Intellectual benefits

The intellectual benefits of social media are in no way automatic. Simply establishing a class blog and then letting the students loose on it will not guarantee higher-order thinking. Rather, a considered design for your use of social media that demands deep processing on the part of the student and – perhaps most importantly – synthesis of various materials or viewpoints is essential if students are to benefit intellectually.

- *Analysis, interpretation, synthesis, critique.* Breaking material up, identifying patterns, and then putting it all back together again to create a new or different meaning are key features of higher cognition. Social media provide a variety and range of tools and services to support these activities.
- *Validation, assessment, evaluation.* Social media can be used to teach students about issues of authority, legitimacy, and authenticity on the web, and can encourage the development of skills of judgement.
- *Traditional literacies.* If tasks and activities are properly designed, social media can readily support the development of traditional literacy (reading and writing) and numeracy through the generation of text- and arithmetic-based teaching and learning episodes.
- *Visual literacy.* Visual material is becoming more and more prevalent in rich-media environments. Using social media can teach children and young people how to decode and interpret such material.
- *Media literacy.* Social media can be used to teach a critical appreciation of the role that media of all sort play in shaping our society and culture.
- *Functional literacy.* Using social media to teach functional social media skills is a recursive process that gives students an operational basis for using social media platforms. Put more simply, using social media teaches students how to create usernames, upload images, manage a profile, and perform other basic functions on the internet.

Benefits for communication, collaboration, participation, and socialisation

One of the most exciting features of social media for education is precisely their socialness. They allow us to break out of the paradigm of the monolithic learner into the more intricate and complex world of constructivist, active, and situated pedagogies.

- *Communication*. Social media are communicative media, pure and simple. They are entirely designed to facilitate connectivity and dialogue.
- *Collaboration and teamwork*. If you design, scaffold, and support educational tasks correctly, social media can be used to encourage students to work together and negotiate their way out of problems.
- *Community and participation*. Engagement in a community of practice has arguably never been easier. Social media provide excellent platforms for people to come together to discuss, share, discover, and network.
- *Audience and participation*. Students are forced to consider issues of audience whenever they publish their work online. In this, they learn about different genres for the presentation of their work.
- *Appropriate online behaviour*. Incidents of unsuitable conduct will doubtlessly arise in any social media environment. Embrace these incidents as excellent 'teaching moments' for the whole class.
- *Peer learning*. By their very nature, social media provide active, socially constructivist learning environments that present students with the chance to formulate questions, express opinions, discuss problems, and share solutions.
- *Diverse perspectives*. Students can use social media to integrate a range of perspectives on a topic – but still make an evaluation of their own at the end.

Motivational benefits

Take a look at what many children and young people do in their 'off time' and you will see that a lot of time is spent using social media (ACMA, 2010; Ofcom, 2011; Rideout et al. 2010). The attractiveness of social media for young people can be harnessed in the classroom.

- *Control and ownership*. Students can create their own social and intellectual presence with social media. In developing their own blog or animation, they are creating something that exists within themselves, not something that is external or in some way 'false'.
- *Increased effort*. Students try harder when they know their work is being published to the world. Having someone other than the teacher accessing and judging their work can provide a high incentive.
- *Audience*. Getting feedback from an audience in the wider world can be very exciting and affirming for students.

- *Self-publication*. Easy self-publication and/or sharing of information makes students want to share their work and to do well at it.
- *Creativity*. Social media provide multiple modes and outlets for creativity, from text to audio to video to animation.

Management and administration benefits

Aside from the educational benefits, social media can also prove useful from a classroom management perspective. Oradini and Saunders (2007) discuss the administrative advantages of using eportfolios in a study at the University of Westminster, but corresponding benefits can also be applied to the use of blogs in the school environment:

- *Ease of feedback*. The majority of social media support some kind of comment or 'wall' function. Teachers can provide specific feedback to a student using these functions and students can learn from reading the feedback on others' sites or pages.
- *Tracking student learning*. Many forms of social media permit for the archiving and searching of student work and you can easily track student learning and progress through time, allowing you to intervene once you've spotted a problem.
- *Accessibility off-campus*. This is useful for both you and the student: you don't have to be in class in order to access school work.
- *Communication with parents*. Parents can view their child's work via the internet and they can get in touch with you (and you with them) to discuss any problems with progress.
- *Easy submission of student work*. By engaging in an online social media task, students will have completed their assignment – no more printing out and handing in paper-based work.
- *Organisation*. An early study by Armstrong et al. (2004) established that students who lack routine and order in their study find blogs useful for organising notes, thoughts, information, and the like. The same can be said for many types of social media: social networks, wikis, bookmarks, and so on.

These many benefits do not just happen on their own: they can only be achieved through solid educational design and a commitment to informed pedagogy on your part. This is why an understanding of theory is important to your everyday classroom practice, and it is to theory that we turn next.

Constructivist approaches to social media use in education

Theories attempt to describe real-world phenomena in abstract terms. In education, they help us explain the complexity of social and cognitive life in ways that allow us to analyse how something works or why something happens as it does. In education there are three broadly accepted theories of learning:

- Behaviourism: learning occurs through changes in behaviour, and in particular is a function of the operations of stimulus-response.
- Cognitivism: learning occurs within the individual mind as learners 'process' and store knowledge internally.
- Constructivism: learning occurs within the mind but is also a collaborative, interactive process in which individuals create knowledge and meaning through experience and incorporate it into their existing frameworks for understanding (or schema).

Although social media can support all three theories of learning, our focus here is primarily on constructivist approaches, not least because contemporary digital media readily support collaboration and interactivity, which are key features of constructivism. At the heart of constructivist approaches to teaching and learning is the learner's active participation in knowledge construction and in the learning process. Learners draw on their own prior knowledge and experience to create new or different understandings of the world – in other words, they build on what they already know. Constructivism encompasses a variety of forms and approaches, all of which are relevant to the informed use of social media in the classroom.

Social constructivism

Social constructivism holds that social relations and social interaction are a key component of learning. This is not a new idea. John Dewey, in *Democracy and Education*, published a century ago, had this to say on the topic:

> ... any social arrangement that remains vitally social, or vitally shared, is educative to those who participate in it. Only when it becomes cast in a mold and runs in a routine way does it lose its educative power. (Dewey, 2004 [1916], p. 6)

Due to their inherently digital nature, social media allow us to 'break the mold and the routine' that Dewey describes to devise social tasks for our students. Wikis, for example, have an architecture that coerces the social construction of knowledge, and social networking explicitly encourages the sharing of information.

Active learning

Active learning states that it is what a student does during a teaching and learning episode that has the most value for learning. The important point here is that 'activity' should not be confused with simple 'busyness' in which no real intellectual furtherance prevails. On this last point, Alfred North Whitehead sounded a warning:

> In training a child to activity of thought, above all things we must beware of what I will call 'inert ideas' – that is to say, ideas that are merely received into the mind without being utilised, or tested, or thrown into fresh combinations. (Whitehead, 1967 [1929], p. 1)

It is exactly these 'fresh combinations' that are essential if learning is to occur. Social media can sustain active learning situations that favour creative and artistic expression. In podcasting, for example, students are heavily engaged in 'learning by doing': not only must they familiarise themselves with the technical intricacies of producing and publishing online audio, they must also learn how to plan a 'radio' show, research a topic, structure an interview, and connect with an audience. None of these things can be achieved by mere repetition or mindless exertion – they require the active, thoughtful engagement of the learner in the creation of something new.

Discovery learning

Social media enable problem solving and encourage independence, two of the key features of discovery learning. Discovery learning is constructivist in nature because it champions the idea that it is the meaning that learners create for themselves that is important to the learning process. As students formulate questions, manipulate their environment, and observe the effects, as they perform experiments, make adjustments, and unearth facts and information, they are engaged in learner-centred, inquiry-based projects that help them construct new knowledge and consolidate the old. To a certain extent, simply using a social media tool or technology will encourage many of these activities as students try to figure out how to make the technology work. But, more explicitly, social media applications such as blogs or bookmarks can be used to foster exploration, innovation, and the communication of newly unearthed ideas and materials.

Peer learning

Like all constructivist approaches to education, peer learning places the student clearly at the centre of the learning venture. With peer learning, students work together to construct and share understanding, something that social media support very well indeed because of their innate interactivity. Whether it's via photosharing, social bookmarking, or gaming, students are involved in activities that promote joint-learning environments and participation. However, certain pre-conditions of positive collaboration and co-operation are necessary if peer learning is to be successful: students must already have had favourable experiences of working with others if they are to learn well (Christudason, 2003, online).

Situated learning

Situated learning is a constructivist theory based on anthropological understandings of culture and society and the 'inherently socially negotiated character of meaning' (Lave and Wenger, 2009 [1991], p. 50). On this model, learners initially participate only at the periphery of an activity in which they are not experts (this is called 'legitimate peripheral participation'). Through ongoing participation in authentic social contexts they build an understanding of the activity. Although the originators of situated learning state that it is not meant to be an educational technique or pedagogical strategy (Lave and Wenger, 2009 [1991], p. 40), it nonetheless can be taken to explain what is going on when social media are used to support student learning. When first entering a 'community of practice' such as a social network, discussion forum, or chat group, newcomers start out on the periphery of the community and, eventually, as they become more skilful and expert, they move towards the centre of the culture. This does not have to apply only to social networks, however: it can also explain how novices become experts in any social media environment.

Special considerations in constructivist environments

John Dewey states that education is 'a fostering, a nurturing, a cultivating process. All of these words mean that it implies attention to the conditions of growth' (2004 [1916], p. 10). As a teacher, it is your responsibility to provide those conditions of growth. In adopting constructivist approaches to the use of social media in your classroom, you need to pay particular attention to three main considerations in supporting growth:

1   *Supporting constructivist approaches takes time*. You must be prepared to carefully plan, implement, and evaluate your chosen teaching and learning strategies without taking shortcuts.
2   *Learners will need a degree of scaffolding*. How much, of course, will depend on the task and individuals' current states of knowledge and understanding – but in order for students to build their own concepts and constructs, you must supply them with materials and supports that will

guide and help them to make meaning of the tasks you set them. See Chapter 2 for more details.

3   *Close monitoring of comprehension*. Because students are being asked to make their own sense of the world, it is essential that you periodically check that their understanding of the task and the topic is accurate. You need to intervene early if there are any misconceptions.

By now it should be clear that social media provide students with the chance to create and not just consume content and to construct their own under-standings of the world, which can greatly enhance existing educational practice. Social media also provide opportunities for students to practise the proto-skills that they will need to succeed in digital environments in the future. But the tools and services supplied by social media should not be seen simply as 'add-ons' to the educational enterprise; instead, they should be regarded as being essential for innovation as well as a part of daily practice within any educational establishment. This is an exciting time for education, and the development of new tools and applications that can be used for teaching and learning is making constructivist educational experiences more than ever a reality for a mass education market.

 Summary

- 'Web 2.0' is a term that is sometimes used to describe social media and the 'second generation' of the internet.
- Traditional media are 'broadcast' media, whereas social media are 'networked' media. The shift in media paradigms is having an effect on how we view and respond to the world.
- Social media tools and services are characterised by participation, collabora-tion, interactivity, communication, community-building, sharing, networking, creativity, distribution, flexibility, and customisation.
- The intellectual benefits of social media are in no way automatic. Social media tasks must be properly designed and integrated into the classroom setting if they are to benefit learning.
- Social media most readily support constructivist pedagogies because they encourage students to construct their own understandings of the world.
- Constructivist pedagogies that are supported by social media include active learning, discovery learning, peer learning, and situated learning.
- Constructivist environments require the scaffolding of student learning, the close monitoring of comprehension, and an investment of time to make sure they succeed.

Resources

Online resources

- Visit the *Using Social Media in the Classroom* companion website for links, discussions, and other materials relating to using social media in education. You can find this at www.sagepub.co.uk/poore

Further reading

- Attwell, G. (2007) Web 2.0 and the changing ways we are using computers for learning: what are the implications for pedagogy and curriculum? Available at http://www.elearningeuropa. info/en/article/Web-2.0-and-the-changing-ways-we-are-using-computers-for-learning%3A-what-are-the-implications-for-pedagogy-and-curriculum. Accessed 13 October 2011.
- Conole, G. (2008) New schemas for mapping pedagogies and technologies. *Ariadne,* 56, July. Available at http://www.ariadne.ac.uk/issue56/conole/. Accessed 13 October 2011.
- Davies, J. and Merchant, G. (2009) Education and Web 2.0: transforming learning – an introduction (Chapter 1), *Web 2.0 for Schools. Learning and Social Participation*. New York: Peter Lang, pp. 1–10.
- Glassman, M., and Kan, M. J. (2011) The logic of wikis: the possibilities of the Web 2.0 classroom, *Computer-Supported Collaborative Learning,* 6(1), 93–112.
- Lankshear, C. and Knobel, M. (2006) Blogging as participation: the active sociality of a new literacy. Paper presented to the American Educational Research Association, San Francisco, USA 11 April 2006. Available at http://citeseerx.ist.psu.edu/viewdoc/download?doi=10.1.1.1 35.3944&rep=rep1&type=pdf. Accessed 13 October 2011.

CHAPTER 2

SOUND EDUCATIONAL DESIGN USING SOCIAL MEDIA

Overview

This chapter focuses on how to design your use of social media in the classroom. In particular, we look at how to define your purposes and how to decide when using social media might benefit your students. We also consider the need to plan out your social media tasks, before turning to the requirement to properly scaffold student learning. The last part of the chapter focuses specifically on details relating to the social media services you might choose to use in your classroom.

Designing the task

The way you go about planning and designing your use of social media will have a huge impact on whether or not you succeed at implementing digital tools into your classroom. Again, we can learn from Dewey:

> We never educate directly, but indirectly by means of the environment. Whether we permit chance environments to do the work, or whether we design environments for the purpose makes a great difference. (Dewey, 2004 [1916], p. 18)

Teachers who are new to the integration of social media into their teaching practice often make the mistake of focusing on a particular tool they want to use with their class instead of on the purposes or intended outcomes of a teaching and learning episode. For example, a teacher may become enamoured of blogs and decide to use blogs for anything and everything, regardless of the suitability of the blogging format for what the teacher wants students to achieve. It is crucial that you determine the broader purpose of the teaching and learning episode first. Only when you have established what it is that you want students to achieve, do, or understand can you go about finding the best way for them to accomplish that. If you decide that using social media *does* best support your purposes, you then need to move on to planning your teaching and learning episode, scaffolding student learning, and writing up rubrics (that is, matrices for success criteria) to clarify your expectations.

Defining your broader purposes

Before you can even consider whether or not social media would support a given teaching and learning episode, you need to do some conceptual groundwork. Start by focusing on your students and ask yourself these three, central questions:

1   What is the *intellectual or conceptual focus* of the episode for students? (Is it comprehension, visualisation, application, analysis, critique, or something else?)
2   What types of '*exchanges*' should students be involved in? (Should it be knowledge sharing, collaboration, networking, dissemination of opinion?)
3   How can students *best accomplish* this? (Is it via social media or some other means?)

You may find that there is some crossover between points 1 and 2; however, it is how you answer question 3 that will determine whether or not you will use social media in your classroom. For example, if the purpose of a teaching and learning episode is to have students demonstrate the development of a line of reasoning using valid arguments backed up by authoritative sources – and you want them to do this individually – then a traditional essay would be the most appropriate tool for you to use. If, however, you want students to demonstrate their comprehension of a topic by collaborating on a knowledge-building project that others can view and discuss, then you might decide that the wiki format best suits your purposes.

Choosing the right social media tools for teaching and learning

But the question still remains, How do I even know *if* social media will support what I want to do with my students? Use Table 2.1 to determine whether or not a social media tool is appropriate for your teaching and learning purposes. Each of the tools is covered in detail in Parts 2 and 3.

Table 2.1 Possible social media tools and the different educational purposes they can support

Purpose: What you want students to achieve	Possible social media tools
Analysis, synthesis, evaluation	• Animation and comic strips • Blogs • Clippings • Games • Mindmapping • Podcasting • Slideshows • Video and videosharing • Wikis
Brainstorming	• IM and chat • Clippings • Mindmapping • Polls and surveys • Skype and VOIP • Social Networking
Collaboration	• Animation and comic strips • IM and chat • Productivity tools • Games • Mindmapping • Podcasting • Skype and VOIP • Social Networking • Video and videosharing • Wikis
Communication and knowledge sharing	• Animation and comic strips • Blogs • Bookmarking • IM and chat • Clippings • Productivity tools • Games • Mindmapping • Photosharing • Podcasting • Polls and surveys • Social networking • RSS

(Continued)

(Continued)

Purpose: What you want students to achieve	Possible social media tools
	• Skype and VOIP • Slideshows • Social Networking • Video and videosharing • Wikis
Comprehension and knowledge building	• Animation and comic strips • Blogs • Games • Mindmapping • Podcasting • Polls and surveys • Slideshows • Video and videosharing • Wikis
Feedback	• Blogs • IM and chat • Podcasting • Polls and surveys • Skype and VOIP • Social Networking
Information seeking, searching, and consolidation	• Bookmarking • Clippings • Productivity tools • Polls and surveys • RSS
Networking	• IM and chat • Games • Photosharing • Skype and VOIP • Social Networking
Object sharing	• Animation and comic strips • Blogs • Bookmarking • Clippings • Productivity tools • Photosharing • RSS • Slideshows • Social Networking • Video and videosharing • Wikis
Opinion building and sharing	• Blogs • Brainstorming and mindmapping • Podcasting • Polls and surveys • Slideshows • Social Networking

Purpose: What you want students to achieve	Possible social media tools
Presentation and dissemination of information	• Animation and comic strips • Blogs • Bookmarking • Brainstorming and mindmapping • Clippings • Productivity tools • Photosharing • Podcasting • RSS • Slideshows • Social Networking • Video and videosharing • Wikis
Storing and managing information	• Bookmarking • Clippings • Productivity tools • Photosharing • RSS • Wikis
Visualisation	• Animation and comic strips • Games • Mindmapping • Photosharing • Slideshows • Video and videosharing

As you can see, there are lots of 'cool' digital tools out there that are suitable for use with your class across many different contexts, but the trick is to choose the *right* cool tool for what you want your students to achieve; don't be seduced by a sparkly website or an awesome application only to find that it doesn't suit your purpose. For example, there would be no point in trying to force a brainstorming task into a social bookmarking service. Similarly, don't decide to use a dynamic simulation environment such as Second Life to deliver lifeless lecture-type virtual classes to a crowd of acutely bored students. And, of course, don't use social media at all if your purpose is to have students demonstrate traditional essay-writing skills. Fitzgerald and Steele perhaps state it most clearly when they point out that

> [t]here is no one tool that provides a social software solution to support learning and teaching, nor is it appropriate to use the one technique for all disciplines or even throughout the teaching of a particular discipline. (Fitzgerald and Steele, 2008, p. 31)

Planning

After defining your purpose and choosing a social media technology or tool that will help you achieve it, your next job is to carefully think through how you will implement your ideas in the classroom. Use the following prompts to get you started – be sure to include specific skills, knowledge, and information, and to write clear, precise statements.

The teaching and learning episode

- What is the purpose of the episode?
- What is the intellectual or conceptual focus of the episode for students?
- What types of 'exchanges' should students be involved in?
- What concepts do you want students to engage with?
- What types of information do you want them to share or contribute?
- What learning outcomes does the episode assess?
- How will you cover the set curriculum?
- What connections should students be making between the curriculum materials?
- What major topics, sections, or materials should be covered?
- What skills should students learn?
- How can students demonstrate their learning?
- How will you assess students' work?

The tool or service

- Why have you chosen to use this tool or service? That is, does it support your purpose?
- Are you using the service appropriately – for what it is designed for (for example, wikis for collaboration, blogs for critique and reflection)?
- How will your use of the tool or service support curriculum or learning objectives?
- Can students choose their own tool or service, or will you choose it for them?
- If students are allowed to choose their own tool or service, then what are the baseline requirements for functionality and security?
- How will you add or invite students to the service?

Students

- What will students be doing with the social media you have chosen?
- How will students identify themselves? First names only?
- What sort of administrative access will students have to the service?
- How frequently should students contribute?

- How will you assess individual or group contributions?
- How will you deal with any poor behaviour in the use of the service?
- What do you need to teach students about privacy, copyright, security?
- What if a student doesn't have access at home? Will you expect them to access the service at school or via a public library?
- Should students' work be public, private, or somewhere in between (for example, public, but not searchable by search engines)?
- Will students need technical assistance with using the service and can you provide this if necessary?

You

- Do you have enough time and energy to manage this project?
- Do you have an appropriate skill level to manage the project?
- What will be the level of your involvement?
- How will you communicate your expectations?
- What level of scaffolding do you need to provide?
- How will you evaluate the effectiveness of using the service in class?

Record your plan and keep refining it as you implement the project. Be sure to keep notes as you go along so that you can make adjustments or improvements on the next iteration. Planning materials can be found on the *Using Social Media in the Classroom* companion website.

Scaffolding

Although many students appear 'tech-savvy' in that they have a facility with, or at least a confidence in using, digital technologies, there is no guarantee that their experience with digital 'genres' goes beyond social networking sites, Google search, Wikipedia, and/or YouTube. There is evidence to suggest that many students – especially older ones – whilst comfortable with using digital technologies to support their personal communication and entertainment needs, are nevertheless confused when teachers ask them to use social media tools in the context of their learning (JISC, 2007). Indeed, students are asking less for instruction on how to operate the tool itself and more for instruction on how the tool supports the educational outcomes the teacher wants for the student (JISC, 2007). Scaffolding refers to the need to provide such instructional supports for learning when introducing students to new materials, tools, or concepts.

To help students understand and successfully complete the tasks you set for them, consider implementing some of the following scaffolding techniques:

- Explain how using this social media tool or technology links into curriculum or learning objectives. Don't underestimate the importance of having this conversation with your students – even the youngest need and want to understand the rationale behind what you are asking them to do.
- Explain your goals for the task.
- Set clear instructions. Provide as much detail as is reasonable about how to complete the task. Be concrete in what students should be doing and when they should be doing it.
- Describe the tool and its main features.
- Provide examples.
- Model best practice by using the media yourself.
- Provide 'frequently asked questions' (FAQs) or 'how-tos'.
- Provide a rubric or success criteria matrix.
- Tell students how you will assess their work.
- Provide technical assistance where you can and need to.

Rubrics (success criteria)

One of the most effective scaffolds to student learning is the rubric or the 'success criteria matrix'. In education, the term 'rubric' refers to a set of criteria by which student achievement is evaluated; these criteria should be linked to your learning outcomes. Some teachers use rubrics only in the assessment of student work as summative, standardising tools that only they have access to. However, rubrics make excellent formative tools, as they help students understand what is required of them before they complete a task. In most classrooms, rubrics should be an essential tool for communicating to students exactly what it takes for them to succeed at different competency levels. Rubrics are also valuable because they force you to clarify what, exactly, you want from students and what constitutes different levels of performance.

To develop a rubric, you need to:

- Determine a set of criteria for assessing the task.
- Consider the range of performance and how your success criteria will be differentiated. Will things range from unsatisfactory to outstanding? Beginning to advanced? Or something else?
- Write up what a performance at each part of the range would look like, according to the criteria.

There is no reason why students shouldn't be involved in the development of a rubric for a task that you have set them, as negotiating about how they will be evaluated can be highly motivating. You will find examples of rubrics throughout this book. You can also search online for rubrics developed by other teachers (search 'Assessment rubrics'). Use these rubrics to get you started, but make sure that your own rubric accurately reflects your own situation. Visit the *Using Social Media in the Classroom* companion website for rubric examples – and consider sharing your own there, too.

Service considerations

Once you are sure that your task has been well designed and that your choice of social media is relevant and justified, you will need to think about what social media service or services best fit your needs, how public or private students' work should be, and how you will handle administrative access to the service(s) you choose.

Choosing a service

There are so many different forms of social media available on the internet that it can sometimes feel overwhelming when it comes to choosing an appropriate service for use in your class. Whilst the functionality of the tool you want to use is important, there are other factors you need to take into account when selecting classroom-based social media. The following points apply generally – for special considerations relating to specific types of social media, refer to the appropriate chapter.

- ☐ The service meets my basic requirements for free.
- ☐ The service provides enough storage and bandwidth to meet my needs.
- ☐ I can make the service or parts of the service private and thus viewable only to those I invite.
- ☐ There is no advertising on the service.
- ☐ There are topic restrictions, such as on hate speech, pornography, and spam.
- ☐ The service has an acceptable Privacy Statement.
- ☐ The service has an acceptable Terms of Service.
- ☐ The service is age- and skill-appropriate to myself and/or my class.
- ☐ There are adequate FAQs, discussion forums, or other forms of help.
- ☐ The service is easy to use.
- ☐ I can set the timezone to my local region.
- ☐ I can export my content (to create a backup).
- ☐ The service is not blocked by my school.

Doing a test run

Once you have hit upon one or two services that meet your baseline criteria, it is time to do some test runs. Create an account with the prospective service(s) and try them out to see how they perform. But don't just do this from home: *it is imperative that you test the service in your school's computing environment* under student (not staff) access conditions across both major operating systems (Windows and Mac) and across the two major web browsers, Internet Explorer and Firefox. You might be surprised by some of the functions or services that are restricted by student firewalls. If you find yourself in a situation where you need to use a blocked service, make a case to have your information technology (IT) people unblock the site from on-campus access – just note, though, that in some environments, it can take up to 24 hours for a site to be unblocked, so be sure to do your testing well ahead of time.

Public or private work?

The vexed question of whether your students' work should be public or private will undoubtedly surface when you consider whether or not to use social media in the classroom. You need to consider carefully your reasons for making your use of social media either public or private; there is no one answer, and how you choose to proceed will depend upon your particular classroom circumstances and your pedagogical aspirations. This topic is covered in more detail in Chapters 16 and 17. But for now, the basic question you want to answer is, 'Who should see students' work?' Here are some subsidiary points for consideration to help you decide:

Use *stronger privacy settings* if:

- You are asking students to post information that might be considered private or confidential.
- You are asking students to contribute work that might be personal or intimate in nature.
- You suspect that the way you are using social media in your classroom might attract internet predators.

Use *weaker privacy settings* if:

- Students need to see or change each other's work.
- You want the general public to comment on or engage with student work.
- You are using social media in a practical sense to teach students about what happens to their data once it goes online.

Most social media services recognise that some users want to keep certain information out of the public realm and so they offer different privacy settings for your data. For example, some services will allow you to make students' work public but not searchable, meaning that anyone with the URL (that is, the direct weblink or hyperlink) to your site can visit it, but if they try to find it via Google or Yahoo or another search engine they won't have any luck.

Ideally, try to find services that support group accounts that do not require you to give away individual student email addresses, or services that do not require sign-up at all (although this will be rare, for the technical reasons described in Chapter 3 under 'Setting up an account'). And always use a service that allows you to delete data once it is posted.

No matter how you choose to control student privacy, you must nevertheless be sure that your students protect their real names, passwords, and usernames: they must not share their personal information with anyone. Having said that, however, students should have a username or display name that at least identifies them to the rest of the class, for example, 'sarahw' or 'leitap'. If they are choosing their own username, they should not choose one that makes it difficult for classmates to know who they are, for example, 'PinkLadyNo3' or 'DirtBikeDemon' or, heaven forbid, '3889274'.

Administrative access

As a teacher you might sometimes wonder whether or not students should be given administrative access to the service that you are using in class. For example, if you have a class blog or wiki you might want to give students administration privileges so that class members can approve posts or pages, customise the site to their liking, and generally keep things tidy. Whilst providing such access gives students a sense of ownership, I would caution strongly against allowing them too much control over a service's settings and administration. This is not because of the potential for mischief (although that surely exists), but rather because a student administrator might accidentally delete other students' work or in some other way make irrevocable changes to the service's operation in your class. In my own case, I do not even allow my adult, pre-service teachers administration access to my class sites: I just don't want them to have the responsibility for any catastrophes that might occur due to user error.

If all of this sounds a bit overwhelming to begin with, don't worry: if you make your way bit by bit through this text, and explore the tools and services we discuss, you will soon build your knowledge and skills.

Summary

- Sound educational design is essential if you are to succeed at implementing social media projects in your classroom.
- Before you begin any classroom-based social media project, you need to carefully define your purpose, plan the task, select the right tools, and scaffold student learning.
- Choosing appropriate privacy settings for your students' social media activities is really important.

Resources

Online resources

 • Visit the *Using Social Media in the Classroom* companion website for links, discussions, and other materials relating to educational design for social media in teaching and learning. You can find this at www.sagepub.co.uk/poore

Further reading

- Fitzgerald, R. and Steele, J. (2008) Digital Learning Communities (DLC): investigating the application of social software to support networked learning. Report. Available at http://eprints.qut.edu.au/18476/. Accessed 13 October 2011.
- Richardson, W. (2006) *Blogs, Wikis, Podcasts, and Other Powerful Web Tools for Classrooms*. Thousand Oaks, CA: Corwin Press.
- Williamson, B. and Payton, S. (2009) Curriculum and teaching innovation. Transforming classroom practice and personalisation. A Futurelab handbook. Available at http://www.futurelab.org.uk/resources/curriculum-and-teaching-innovation-handbook. Accessed 1 November 2011.

CHAPTER 3

COMMON ASPECTS OF SOCIAL MEDIA FUNCTIONS AND PRACTICE

Overview

In this chapter we investigate some of the fundamental operational features and characteristics of social media environments, including RSS, tags, hyper-links, widgets, and embed code – all of which are part of the technical territory of social media. We also look at how to set up an account and how to create a secure password. Backups and testing are also covered as part of your essential practice when using social media in the classroom. Finally, we identify some of the key personal attributes and qualities that will help you to succeed in your educational use of social media.

Functional commonalities

Most of the social media sites, services, tools, and applications that inhabit the internet share some basic characteristics or requirements when it comes to how they operate. This section introduces you to the most common. Sometimes the names of the functions are a little different, but they nevertheless work in the same way. In any case, don't worry too much about learning everything all at once or about 'getting it right' – the best way to become familiar with social media is to just start using them, so jump in and experiment a little.

RSS: the 'backbone' of social media

There is some confusion about what the letters 'RSS' actually stand for, but most sources cite the abbreviation as either standing for 'Really Simple Syndication' or 'Rich Site Summary'. Regardless, RSS aggregates or 'feeds' material from the web into one spot and it is one of the key technologies in the distribution of social media content.

RSS feeds enable you to subscribe to content on the web so that it comes directly to you in the one place; whenever you 'follow' someone on Twitter or Facebook, or whenever you subscribe to someone's channel, you are using RSS, whether you realise it or not. RSS means that you don't need to visit your favourite websites or 'people' every day to check to see the latest updates – instead, the updates come straight to you. You can subscribe to news, blogs, weather reports, even other people's bookmarks, tags, or photos.

> ### Video clip. RSS in Plain English
>
> View the video 'RSS in Plain English' on YouTube (search 'RSS in Plain English') to get a visual representation of how RSS works.

Many people use what is known as a 'feed reader' or 'aggregator' to collect all their RSS feeds into the one place. To subscribe to a feed in this way, you must first make sure that a site or service actually has a feed. If you find a small, square, orange 'RSS' icon or some text that says 'RSS' or 'Subscribe' or something similar, then the page has a feed attached to it. Here are the basic steps to follow when aggregating feeds:

1 Set up an account with a feed reading service, such as Google Reader, Netvibes, or Pageflakes.
2 Visit the site you want to subscribe to (say, BBC world news) and find its RSS feed. (If you are using the Firefox browser, the little RSS icon will appear in the address bar indicating that this web page has an RSS feed.) Click on the feed link. Often, the feed will look like a strange bunch of code or like a really plain or ugly web page. Copy the URL or web address of this page. This is the RSS feed address.

3   Go back to your feed reader and look for the 'add content', 'add subscription', or 'add feed' area. Paste in the feed address. You should now be subscribed to the feed.

Although you might never choose to subscribe to RSS feeds in this way, you should nevertheless be aware of how RSS works.

Setting up an account

In order to use most social media services you will have to create an account with a service provider. When you create an account, you are actually setting up your own personal folder and file space on the provider's servers; your account details are associated with your personal space so that when you log back in, your data and materials can be retrieved.

In order for this to occur, you need supply no more than:

1   A username. This must be unique because two different users of the same service cannot have the same username.
2   A password. This needs to be strong – the name of your cat is probably not secure enough.
3   An email address. You might have to confirm your account via email, so be sure to check your inbox immediately when you sign up.

Anything else is redundant in a technical sense.

Before you sign up, make sure you read, understand, and agree with the Terms of Service (or similar) and the Privacy Policy of the service you are signing up for. Most of us just click on 'accept' as a matter of course when registering an account with a service, but this is not good practice. See Chapter 16 for advice on how to interpret Terms of Service and Privacy Policies to make sure that you are not giving away important rights to your data. Once you have agreed to accept a Terms of Service, follow these steps:

1   Look for the 'sign up', 'register', 'join', or similar button.
2   Follow the instructions. At base you should have to create a username, create a password, and provide an email address.
3   Write your account particulars down in a safe place if you think you will have trouble remembering what they are – you will need your username and password to sign in to your account in the future.

Some important points to note:

*   You will not be able to change your username later, so choose carefully; you will, however, be able to change your password and email address.

- If possible, try to use the same username across the internet so that you don't have to create and remember lots of different usernames. Just be sure to choose a username that is likely to be unique. For example, jsmith might already be in use by other people, whereas jksmith497 might be available on most services.
- Some sites ask for your date of birth when you sign up, especially if there are age restrictions associated with use of the service. You need to take this into account if you are asking children in your class to sign up for a particular service.
- You can usually change your password and your email address in your 'settings', 'manage', or similar administration area.

Creating a secure password

Password security is something that most of us don't take seriously enough. You must use a secure password, use a different password for each site or service you sign up for, and change your password on a regular basis.

There are many ways to create a secure password that you will remember. Primarily, you want to create a master password that you can add different things to according to the site you are visiting. Use a formula to help you develop a password:

- Start with a word that you will remember. For example, 'falafel'.
- Reverse it: 'lefalaf'.
- Add some numbers, perhaps the year you graduated from high school (birth years aren't always secure as you have probably provided that information already to Facebook and other services): lefalaf08.
- Add some symbols: lefalaf*08$.
- Add some more numbers, perhaps the year you started primary school: lefalaf*08$94. This is your master password.
- Now, add in a different set of site-specific letters for each site you visit – perhaps the first two and last two letters of the site, in capitals and sentence case, respectively. So, for Facebook, your password would be FAlefalaf*08$94ok; Google would be GOlefalaf*08$94le.

You now have a unique password for every site, and one that you can remember. Some final points:

- Don't forget to log out of any open account when you are finished. This is especially important when using non-private computers such as computers at work, university, or school.
- Internet security is really important.

Hyperlinks

A hyperlink can be described as a referral to a document, image, or other object elsewhere on the internet. Most people know how to use hyperlinks when they are browsing the web, but there is some etiquette around how to add them to your site:

1 When adding a link, look for the link icon. It's a small picture of a chain link or an Earth's globe with a chain link in front of it.
2 Click on the icon and follow the instructions.
3 Add the link *behind* the text, i.e., CORRECT: <u>Visit the Social Media in the Classroom homepage</u> // WRONG: Visit the Social Media in the Classroom homepage http://www.sagepub.co.uk/poore.

For accessibility reasons, you should also avoid hyperlinks that state only 'click here', that list consecutive one word links, and that open in new windows.

Tags and tag clouds

Tags (also known as 'labels' in some systems) are keywords that are added to objects and information on the web – they help you to navigate websites such as blogs, YouTube, Flickr, and Twitter. Tags also provide a way for you to classify your own content on the web and they are essential if visitors are to find material on your site.

Tags are nimble, dynamic, and often idiosyncratic, and, importantly, more than one tag can be added to a single resource. For example, if I were to post a picture or a story about a beagle puppy, I might tag it as 'beagle', 'puppy', and 'dog'; a 10-year-old girl, on the other hand, might tag the same photo as 'cute', 'doggie', 'Ralphie', and 'fun'.

A tag cloud is a visual representation of all the tags on a website (see Figure 3.1). In a tag cloud, some words appear bigger than others: the bigger the appearance of the word, the more often it has been used on the site.

Widgets and embed code

Widgets (sometimes called 'gadgets') are used to display dynamic content such as videos or RSS feeds from another website or service on your own website – they're similar to 'applications' in Facebook. Typical widgets include video widgets, calendar or map widgets, tag cloud widgets, and RSS widgets. So, when you show a YouTube video or other dynamic object on

animations assessment rubrics
assignments audios coffee
constructive alignment copyright
cyberbullying cybersafety
digital divide digital literacy
learning outcomes lectures
literacy new media
literacy privacy professional
experience research journal risk
management self-
portraits slideshows stats study
guides summaries teacher identity
teacher roles tutorials videos
week 1 week 2 week 3
week 4 week 5 week 6
week 7 week 8 week 9 welcome

Figure 3.1   A tag cloud

your own site or page, you are doing so via a widget; the video itself still 'lives' on YouTube – it's just that you are displaying it on your own site.

To add a widget to your site, you first need to find the embed code for the original object (video, map, slideshow, whatever) you want to display. The embed code is a small piece of html code that tells your widget (1) where the original object can be found on the web, and (2) how to display it on your site. Say, for example, you want to display a YouTube video on your own website – perhaps your blog or wiki. Here's what to do:

1   Figure out where you want to display the video on your own site.
2   Go to YouTube and locate the video you want to embed.
3   Look for the video's embed code by searching for the word 'embed' or 'share' on the page. The embed code might look something like this: <iframe title="MP video player" class="mp-player"type="text/html" width="280"height="130"src="http://www.mp7238.com/embed/video" frameborder="0"></iframe>
4   Copy the embed code.
5   Now, go back to your own site and paste in the embed code using the 'add widget' or 'add video' or similar function.

6 Click 'save' on your own site.
7 Refresh the page to make sure that you are looking at the latest version of your site. You should now be able to see and play the YouTube video on your own site.

The same principles apply for any object that you want to embed, not just YouTube videos.

Saving your work

When you use social media you are writing or creating material directly on the internet. As stated in Chapter 1, you don't need to know how to write html code when using social media, and that is because the system or service you are using is actually writing it for you 'behind the scenes'. Many services have an automatic 'save' function that saves your work periodically. Don't rely too heavily on this, however. Just as you frequently and 'manually' save your work when using Word or PowerPoint or similar programs, so should you manually save your work when using social media.

If you believe you have clicked 'save' but the service does not appear to be displaying the latest version of your work, simply refresh the page you are looking at so that you are sure to be looking at the latest saved version of the page.

Creating backups

As the administrator or owner of a site, it is your rwesponsibility to create backups regularly. Backing up is not the same as saving your work: backing up means taking a whole copy of the site and placing it in, ideally, two different digital locations. Saving simply means keeping a single local copy of the site or file or whatever object you are working on.

> Backing up any site you manage is your responsibility.

Backing up regularly is a critical part of your risk management routine for using social media (see Chapters 16 and 17) in the classroom: if students' work is hosted on an external social media service and, for whatever reason, the work disappears, you need to be able to access a recent version of that work. If possible, you should choose services that allow you to easily export, via your administration or settings area, your content to your local desktop or other location of your choosing. If, however, your web service does not offer a backup option, there are other solutions:

1 Take an html ('web code') copy of your work via your internet browser. Go to File > Save As and save your work locally. You will be able to open and read a local copy of the page you have saved by opening it in your browser software.
2 Use a tool such as HTTrack for PC (search 'HTTrack') or SiteSucker for Mac (search 'SiteSucker') to get an html copy of your entire site(s).

Once you have your backup, you should save it in at least two separate digital places; keeping it on your local hard drive, on another internet service (see Chapter 12 for file hosting services or 'dropboxes'), on a DVD-ROM or CD-ROM, on an external hard disk, or even on a flash drive would all be acceptable.

Testing social media for your class

Social media sometimes work differently in different digital environments. For example, a service might work well using PCs but not so well using Macs. Similarly, it might display best in Firefox but quite poorly in Internet Explorer. As mentioned in Chapter 2, you should test the service(s) you are hoping to use in your school's computing environment under student – not staff – access conditions, across both major operating systems (that is, PC and Mac), and across the two major web browsers, Internet Explorer and Firefox. There is nothing more frustrating to students than finding that a widget works just fine on their home machine but fails to load at school.

A word on Word ...

Neither you nor your students should be using Microsoft Word to construct work before pasting that work into a class social media site. There are two reasons for this.

1 The cognitive style you adopt in Word will be different from the style you adopt when contributing straight into a social media interface. We tend to associate using Word with writing essays, which may encourage you or your students to adopt an inappropriately formal style and tone for online work.
2 You are likely to come across formatting problems: the transfer across media formats may mean that when you paste your Word document into the web service your class is using things may look peculiar – and you will

just end up reformatting things, anyway. (It's a form of double-handling.) These types of formatting problems also occur when you transfer material across Microsoft programs, for example, when you move text from MS PowerPoint into MS Word, which is only one of the reasons you would never construct a PowerPoint presentation in Word and then paste it into PowerPoint when you have finished.

You may think that writing something in Word provides you with a form of 'backup' if you or your students are writing a long or complex piece on a site or service. To a certain extent this is true, but it is probably better to use Word only to paste *into*, and not *from* (for the reasons outlined above). In other words, if you or your students are writing a tricky piece, then it might be a good idea to copy what you've written on the site and just 'store' it in Word or a text editor every now and then until you have finalised your piece and published it online.

Personal qualities for successful engagement with social media

Books and websites about social media too frequently focus only on the functional or technical skills you need to navigate digital tools and technologies. But having the right attitude and knowing how to problem-solve your way out of difficulties are both essential if you are to become a confident, competent, thoughtful, reflective practitioner of social media in the classroom.

Attitude

The attitude you bring to social media environments is perhaps the single most important pre-condition for successful teaching and learning with digital technologies and tools. For those already used to communicating via social networks, and who embrace them naturally, there may need to be some tempering of enthusiasm, as well as an acknowledgement that social facility with these media does not automatically suggest expertise in educational application. Confidence and facility with technology should not be confused with competency or with the critical deployment of such resources for educational purposes. It can help if you keep an open mind to your own *actual* levels of knowledge of social media systems, and be willing to expand your repertoire.

In contrast to this, you might feel intimidated by the thought of using social media in your classroom and unnerved by the notion of what might be happening to your data once you send it out onto the internet. It is good to be sceptical of the digital environment, but don't base your scepticism on ignorance. Acknowledge that social media are here to stay and that you do need to educate yourself about how they work. Only once you have a proper understanding of digital environments can you make informed decisions about what is and is not appropriate in the educational context.

You might also wonder to yourself, 'How on earth will I learn all this stuff?' Some essential points:

- *You can't break it.* Some more mature-aged users have been discouraged from using social media because of prior bad experiences with 'Web 1.0' digital tools. Perhaps you tried to publish something online using an 'old' internet technology only to find that the system collapsed and you lost all your hard work; or perhaps you clicked on the wrong button and your organisation's website disappeared. But the new 'Web 2.0'-based social media are designed to make it easy for you to publish on the internet, which means that the ability to crash entire systems has been taken out of your hands. So, don't be afraid – just get in there and play around: click on things and see what effect it has; make a comment on someone's blog; make a movie, whatever – you can always delete it later.
- *Social media largely work on similar principles.* Although each tool or service is a little different, there are nevertheless enough similarities between them that, after having learnt how one system works, you can transfer a lot of that knowledge into the use of another system. For example, once you know how widgets and embed code work, you will find similar protocols across services.
- *Get some 'quick wins'.* Start small. Don't feel as though you have to have a full-blown class podcast established within two weeks – that's too much pressure even for the most adept. Why not start with creating an online animation? It sounds difficult, but, as you will see in Chapter 8, all you have to do is drag-and-drop a selection of objects into a template, hit 'save', and then watch your cartoon characters do exactly what you told them to do. Quick wins can give you a sense of accomplishment, which, in turn, leads to increased confidence and understanding in how social media work.
- *Remember: using social media is easy.* Relax a bit. People don't use social media because they're difficult – they use them precisely because they're easy and created with real-life users (that is, you) in mind.

Being your own helpdesk

Social media services work on a different model of support from the one that many of us – particularly older users – grew up with. First, such services often do not have a dedicated helpline – after all, the service is being supplied for free. This means that you cannot pick up the phone or send an email to get a response to your question or problem. Similarly, you won't find an instruction manual accompanying the service you've signed up for. This is because the instructions are already on the screen, and you should be able to follow them quite easily: let the system teach you. Moreover, the service is usually in 'beta' mode, that is, the developers are making small changes to the software all the time, so writing and re-writing instruction manuals over and over again simply isn't realistic. Instead, social media services primarily use FAQs and discussion forums to provide help and support to users.

So, when using a social media service, you might need to change the model of support that you currently have in your head. You need to move from a 'helpdesk' model to a 'help yourself' model. In fact, the more you 'help yourself', the more quickly you'll learn how the service works – and you'll become a better problem solver, too.

Here are some tips for helping yourself:

- *Read the FAQs.* FAQs are usually written in informal and simple language. Generally, you would use the FAQs for questions about how the service works, such as 'How do I invite people to view my wiki?'
- *Search the service's discussion forum.* Use the discussion forum for information about any problems you are having with the service. You will see discussion forum posts with titles such as 'Acme podcast plug-in won't read my MP3 file' or 'Cannot display two images side-by-side'. If you find a service that has a robust community of users, then you can be pretty sure that someone else has already had the same problem that you're having, and that the community has worked together to solve the problem for you. At the very least you can get suggestions for where to start.
- *Google a solution.* The service's discussion forum won't be the only place where people are providing answers to your questions. A full-phrase search (such as, 'Why can't I see my visual editor in WordPress?') can often get you good results.
- *Find a video tutorial on YouTube.* There are many excellent, clear video tutorials on YouTube. If you don't know what a blog is, for example, search YouTube and watch a video.
- *Discover for yourself what is and is not possible.* If you can imagine doing something on the web, then you probably can – you just have to google it. For example, if you think it would be a good idea to store your files on the web so that you don't have to email documents to yourself all the time, then search for something like 'online file storage'. If you want your students to make a cartoon strip of a class topic, google 'online cartoon

creator' and see what comes up. Your starting point should be, 'If I want to do it, then I probably can'.

In addition to this, it is important that you take the pressure off yourself:

- *You don't need to know everything up-front.* Take your time exploring a new site or service. Learn to do the basics first and then build on that.
- *Remember: you can't break it.* . . . Not unless you *really* know what you're doing and you start messing about with code and things that sit behind social media services. But that's not most of us, and it usually requires some form of criminal activity to get to that stage. So, feel free to play and explore and create – just don't forget to save!
- *It's not the software, it's YOU!* If you feel intimidated by the web, then you might end up blaming your computer, the system you're using, the people who run the service, or some unnameable outside entity when things go wrong. You can go a long way to reducing your anxiety by deciding that it's 'user incompetence', not system error, that is the most likely explanation for your problems. When something 'goes wrong' or 'doesn't work' go back and check for the mistake that *you* probably made: maybe you forgot to fill in an essential information field; perhaps you typed two different things when asked to confirm your password; conceivably you made a typo when entering your email address; or, you forgot to save. Realising that the problem is probably with you, and not with the machine, is a stress-reduction technique that can really work.

▢ Summary

- RSS is a key technology in the distribution of social media content. It allows users to aggregate 'feeds' into one place.
- Most social media share common features such as tags, hyperlinks, widgets, and embed code.
- When setting up an account with a social media service, you need to pay attention to the Terms of Service and the username you choose and you must use a secure password.
- You must save and backup your work regularly when using social media services.
- It is essential that you test any intended use of social media both in the physical classroom environment and under student login conditions.
- The type of attitude you bring to using social media will go a long way to determining your level of success in implementing social media projects in the classroom.

Resources

Online resources

- Visit the *Using Social Media in the Classroom* companion website for links, discussions, handouts, and other materials relating to the common aspects of using social networks for teaching and learning. You can find this at www.sagepub.co.uk/poore

Further reading

- Anderson. P. (2007) What is Web 2.0? Ideas, technologies and implications for education. JISC Technology and Standards Watch, February 2007. Available at http://www.jisc.ac.uk/publications/reports/2007/twweb2.aspx. Accessed 1 November 2011.
- Bell, A. (2009) *Exploring Web 2.0: Second Generation Interactive Tools – Blogs, Podcasts, Wikis, Networking, Virtual Worlds, and More.* Georgetown, TX: Katy Crossing Press. Chapters 1–3.
- O'Reilly, T. (2005) What is Web 2.0. Design patterns and business models for the next generation of software. Available at http://oreilly.com/web2/archive/what-is-web-20.html. Accessed 1 November 2011.

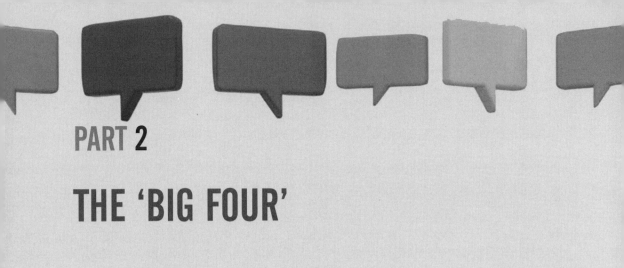

PART 2

THE 'BIG FOUR'

Part 2 of *Using Social Media in the Classroom* addresses the 'big four' of social media: blogs (Chapter 4), wikis (Chapter 5), social networking (Chapter 6), and podcasting (Chapter 7). This part shows how teachers can use these tools to support longer-term class projects and describes basic technical features alongside benefits and special considerations for each.

CHAPTER 4

BLOGS

Overview

Blogs are one of the most powerful social media applications to have arisen in recent years. Like most social media tools a blog is, at base, simply a website – but it is a website that has certain characteristics and functions. This chapter introduces you to blogging basics: what blogs are, how they are structured, and how to set one up. We will also look at some of the educational benefits of blogging and introduce you to some blogging models. Finally, we'll cover some of the special considerations for blogging in the classroom, paying particular attention to questions of navigation, privacy, and scaffolding.

What is a blog?

Blog basics

A blog is a website where you make regular entries (called 'posts') on a topic or range of topics. Some blogs are similar to personal journals or diaries, whilst others – such as those used for educational blogging – have a more 'professional' or subject-based focus. Blogs are most commonly written by individuals.

The word 'blog' is a contraction of the term 'web log'.

The core of your blog is made up of your blog posts. Posts might include opinion, links, observations, commentary, reflections, discoveries, tips, announcements, advice, or anything else of interest or relevance to your readers. You can also add rich media (such as images, video, photos, audio, and graphics) to your post. Posts are automatically dated, archived, and displayed in reverse chronological order, that is, the latest material is displayed at the top of the page, whilst older material gets shunted further down the page with each new post you publish (this is what makes blogs 'dynamic' in nature). Posts are typically brief and concise (often a short paragraph or two), and Standard English is the most acceptable form of blog writing – both 'text speak' and formal, academic English are typically avoided.

Video clip. Blogs in Plain English

To get a succinct overview of how blogs work, watch CommonCraft's 'Blogs in Plain English' video on YouTube (search 'Blogs in Plain English').

Tags (see Chapter 3) are used to identify each post with multiple keywords so that readers can search for and retrieve content from your blog. Good tagging is essential to successful blogging, as it provides your readers with the most effective means to navigate your blog. If you do not tag up your posts, readers will find it difficult to locate material and they will quickly lose patience with your blogging efforts.

Once you have written a post, your readers can comment on it. Readers normally respond to the initial post and generally not to each other's comments (unlike in a discussion forum, where members respond to the discussion as a whole – although this distinction can be delicate at times).

Setting up a blog

It is easy to set up a blog. First you need to choose a blogging service (see 'Special considerations' towards the end of this chapter). Your school or institution may already have a blogging platform as part of its learning management system (LMS) and you may wish to use that. If, however, you want to use a 'real-life' bogging service that provides students with an authentic online experience and that is free, then you may wish to choose between the following popular blog hosts:

- *Blogger.com*. Fairly easy to use with enough tools and functions to support most needs. Blogger is a Google service, so if you already have a Google account then you already have access to Blogger.
- *Tumblr.com*. A very simple blogging tool, almost perfect for journalling. It does not allow comments, though, and does not automatically support a tag cloud. This is a good choice for younger students and those who want a gentler introduction to blogging.
- *WordPress.com*. A very powerful blogging tool with excellent functionality – you can do just about anything with it. Suitable for older students or those with good confidence and skill levels.
- *Kidblog.org*. A WordPress-based service, but massively streamlined, so only the basics are included. Designed with safety and simplicity in mind for primary and middle school users. Allows you to set up a class blog without having to use student email addresses.

> ### To think about. Hosting blog software on your school's server
>
> If you are having trouble convincing your school leadership that 'external' blogging can be a safe option for your school, then you might want to suggest that your IT services people download and install the WordPress software from WordPress.org (this is a different service from WordPress.com, although it is run by the same company). The software is free and can be hosted on your school's intranet.

Once you have decided which service to use, you will need to create an account (see Chapter 3). This, in turn, will generate a blog for you. Essentially, your blog has two parts to it: (1) the 'front page', which regular visitors to your blog can view, and (2) your dashboard or 'control panel', from where you build, write, and manage your blog as the blog's main author and administrator. Only the blog author(s) can view the dashboard.

As stated in Chapter 3, let the system teach you. Play around a little: write a test post – try adding images, links or video as well as text – and then go and view it on your front page. Remember, you can always delete material later.

Dos and Don'ts. What to add: essential widgets

Add these widgets to your blog's 'appearance' or 'design':

- Tag cloud
- Archive
- Search box
- Pages (if using static pages)
- Links.

You will notice in your dashboard that you have a variety of settings for your blog: for example, you can make it public or private, you can change its theme, design, or appearance, and you can control comments and discussions. Again, have a look around your dashboard and explore the full range of functions available to you.

 ### Activity. Set up your own blog

Create an account with one or more of the blogging services recommended above and get a blog. Visit your dashboard or administration area and try some of the following:

- Write a test entry, add tags to it, and publish it.
- Write further entries, this time adding images, links, and 'widgets' (for video and the like). You can always delete things later.
- Customise the appearance or design of your blog.
- Add a friend as a 'user' of your blog or ask them to make a comment on your blog.
- Explore the privacy and discussion settings.

Tip: Keep two tabs open in your browser (if you don't know about tabbed browsing, then google it to find out) – one for your dashboard and one for the public face of your blog (that is, the front page of your blog site itself).

Switch between your dashboard and your site to make sure that the changes you *think* you have made in your dashboard are actually showing on your site. Don't forget to refresh the screen to be sure that you are viewing the latest saved version of your site.

Educational benefits of blogs

Pedagogy

Blogs are excellent for soliciting critique and reflection from students and, because of their dynamic nature (that is, because new posts are always being added and commented on), students can build their understanding of a topic at the same time as refining that understanding. This makes blogs excellent for constructivist pedagogies. As a teacher, this also provides you with a perfect opportunity to track the development of a student's thinking over time and to provide both formative and summative feedback on the student's work; it also helps you to identify struggling or disengaged students.

In general, blogging encourages students to evaluate ideas, advance positions, and to explore diverse perspectives on a topic. And even though blogging services support a variety of rich media, most of the material contained on blogs is text-based. Higher-order thinking skills such as assessment, interpretation, validation, analysis, critique, synthesis, evaluation, creativity, and imagination can – and should – be encouraged through writing blog posts.

Audience, writing, and community awareness

Because blogging provides an authentic link into a broader online community, students become aware of what it means to write for a public audience. This means that they have to make informed decisions about a number of things, including:

- *Writing*. Tone, style, length of post, readability.
- *Content*. Appropriateness, relevance, interest factor, accuracy of data or reasonableness of arguments, effective communication of ideas.
- *Presentation*. Organisation, appearance, use of rich media (videos, hyperlinks, slideshows, and so on) to enhance readability, relevance of media, post frequency, correct grammar and punctuation.

> ### Dos and Don'ts. What to avoid
>
> - Blogs are their own 'genre': don't use them as email lists, discussion groups, or listservs.
> - Don't use blogs to get students to post mini-essays or the like. If you want students to write a mini-essay, then ask them to write a mini-essay.

The flow-on effect of this is that many students tend to take a little more care over their writing and the communication of their ideas (Bell, 2009, pp. 89–90; Solomon and Schrum, 2010, p. 18) than they sometimes do when putting together something that only their teacher will read: blogging can motivate students to try harder when they know that their work is being published to the world. Student blogging, therefore, is community-oriented but learner-centred, and helps students to cultivate networks with others.

Creativity and flow

The blogging format can be used for student bloggers to express themselves creatively and intellectually. Because the format itself readily stimulates ongoing engagement with a topic, students are at liberty to expose the development of their thinking, to go off on the occasional tangent, and to take the initiative in communicating new thoughts and discoveries. And because they can blog what they want when they want, a certain level of 'flow' can be reached: if they are particularly focused on a topic, it is not unusual to see several posts appear within short succession.

> ### Ideas. Blog ideas
>
> - **Blog questions or problems** for students to consider.
> - Use a class blog for students to **share their discoveries or opinions** on a topic.
> - Use a blog as a **class management tool** to post announcements, assignment info, feedback, tips.
> - Ask students to **comment on other students' posts**. You might decide to form students into small 'feedback groups' where they are responsible for posting a certain number of comments on two or three of their classmates' blogs.
> - Get students to keep their own blog on a class topic. At the end of the module or teaching episode, ask them to **share their five (or whatever number) best posts** with the rest of the class.

Individual responsibility

In taking on a personal blog, students also take responsibility for it: it is theirs to design, manage, and exploit as they wish (within bounds that you set, naturally). Students learn quickly that if they are going to have a successful blog, then they need to publish regularly with material that is engaging, insightful, and useful to readers.

Administration

Blogs are ideal for use as a classroom management or administration tool. As a teacher, your blog can be the central repository for all class-related information and news. Blog posts can especially be effective as a way of both communicating announcements and providing general advice, tips, and feedback to the class as a whole. Further, you can set up static pages to contain core information such as contact details, syllabus or curriculum information, assignment details, and so on, and students and parents can also leave questions and comments on your posts, allowing you to respond as appropriate.

Blogging models

There are many ways you can use blogs with your class. Richardson (2006, pp. 40–4) suggests using blogs to showcase student work, to develop student eportfolios, or to create an online book club, but you might also want to choose from one of the main models listed below to get you started.

Administration blog

On this model, only the teacher writes blog posts and the main purpose of the blog is to use it as a learning management system. To this end, you might want to post class announcements, assignment instructions, tips and advice, or other class administration information. This type of blog also provides a great way to keep parents up to date with class goings-on, and to get parental feedback via comments. Students and parents may be permitted to make comments, but the focus is on what the teacher wants to communicate. This model can be combined with the class blog model, described below.

Class blog (learning-focused)

You might decide that you want just the one blog that all class members contribute to, in which case all students are added as 'authors' to a central blog.

The idea here is that they write posts on the topics you set or that are relevant to the class as a whole. As the teacher, you take the lead on posting, but students are also encouraged to come up with their own (focused and relevant) posts. Miss Baker's Extreme Biology blog (search 'Miss Baker's Extreme Biology blog') provides an excellent model for this type of blogging. Make sure you can clearly identify students through either their first name or username (see Chapter 2, 'Public or private work?') and that you can delete inappropriate posts if you have to.

Ideas. Be inspired!

Visit these class blogs to see how other teachers are integrating blogging into their classrooms.

- *Climb High*. A Grade 3 blog from the Comox Valley in British Columbia, Canada. An excellent example of how teachers can use blogs to communicate their class activities to a broader audience (search 'Climb High Comox').
- *Extreme Biology*. Miss Baker's class blog has won several awards over the years. Miss Baker's entire class contributes to the blog as authors (search 'Miss Baker's Extreme Biology blog').
- *Huzzah!* Another blog from the Comox Valley, BC. *Huzzah!* is a Year 6 blog with links to the entire class's individual student blogs (search 'Huzzah Comox').
- Visit the Edublog Awards pages for more examples (search 'Edublog awards').

Individual student blogs (learning-focused)

In this blogging arrangement each student in your class has their own blog. This format requires a little more administration on behalf of the teacher as you have to find a way to keep track of each student's blogging efforts. An easy way of doing this is to add each student's blog RSS feed into a feed reader such as Netvibes (see Chapter 3, 'RSS: The "backbone" of social media'). That way, you can track new posts, see who is having difficulties, and – best of all – aggregate and view all student blogs in the one spot. This model gives students control and ownership over their blogging environment and can be good for those who feel a little shy about contributing to a broader class blog. It can also encourage a certain level of creativity and experimentation amongst students that they might not otherwise feel comfortable with. Perhaps the biggest advantage of students each having an individual blog, however, is that it can be used as a lifelong eportfolio in which students provide examples of their work, share their discoveries, post observations, embed and comment on media that excites or interests them, and tag it all up for easy navigation. Ideally, the student would continue to use this site in future classes (not just yours – you can co-ordinate this with teacher colleagues) and even maintain it into adulthood.

Regardless of how you decide to use blogs in your classroom, there are a number of issues that must be taken into consideration before you embark on your project. We now turn to them.

Special considerations for blogging

There are a number of things to take into account when embarking on a blogging project with your class. In addition to the matters discussed below, make sure that you have enough time, energy – and enthusiasm – to implement using this form of social media in your classroom.

Choosing a blogging service

Don't rush into choosing a blogging service. Take time to evaluate several different blogging platforms before deciding upon one that best suits your purpose. Sites such as WeblogMatrix.org can be useful in this regard, as they allow you to automatically sift and compare services.

Use the checklist below in addition to the general points listed in Chapter 2 under 'Choosing a service' to help you or visit the *Using Social Media in the Classroom* companion website for the consolidated list.

- ☐ The dashboard is easy to use.
- ☐ Posts can be tagged and archived.
- ☐ Video, images, and hyperlinks can be added to posts.
- ☐ The service supports widgets.
- ☐ I can add static pages if I want to (for information that students need to access on a regular basis).
- ☐ I can invite, add, and delete users as I need to.
- ☐ I can moderate and approve comments and delete them if necessary.
- ☐ I can set the timezone to my local region.
- ☐ I can export my content if I wish (to create a backup).

Once you have found two or three services that appear acceptable, create an account with each and do some 'test runs' to see how they perform. If your students are creating their own, individual blogs, then why not give them a range of services to select from? Some might feel comfortable using the fully featured WordPress, whilst others might prefer the simplicity of Tumblr. If you have done the above groundwork correctly and found a selection of suitable services, then there should be no harm in letting students choose what suits them best (but see Chapter 17 for more information).

Activity. Compare blogging services

Set up a blog on at least two different blogging sites (say, WordPress and Blogger). Explore the functionality of each, especially noting:

- What sort of support is provided? FAQs? Forums?
- Can you moderate comments?
- Can you remove posted information quickly?
- What are the Terms of Service that govern use of the blog?
- Can you customise the look of the blog?
- Can you add widgets?
- Can the blog have multiple authors?
- How much space is your blog allocated by the service provider?
- Can you set up static pages?
- What are the privacy options?
- Can you delete the blog?
- Can you export the blog to create a backup or transfer it to another service?

Note anything else that you think will be important in helping you decide on a suitable blogging platform for your class. See the *Using Social Media in the Classroom* companion website for a blogging plan.

A public or private blog?

Because blogging is often a personal, individual enterprise, attentiveness to student privacy, exposure, and vulnerability is particularly important. Thankfully, with blogging you have a number of options available to you:

1 *You can lock everything down so that a student's blog is visible only to yourself and the student and no one else.* This might be a good option if you want the student to blog some quite personal reactions to course content, or if there are potential issues related to the visibility of students' work to others (see Chapter 17), but it does depend on the student being diligent in adding you as a viewer of the blog.

2 *You can lock everything down so that a student's blog is visible only to yourself and the rest of the class.* You might use this option if you have

genuine concerns about privacy for your class, or if you want only class members to be able to comment on the class's blog(s). This option, however, can be quite time-consuming from an administration point of view as you typically have to invite each and every individual student via their email address and then rely on them to register with your blog *using only that email address and not another* (because the invitation system will only recognise addresses that you have keyed in). If students have a school email address you should invite them using that address – they can always change it to their Hotmail or Gmail or other address later if they wish. Even better if the blogging service you have chosen allows you to create bulk user accounts without using email addresses.

3 *You can open things up so that anyone with internet access can see your students' work and (potentially) comment on it.* This option makes the best use of the power of blogging in that it allows people in the online community to comment on students' work, thus exposing their work to more opinions (and therefore helping them form their own) and giving them a sense of legitimacy. But it also exposes students to potential security and privacy risks (see Chapters 16 and 17). You can control for these, however, through comment moderation functions and the like.

If you have chosen your blogging service well, then you will have even more options for controlling privacy (for example, some services, such as WordPress, allow you to make your blog public but to simultaneously block search engines, meaning that people will only find your blog if they have the blog's URL or if it is linked to from some other site). However you go about it, pedagogical as well as security considerations should inform your decisions about the visibility of your students and their work.

Navigation

Certain readers find blogs hard to navigate because not everyone is used to the fluid, dynamic structure of blogs. In particular, it can be confusing for some to make their way around a website that does not have traditional static pages and a conventional left-hand menu. The main problem, here, is not that blogs are unstructured, but that some visitors do not understand what tags are and how they work to structure blog content (see Chapter 3); it is essential that students understand the importance of tagging up all their content with useful keywords and then displaying a tag cloud or list of tags on their blog.

Navigation can also be improved by placing your content in categories that, like tags, classify your posts and help your readers find material on your site. Categories, however, are generally fixed and are more formal than are tags, and they basically serve as a table of contents for your blog. For example, you might tag up a post about scissors with tags such as 'cutting', 'sharp', 'blades', 'useful', 'shears', 'sewing', 'kitchen', 'paper', and 'hairdressing', but assign the post to the broad category of 'Household implements'.

Finally, blog navigation can be helped by the addition of an archive of your posts and a search box. All these navigational aids can usually be easily added as widgets.

Blogs versus discussion forums

I'm often asked about the difference between a blog and a discussion forum. The answer is simply this: a blog is usually written by a single person who contributes an original blog post and then gets comments (or replies) from people about the original post; with a discussion forum, however, anyone can make an initial contribution, and replies generally move the discussion forwards – that is, people don't just respond exclusively to the issues raised in the original post, but to the conversation as it develops. Don't worry too much about the subtleties of all this, because there is often some cross-over in how these online tools are used. The important thing is that you are using a tool that gets students engaged in the topic at hand.

> **To think about. Getting parents and other staff on board**
>
> Mr Sloan of Ferry Lane Primary School in Tottenham, UK, has a special page on his blog where he explains his blogging project to parents and carers. This is an excellent **strategy for communicating your rationale for blogging** in the classroom and helps to address any privacy and security concerns that parents might have (search 'Ferry Lane parents').

Static pages

Although primarily about dynamic content that is presented in reverse chronological order, there is nevertheless a place for static pages on most blogs. Static pages typically contain material that is unlikely to change and that readers need to refer to often – and they are essential if you are using your blog as a class administration tool. Consider using static pages for assignment information and instructions, assessment rubrics, tips and tricks, key resources, and any other essential items that students need to access regularly.

Scaffolding student blogging

It has to be stated up front that the blogging instruments included on social networking services (such as Facebook or Ning.com) or on the school's learning management system are usually only pallid imitations of genuine blogging tools. So although young people might be familiar with the term 'blog' there is every chance that a class blog will be the first 'real' or 'proper' blog your students have contributed to.

Because of this, you need to be clear with students about your blogging enterprise – what it consists of and what you hope they will gain from it. It also means that you have to strongly scaffold their learning. In addition to giving students 'FAQs' or 'how-tos', setting clear instructions, and providing examples (see 'Scaffolding' in Chapter 2 for more information), be sure to do the following:

- Tell students why you have chosen to blog in your class.
- Describe what a blog is as well as its main features. In particular, let students know that posts are displayed in reverse chronological order, and explain the value of tags.
- Talk about the types of posts or comments you want to see on the blog. Especially explain what constitutes acceptable content and acceptable topics for discussion.
- Encourage students to critique and reflect upon class topics and key themes in their posts and/or comments.
- Advise students on what makes a good blog post. Tell them to choose a catchy title for their post, to keep it short and coherent, and that bullet points and lists are OK. Encourage them to add rich media such as video if it helps them get their point across, and to link out to interesting material.
- Explain that blogging is its own genre of writing: that paragraphs are usually kept short, that clear, simple, and jargon-free language is expected, and that blogging is an exercise in focused writing. Insist that they proofread and edit their posts.
- Remind students to express their (considered) opinion and to put some 'personality' into their writing.
- Discuss the importance of audience.
- Prompt students to think carefully about tags and categories.
- Give suggestions.
- Tell students that they should take as much care with their comments as with their posts. They should understand that comments need to be short, concise, and on-topic. Further, they need to be friendly, polite, and constructive.
- Tell students how you will assess their work.

- Model good blogging. If you have your own blog, use it as an example of best practice. Make sure you model the type and style of writing you expect from your students, as well as the standard of content and presentation you want.
- Provide examples. Link to previous students' blogs (if you have any) or to external blogs to give students a sense of how blogging works in the educational environment, to let them know what you expect them to accomplish, and to give them ideas for how to accomplish it. Discuss these examples in class or get students to analyse them as part of the blogging task itself.
- Ask students to review and comment on each other's blogs. This acts as a form of peer-review and can be one of the most effective ways to enhance student learning of both content and process.

How much do you assess?

Because blogging is an ongoing process, students may end up either writing scores of posts on their individual blogs, or making dozens of comments on a class blog. Manifestly, you will not have the time to mark each and every blog post or comment your students make. Strategies for dealing with this situation include setting an upper limit to the number of posts or comments students can make, or asking students to submit their 'best five' posts or comments (or whatever number you choose) for assessment. Students also often want to know what your minimum expectations are for the length of a post or comment. Although you may prefer not to set such limits for fear that it will stifle creativity, you could still consider setting 'suggested minimum' limits.

Blog rubrics (success criteria)

You might want to consider the following areas for your blog rubric or success criteria matrix – of course, your final rubric or matrix should be presented at a level appropriate to the age of your class (even better if you can get the students to help develop the rubric, based on the learning outcomes – see Chapter 2):

Content

- Comprehension
- Development of ideas
- Intellectual engagement with subject matter
- Critique and analysis of key topics
- Reflection on core themes
- Demonstration of creative thinking or approaches
- Accuracy of data or information presented

Communication and posts

- Writing/communication quality
- Relevance of links or embedded media
- Post frequency
- Encouragement of community contributions

Design and administration

- Organisation (for example, use of tags, archives, categories, feeds)
- Appearance
- Use of enhancements (especially if using widgets)
- Management and administration of blog
- Navigability of blog

Once you have developed your rubric (preferably with input from students themselves), be sure to make it available to your students and encourage them to refer to it often as they complete their assignment. See Table 4.1 for a sample blogging rubric or success criteria matrix.

 Activity. Develop a blogging assessment rubric/success criteria matrix

Write up a rubric for your class's blogging project. What criteria will you be measuring? Writing? Intellectual engagement? Writing and communication? Comprehension? Appearance of the blog? What performance ranges will you be using?

Writing a rubric is not as easy at it sounds – but you don't have to start from scratch (although you may wish to). Do a web search for 'assessment rubric' or visit a site such as Rubistar.4teachers.org to get a sense of how other teachers have tackled the task. You might like to share your own blogging rubric on the *Using Social Media in the Classroom* companion website.

 Activity. Work on your blogging plan

Use the blogging plan template found on the *Using Social Media in the Classroom* companion website to develop a class blogging project. Be sure to take into account the general planning considerations outlined in Chapter 2 under 'Planning', as well as the concerns that are specific to blogging.

Table 4.1 Sample blogging rubric/success criteria matrix

Category	Beginning	Emergent	Proficient	Advanced
Comprehension	Little evidence of knowledge or understanding of the topic. Considerable confusion about the topic.	Minimal engagement with, and descriptions of, the topic, with reference to some specific aspects. Limited confusion about the topic.	Detailed engagement with, and descriptions of, the topic, with reference to specific aspects of the topic. No significant confusion about the topic.	Careful, broad and deep engagement with, and descriptions of, the topic. Inconsistencies and differing positions or approaches are noted and accounted for. Clear comprehension of the topic.
Writing and communication	Entries are poorly structured and confusing to read. The reader has no clear sense of what the topic is about. Grammar, spelling, and punctuation are poor.	Entries sometimes lack relevance and the reader sometimes has trouble following the main point or points being made. There are lapses in grammar, spelling, and punctuation.	Entries are on-topic, relevant, and structured so that the reader can follow the main point or points being made. There are few errors in grammar, spelling, and punctuation.	Entries are relevant, well structured, and the writing clearly expresses the complexity of the topic. Grammar, spelling, and punctuation are nearly flawless.
Relevance of rich media	There are no rich media added, or the rich media added cannot be clearly linked to the topic.	Rich media are included, but they sometimes do not clearly link to the topic.	Rich media link to the topic and support the main points being made.	Rich media clearly support the main points being made and enhance the reading experience.
Navigability	Almost impossible to access and navigate blog content. No use of tags or other organising devices. Titles poorly used or meaningless.	Blog content can be accessed via tags or other organising devices. Titles used well. Links and media (such as videos) are adequately embedded.	Easy access to blog content. Good use of tags or other organising devices. Links and media (such as videos) are adequately and accurately embedded and show a good understanding of web authoring etiquette.	Excellent access to blog content of all descriptions. Extended, relevant, and sensible use of tags or other organising devices. Links and media (such as videos) are intelligently and accurately embedded and show an excellent understanding of web authoring etiquette.

▢ Summary

- Blogs are websites that allow you to write and publish posts on a certain topic and to get feedback on your posts in the form of comments.
- Blogs are characterised by dynamic content that is displayed in reverse chronological order and by posts, comments, and tags.

- Blogging is good for critique and reflection, for sharing opinion and discoveries, and encourages creativity and flow.
- There are three main models of blogging: (1) the administration blog, (2) the class blog, and (3) the individual student blog. These last two are learning-focused.
- Special considerations for blogging include whether or not student blogging should be public or private, how to scaffold student blogging, and how to assess student blogs.

Resources

Online resources

- Search 'Blogs in education' to find tips and advice on how to start your class blog.
- WeblogMatrix.org will let you compare blogging services.
- Edublogs.org provides blogging services as well as information on, and resources for, using blogs in the classroom.
- There are blog handouts, FAQs, and planning materials on the *Using Social Media in the Classroom* companion website. You can find this at www.sagepub.co.uk/poore

Further reading

- Byington, T. A. (2011) Communities of practice: using blogs to increase collaboration, *Intervention in School and Clinic,* 46(5), 280–91.
- Laia, H. and Chenc, C. (2011) Factors influencing secondary school teachers' adoption of teaching blogs, *Computers & Education,* 56(4), 948–60.
- McGrail, E. and Davis, A. (2011) The influence of classroom blogging on elementary student writing, *Journal of Research in Childhood Education,* 25(4), 415–37.
- Sawmiller, A. (2010) Classroom blogging: what is the role in science learning? *The Clearing House,* 83, 44–8.

CHAPTER 5

WIKIS

Overview

Like blogs, wikis are websites that have certain features and attributes, all of which can be applied to a variety of educational conditions. In particular, wikis have the potential to enhance the student learning experience by encouraging group, rather than individual, approaches to learning. In this chapter, we explore wiki basics before moving on to examine the collaborative, constructivist pedagogies that wikis can be used to promote. Wikis support administrative as well as learning-focused activities but, if you choose to use wikis in your class, then there are some things that will require your attention, such as how to scaffold student wiki contributions, how to create a successful wiki, and how to deal with 'edit wars'.

The word 'wiki' is short for the term *'wiki wiki'*, which means 'quick' in Hawaiian.

What is a wiki?

A wiki is a website that allows people to easily edit, add to, and delete web-pages and/or their contents. You can make your wiki public or private: it can be editable either by anyone (usually anyone with a username and password) or by only those people you invite. This is what makes wikis a social media technology: the ability for writers and readers to participate directly in a digital space. Unlike blogs, which are clearly 'dynamic' in the way they present their content (in reverse chronological order), wikis display as 'static' to their readers, despite their 'work-in-progress' nature.

Video clip. Wikis in Plain English

CommonCraft's video 'Wikis in Plain English' can be viewed on YouTube (search 'Wikis in Plain English').

Wikis can be on any topic. Some wikis are about rally cars, others about cancer research or colonialist literature, and still others are about Joss Whedon's TV shows. Class-based wikis tend to be focused around key subject areas or topics that are covered in the curriculum. Wikis are typically created by groups, not by individuals.

Key point. What about Wikipedia?

Wikipedia is probably the best-known example of a wiki. Wikipedia is a website that anyone in the world can contribute to by creating and editing articles on any topic. It is important to understand that Wikipedia is just an example of a wiki – not all wikis are Wikipedia.

Wikis are first and foremost made up of pages that are focused around certain topics (or aspects of a topic). Contributors to the wiki make changes or edits to the pages by adding or deleting information in order to build an understanding or representation of a topic. Unlike a blog, a wiki does not have a dashboard – you write your pages directly into the WYSIWYG (What You See Is What You Get) editor. Edits are made by clicking on an 'edit' button at the top of the page. This turns the page into something that resembles a Word document: you can change fonts, add bullets, hyperlinks, images, videos, widgets, tables, and do many of the things that you can do in a regular Word document or other digital writing environment. Once you have made your edits, you need to make sure you save the page. Wiki pages can be moved, deleted, or 'protected' so that only those with full administration access can edit them.

Dos and Don'ts. Essential wiki tips

When working with wikis, be sure to do the following:

- Save your wiki work often – just as you do when writing something in Word.
- Make sure you 'monitor' your class wiki. This means you get updates sent to your email each time an edit is made to a wiki page. You can organise this through your account settings.

Aside from the obvious ability to create and/or edit pages, wikis have three other distinguishing features:

1   Each wiki page automatically comes with a discussion forum or comments area added to it so that background conversations about the page can go on.
2   Wikis also have a 'history' function attached to each page, meaning that you can follow what edits were made when and by whom, and compare different versions of the page. This is indispensible when you want to track which students have been making substantive changes to the content of the page, as compared to those who have simply fixed punctuation errors.
3   Finally, if you don't like the current version of a page – or if someone has 'vandalised' the page – then you can restore it to an earlier version.

Wikis allow you to set different 'permissions' for contributors. As the creator or owner of a wiki you automatically have all the administration rights possible, allowing you to choose levels of access for other users. You might, for example, want students to be able to add and delete pages (in other words, to have fairly high-level permissions). Or you might prefer that they simply edit the pages you have already set up (most likely in the school setting, unless students have their own, personal wiki). In any case, choose carefully the permissions you give to other users.

To think about. Hosting wiki software on your school's server

MediaWiki is the software that powers Wikipedia. If your school administration is concerned about using external services, then consider asking a school IT specialist to instal MediaWiki on a school server. MediaWiki is not as easy to use as web-based services, but it does have quite good functionality. The software is free and can be downloaded from MediaWiki.org.

As is the case with blogs, you can customise the look and feel of your wiki, manage members and discussions, attach files, and add tags. You can also 'monitor' your wiki, meaning that you can get notifications of when new content has been added to your wiki, or when someone has contributed to a discussion forum.

There are many free wiki services available on the web. All you need to do to get a wiki is to sign up with a wiki service by creating a username and password, and generate your wiki: you could be wikiing in seconds from now!

In terms of wiki services, both Wikispaces.com and PBWorks.com are popular with educators, and both offer easy-to-use, good-looking wikis with excellent functionality. School teachers can create ad- and cost-free K–12 wikis, and, in an excellent move for protecting student privacy, you can generate bulk student accounts without using email addresses.

 Activity. Set up your own wiki

Get an account with a wiki service such as Wikispaces.com or PBWorks. Once you have created a wiki (just follow the instructions on the screen), click the 'edit' button on the wiki page and add some content to your wiki:

- Write a welcome message on your wiki homepage. Click 'save' to view your message.
- Go into edit mode again, and this time try adding images, links, and 'widgets' (for video and the like). You can always delete things later.
- Add some new pages to your wiki. Create a navigation menu and link to them.
- Explore your 'manage wiki' or 'settings' area: customise the appearance or design of your wiki and invite some people to contribute to your wiki.
- Explore the privacy, editing, and discussion settings. Practise making your wiki public or private.

Educational benefits of wikis

Pedagogy

Collaboration is at the heart of the wiki medium: a wiki proper simply cannot be built without the ongoing co-operative efforts of a community of users who seek to build and communicate knowledge and information. Wikis therefore easily lend themselves to socially constructivist approaches to teaching and learning at the same time as encouraging high-level cognitive engagement with analysis, synthesis, and evaluation skills amongst students. Further, wiki-style collaboration provides a clear demonstration of situated learning theory in action: students start on the periphery of an activity (or 'culture' if you will) and through the ongoing mediation of social relations they become more and more proficient in that activity.

Wikis are suitable for ongoing, investigative group projects that ask students to explore a topic in-depth, synthesise their discoveries, and then disseminate their findings to a wider audience. The medium particularly allows students to demonstrate higher-level thinking skills through the selection and presentation of information – especially if you ask them to justify their reasoning behind their decisions in the discussion forum.

Teamwork, collaboration, and online behaviour

Most of the educational benefits of social media described in Chapter 1 apply to wikis: they are collaborative, participative, encourage socialisation, and give students a sense of ownership over their work. But because they compel students to work together, wikis are also particularly effective in teaching students negotiation and teamwork skills, as well as how to integrate diverse perspectives or ideas into the construction of a final intellectual product.

In this way, wikis can also be excellent for reinforcing appropriate online behaviour. Occasionally, disagreements will arise between students about the content or format of a group wiki space. The result is often an 'edit war' (discussed in more detail, below), in which one party will make changes to the wiki, only to have the other party change things back (perhaps using the wiki's 'revert' function, mentioned earlier). Ideally, students should be encouraged to work through any differences themselves in a mature fashion either in person or via the page's discussion forum. Realistically, however, this edifying scenario could prove uncommon. More likely, this back-and-forth pattern will continue until an administrator (that is, the teacher) decides that enough is enough and that the page should be locked from further editing. These situations, although often disappointing to a teacher who has spent so much valuable time and effort in getting a wiki under way in class, nevertheless provide a terrific opportunity to stop the class and have a time-out to discuss acceptable dispute resolution methods. It also gives you the chance to remind students that poor online behaviour has consequences.

Communication, organisation, and acknowledgement

In terms of audience communication, wikis can be used to teach students about the genre of professional writing. Standard, jargon-free English is the norm for wikis, and that means students should be expected to use correct spelling, grammar, and punctuation. Moreover, they should be encouraged to edit their own and others' work for style, tone, grammar, spelling, and focus.

Ideas. Be inspired!

- *Room 25.* Mr McLean teaches Year 6 at Katikati Primary School on New Zealand's North Island and runs a multi-purpose wiki for his class. Individual student wikis are linked to as 'student eportfolios' (search 'Room 25 Katikati').
- *Digie-xplorers.* A wonderful example of a wiki being used to support a narrative 'pick-a-path' writing project for 9-year-olds. From Lynmore School, Rotorua, New Zealand (search 'Digie-xplorers pick-a-path').
- *Ah Bon?* Mme Thomas uses wikis to deliver resources to her middle school students. Follow the links to find all of Mme Thomas' wiki projects (search 'Ah bon French wiki').
- Many more wiki examples can be found at Educational Wikis, hosted by Wikispaces (search 'Educational wikis Wikispaces') and at the Edublog Awards for Best Educational Wiki website (search 'Edublog awards wikis').

Wikis also force students to think about how to best structure their work. Unlike blogs – the format of which can foster a 'stream-of-consciousness' type of communication – wikis demand a clear and obvious structuring of content so that wiki readers can quickly locate information. Part of this structuring includes having students make decisions about the relevance of content, including images, videos, links, and other media.

Additionally, wikis can be used to get students into the habit of acknowledging their sources. Because wikis are largely about the construction and presentation of knowledge, the material used by students in building their wiki will often come from elsewhere. Although a good deal of internet culture is about 'mash-ups' and quick cut-and-paste jobs, wikis are a little different in that they require a higher level of acknowledgement if the information contained in them is to be trusted and verified (note how Wikipedia requires proper citation of sources). A simple hyperlink to the original source may be all that you require of younger students, or a full-out reference and quote marks from older students; either way, students need to understand the importance of giving due recognition to the work created by others.

Administration

Finally, it has to be said that the administrative or classroom management benefits of wikis are considerable. Wikis are extremely easy to use, and are excellent resource repositories, thus making them good learning management systems for those who simply want to make content available to students. If, however, you are using wikis as educational tools, they have added benefits in that both you and the students can track learning progress through time via the page history function (which also acts as version control), and you can receive email notifications of changes made to the wiki. Further, the effortlessness of self-publication on a wiki is not only very motivating for students, it also means that you, as the teacher, spend less time answering technical or operational questions as they relate to how to use the wiki service.

Ideas. Wiki ideas

- Use a wiki as a **class management tool**. Create areas for class details (such as syllabus, assignments, tips, instructions), class topics (topic 1, topic 2, and so on), study guide, resources.
- Ask students to form into small groups and to **build a wiki space around a set topic**. Use the history function to check individual students' progress – for example, you can see who has been making substantive contributions to the wiki, and who has just been adding commas. Have students present their wiki to the rest of the class.
- Ask students to use the page's discussion forum to **justify their selection of page content**.
- Get your class to **write a Wikipedia article** on a topic that doesn't have a page yet. Get them to start the page themselves.
- Send students to Wikipedia and have them **analyse the development of an article on a controversial topic** (for example, the Israeli-Palestinian conflict or

George W. Bush). Ask them to look through the discussions that sit behind the article and have them trace major sticking-points or the ways in which consensus was achieved. Get them to write a report on the issue and to publish it on the class wiki.

- Get students to build **resource collections**, FAQs, or glossaries around class topics. Use a wiki to share the information, videos, links, and images that make up the collection.
- Create **chain stories** using a wiki. Put students in pairs and get them to start a story on a wiki. Get other pairs to continue the story lesson by lesson.

Wiki models

Wikis lend themselves to multiple educational uses thanks to the many and varied features they support. However, there are three main types of wiki that teachers use in the classroom, as described below.

Administration wiki

Because wikis are highly flexible content management systems they are ideal for use as a class administration tool. You can use them to create pages for assignments, study resources, topics covered in the syllabus, homework, announcements (these could be placed on the wiki's homepage), or anything else related to the day-to-day running of your class. Students and parents both can view your class administration wiki and make contributions to, or ask questions via, the discussion forums for various pages. Some teachers use wikis for classroom administration and communication whilst others use blogs. Neither is particularly better than the other for this purpose: it is just a matter of personal preference which one you choose.

Class wiki (learning-focused)

Many teachers use wikis as the basis for collaborative student projects. Students can be formed into groups and asked to build a wiki space around a set topic, or to contribute to a class wiki as a whole. The focus in this type of wiki is on student learning, not on the day-to-day management of the classroom environment. Individual student contributions can be traced through both the page history function and the wiki's discussion forums.

Individual student wiki (learning-focused)

Although wikis are primarily designed for collaboration, many teachers have found value in giving each student in their class their own, personal wiki. This individual wiki acts as a learning portfolio for the student and can easily be linked to from the main class (or teacher) wiki.

Many teachers choose to combine models – that is, they have a whole-of-class wiki that serves both administrative and pedagogical roles, or they might have an administrative wiki that also links to individual student wikis. The format you choose will depend on your purpose for using wikis in your class and on your confidence in using wiki tools.

Special considerations for wikis

For your wiki venture to be successful you need to be aware of some of the peculiarities of wiki use in the classroom. Chapter 2 takes you through the general planning and other issues for any social media initiative you might implement in your class, but wikis require some additional groundwork.

Choosing a wiki service

Because of the large number and variety of wiki providers available on the web, you may find it difficult to choose which service is best for your classroom situation. Use WikiMatrix.org or a similar wiki comparison site to help you sift and compare the functions of different services. As with all uses of social media in the school environment, however, you should be looking for an ad-free service that has protections for privacy built in to the system.

 In conjunction with the general checklist items for choosing a service (see Chapter 2), use the guide below to help you work through some of the items you need to consider when choosing a wiki service for your classroom. You can also visit the *Using Social Media in the Classroom* companion website for the consolidated list.

- ☐ I can create bulk student accounts without using email addresses.
- ☐ The wiki edit function is easy to use.
- ☐ I can lock pages if I want to.
- ☐ Pages can be deleted if necessary.
- ☐ Rich media can be added to pages.
- ☐ The service supports widgets.
- ☐ I can monitor changes made to pages.
- ☐ I can delete discussion topics.

As with any social media that you hope to use in class, be sure to conduct some trial runs of the service(s) you are thinking of using. Compare the wiki(s) across both Internet Explorer and Firefox browsers, and be sure to test them in the student computing environment at your school. See Chapter 17 for more information.

 Activity. Compare wiki services

Set up a wiki on at least two different wiki sites (say, Wikispaces and PBWorks). Explore the functionality of each, especially noting:

- What sort of support is provided? FAQs? Forums?
- Can you moderate discussions and delete discussion topics?
- Can you remove posted information quickly?
- What are the conditions of use of the wiki?
- Can you customise the look of the wiki?
- How easily does the service support widgets?
- How much space is your wiki allocated?
- How easily can you create new pages and link to them?
- What are the privacy options?
- Can you delete the wiki?
- Can you export the wiki to create a backup or can you transfer it to another service?

Note anything else that you think will be important in helping you decide on a suitable wiki platform for your class. Visit the *Using Social Media in the Classroom* companion website for more planning materials.

Successful wikis

Wikis are rather like garden plants: to flourish, they require cultivation, nurturing, nourishment – and perhaps the occasional word of encouragement. Successful wikis are built on strong communities, as articulated by Jonathan Davies (2004):

- *Wikis must have a common goal* (Davies, 2004, p. 64). Users need to be clear about both the wiki's purpose and their role in its construction. Uncertainty leads to unfocused and/or low-level contributions.
- *Trust is everything* (Davies, 2004). Any effective teamwork is built on relationships of trust. Team members need to feel that they can rely on others

to contribute equally and behave appropriately, and that any concerns or differences can be raised in a collegial, supportive atmosphere.

- *Wikiing must be valuable on a personal level* (Davies, 2004, p. 66). Although wikis are about group collaboration, individuals must nevertheless gain some kind of individual satisfaction from contributing to the combined effort.
- *Encouragement is essential.* Users should inspire each other in their wiki efforts. As the teacher, it is also important that you take an active role in motivating students to assemble the best product possible.

Problems of collaboration and ownership

Wiki writers sometimes worry about the absence of 'individual credit' (Davies, 2004, p. 21) given to their contributions. This can mean a lack of collegiality and collaboration on a wiki, and can result in students dividing the work up amongst themselves, in effect saying, 'I'll do this bit, you do that bit, and you do that other bit'. Students often take two approaches to 'farming out' the work: (1) they either divide things up by content area – meaning that each student tackles a different content area and is responsible for it and it alone, or, less often, (2) they allocate tasks according to the different types of duties to be performed on the wiki – one student contributes the substantive content to the wiki, another deals with structuring and organising the wiki, and yet another takes over editorial duties by fixing grammar and punctuation errors. Neither situation is satisfactory if your wiki's purpose is to engender co-operation amongst class members. To mitigate against these scenarios, consider doing the following:

- Reiterate the point that a wiki or wikispace should be owned by all in the group – not just by individuals.
- Remind students that you are looking for evidence that they can work in a collaborative fashion in a team-based environment – and that, if they are still worried, their individual contributions can be easily tracked through the wiki's 'history' function.
- Let them know that if they farm out the work, then their wiki is likely to end up a mess of incoherent, unfocused, unlinked ideas and content, all of which will be reflected in their final grade for the project.
- Tell them to aim for a balance in their contributions to the wiki, that they should be (1) adding substantive, topic-related content, (2) working with the group to organise that content, and, (3) making an effort to 'polish' the site in terms of grammar, punctuation, and spelling, as well as how the site looks.

Not all collaboration problems come about because of concerns over provenance, however. In some cases, students are genuinely reluctant to edit others' work because they don't feel that they have the 'right' to change material created or added by classmates. Again, you need to remind students that it is expected that a wiki will undergo numerous revisions.

Visit the wiki pages on the *Using Social Media in the Classroom* companion website for a handout you can adapt to your purposes and pre-empt some of these problems.

Edit wars

These can start up when users disagree over a wiki's development and/or content. In edit wars, contributors repeatedly wipe out another's work and restore their own version of the page. If this kind of exchange occurs on a page, then editing should cease and a discussion should be started in the page's discussion forum about why certain content should or should not be included. Students should be urged to reason and argue for their position and to work towards a consensus on what is the best content for the wiki – it shouldn't be about personalities or ego.

Concurrent editing

Because only one version of a wiki page can be saved at any one time, problems can arise when two different users attempt to edit a page concurrently. This doesn't occur with too much frequency, but it can still be an obstacle. If this happens, you will likely receive an onscreen message that lets you know that concurrent editing is occurring. If there are no conflicts, the system will simply merge the changes. If there are conflicting changes, however, the system will give you a number of options for resolving the conflict; for example, you might choose to remove the conflict before saving, or overwrite the other users' changes altogether. Problems of concurrent editing should not be confused with edit wars, the latter of which are rather more intentional in their effects.

Scaffolding student wiki contributions

Members of your class may never have contributed to a wiki before, so you will need to scaffold student learning in very explicit ways. Always – *always* – be up front about your expectations for the wiki, and be sure to set clear instructions and provide examples (see Chapter 2).

Create a specific section on your class wiki that tells students everything they need to know. You might want to treat it as an FAQ, and, ideally, any information you provide should be easily printable or available also in PDF format. See the wiki FAQ available on the *Using Social Media in the Classroom* companion website for the type of information you might provide to students. In particular:

- Tell students why you have chosen to use a wiki.
- Describe what a wiki is and how it is organised.
- Talk about the 'philosophy' of a wiki, that is, that it is about collaboration and knowledge building and that the content constantly changes.
- Clarify what your wiki will be about and what your goals are for it.
- Explain who can contribute to a wiki and how.
- Tell students that it is OK (indeed, that it is expected) to change other people's content, to add their own, and to fix any errors that appear on the wiki. If they think that a change might be controversial, then they should justify their edit in the page's discussion forum.
- Tell them not to take it too personally if their content is edited by another community member and to take a step back and reconsider: did their addition really add to the wiki, or was it, in fact, irrelevant or poorly done? But, at the same time, …
- Detail what will happen if an edit war starts up.
- Give suggestions as to how students might plan and structure their wiki, and let them know that clear structure and organisation are vital.
- Explain the importance of good writing, the value of including relevant rich media (such as links, videos, and images), and of the need for the appropriate acknowledgement of sources – all of which contribute to a wiki's plausibility.
- Tell students not to 'farm bits out', that is, they shouldn't carve up the work amongst themselves, topic-by-topic or task-by-task (as described above). Strongly reiterate that you are looking for collaborative efforts, not individual ones.
- Explain that students should aim for a balance in their contributions to the wiki: that they should be (1) adding substantive, topic-related content, (2) working with the group to organise that content, and, (3) making an effort to 'polish' the site in terms of grammar, punctuation, and spelling, as well as how the site looks.
- Give the class easy assignments to start with so that they get used to the wiki format. Increase the level of complexity as you go (Hennis and Ubacht, n.d., online).
- Tell students how you will assess their work.

Assessing wikis: individual versus group grades

One of the first factors to consider when assessing wikis is whether or not to give students individual or group grades, or both. As previously mentioned, many students express concerns about whether or not they will get individual credit for their contributions to a group wiki. Perhaps the best way to address such issues is to award both individual and group marks for wiki work – you might even want to consult with students themselves about how to apportion grades for both types of contribution. But regardless of how you decide to break things up, you need to make sure that your expectations and assessment criteria are clearly laid out, and that you are meeting your curriculum and/or learning objectives with the assessment.

Wiki rubrics (success criteria)

Develop an assessment rubric (or success criteria matrix) for each wiki project you ask your students to undertake. You will need to develop separate rubrics for individual and group grades. Visit the *Using Social Media in the Classroom* companion website to share your own rubric. Some general areas for consideration might include:

Content

- Ideas
- Comprehension
- Intellectual engagement with core themes
- Use of data
- Information sharing
- Focus
- Development of content
- Acknowledgement of sources

Pages

- Writing quality
- Relevance of links or embedded media
- Frequency and quality of page edits
- Relevance of discussion topics
- Design and administration
- Structure and organisation

Appearance

- Use of enhancements (especially if using widgets)
- Management and administration
- Group work
- Quality of teamwork
- Wiki etiquette
- Distribution of tasks

Table 5.1 provides an example of a wiki rubric or success criteria matrix for a group activity.

Table 5.1   Sample wiki rubric/success criteria matrix for a group activity

Category	Beginning	Emergent	Proficient	Advanced
Quality of team work	Little evidence that group members have worked together. The work has been divided up amongst group members. No discussions about wiki contents. No encouragement of other members.	Only one or two wiki members have notably contributed to the wiki's development. Wiki contributors have tended to focus on only one type of task (for example, proofreading, adding images, or finding links). Few discussions about wiki contents. Little encouragement of other members.	All members have contributed to the wiki's development. Wiki contributors have engaged in a variety of tasks. There are discussions relating to the development of the wiki's contents. Members encourage each other.	All members have made significant, broad and deep contributions to the wiki's development. Contributors have engaged in a variety of tasks. Discussions relating to the development of the wiki's contents are focused and insightful. Members encourage each other and offer help and suggestions to others.
Content	Content on the wiki is irrelevant or inadequate. It does not focus on key themes and is trivial or superficial.	Content is broadly relevant to the topic and the key themes but does not consistently meet the learning curriculum for the task.	Content is relevant and focused. The wiki demonstrates a clear appreciation of the topic and the key themes. Meets curriculum objectives.	Content is relevant, focused, and demonstrates a perceptive understanding of the topic and key themes. Exceeds curriculum objectives for the task.
Structure and organisation	The wiki has no discernable structure. The wiki is disorganised with extraneous content appearing on pages. No sense of how the pages connect or how topics or themes are linked. No logic to the wiki.	The wiki has a loose but often confusing structure. Some content is organised on the correct pages, but other content is peripheral to the page's focus. Pages and topics are vaguely connected. Little logic to the wiki.	Clear structure to the wiki in which content is well organised and presented. Connections between themes and topic are coherently made.	Wiki content is clearly and logically organised. Structure is logical and coherent. Key themes are kept discrete but connections between them are made explicit.

Activity. Develop a wiki assessment rubric (success criteria matrix)

Write up a rubric or a success criteria matrix for your class's wiki project. What criteria will you be measuring? Development of content? Structure and organisation? Quality of teamwork? Comprehension? Use of data? What performance ranges will you be using? You might want to search online for examples of wiki rubrics that other teachers have already developed, just as a way of getting started.

Wikipedia

In 2011, Wikipedia celebrated its tenth birthday. Both revered and condemned as an encyclopedic knowledge source that (in theory) anyone can edit, Wikipedia often polarises teachers as to whether or not it should be used with students. Many, if not most, teachers impose a blanket ban on Wikipedia – and many, if not most, students use it anyway.

Although there have been infamous hoaxes perpetrated on Wikipedia (search 'Seigenthaler incident' to learn about an edit made on the site that falsely stated that American journalist John Seigenthaler had been under suspicion for the Kennedy assassinations), Wikipedia nevertheless is a *generally* reliable source of basic, factual information. It is especially strong, for example, on the more quantitative, scientific disciplines, although articles written for the humanities are also gaining in breadth and depth.

Wikipedia has three core content policies that guide the writing of articles:

1 *Neutral point of view*. This means making a fair representation of the arguments, research, findings, or views discussed in the article.
2 *No original research*. All material must be able to be backed up by reliable, already published sources.
3 *Verifiability*. Anything likely to be challenged must be backed up by reference to reliable sources.

If an article is in dispute, or if an edit war erupts, editing on the article can be suspended and the dispute shifted to the discussion area until it is resolved. Wikipedia also indicates to readers when an article lacks citations or readability, when it might be overlong (requiring it to be split into smaller articles), or when it might be out of date or ambiguous, all of which prompts editors to fix them. From this, Wikipedia can be used to teach students about reliability, verifiability, veracity, and peer review in research, and one of the best points to start at, here, is with Wikipedia's own 'About' pages.

Like all social media sites and services, though, Wikipedia should be used wisely. This might mean advising students that it is OK for them to *start* with Wikipedia, but that they will need to expand their research to cover other sources (and not just those listed at the end of a Wikipedia article, either), that you will not accept Wikipedia in any list of references, and that you will be checking Wikipedia entries against students' own work for plagiarism.

Wiki and blog comparison tables

The question of 'Should I use a wiki or a blog?' often arises when you are considering which social media tools will best support your classroom activities. It can help to have a source of comparison between the two because there are, in fact, major differences between wikis and blogs both in terms of concept and function. The tables (Tables 5.2–5.5) below should help to clarify the differences between these two main social media formats. Take care not to use a wiki for a task that would actually best be suited to blogging, and vice versa.

General comparisons

Table 5.2   Comparison of general characteristics of blogs and wikis

Blogs	Wikis
Process	Product
Individual	Collective
Dynamic (latest content at top)	Static (but continually updated)
Lengthy scrolls down the screen	Pages and links
Monological	Community based
Temporal	Atemporal
Show change in thinking	Show development of knowledge
One-to-many	Many-to-many
Immediate, in the moment	Mediated
Critique and reflection	Topic and content focus
Publication	Constant revision

Functional characteristics

Table 5.3   Comparison of functional characteristics of blogs and wikis

Blogs	Wikis
Posts	Pages
Comments	Discussion forums
Tags	Navigation menu
Dashboard	WYSIWYG editor
Archive	History and page reversion; restore function

Educational benefits

Table 5.4   Comparison of educational benefits of blogs and wikis

Blogs	Wikis
Critique and reflection	Collaboration, negotiation, teamwork
Track developments in thinking	Track developments in knowledge construction and comprehension
Individual control and ownership	Synthesis of research, scholarship
Easy sharing of opinion and discoveries	Easy sharing of information and data
Allow for creativity and flow	Structuring and presentation of knowledge is explicit
Writing skills, integration of diverse perspectives, communication, appropriate online behaviour, motivation, engagement in the community, higher-order thinking, audience, students try harder	Writing skills, integration of diverse perspectives, communication, appropriate online behaviour, motivation, engagement in the community, higher-order thinking, audience, students try harder
Constructivist	Constructivist

Classroom issues

Table 5.5   Comparison of classroom issues for blogs and wikis

Blogs	Wikis
Creating individual student blogs	Creating bulk accounts for the one wiki
Individual responsibility	Common responsibility and team work
Safety and freedom of expression	Trust in others
Personal value	Personal and group value
Feedback	Encouragement
Sharing and access	Collaboration, ownership, provenance
Administrative control over individual blogs	Edit wars
Identifying how much to assess	Assessing individual and group contributions
Easily view individual work all in the one place	Track individual contributions to group work
Clarifying expectations	Clarifying expectations
Scaffolding student learning	Scaffolding student learning

 Activity. Work on your wiki plan

Use the wiki plan template found on the *Using Social Media in the Classroom* companion website to develop a class wiki project. Be sure to take into account the general planning considerations outlined in Chapter 2 under 'Planning', as well as the concerns that are specific to wikis.

Summary

- Wikis are websites that anyone can edit – depending on how you set them up.
- Wikis are characterised by collaboration on static pages (which are continually updated) that wiki contributors edit.
- Each wiki page comes with a discussion forum, a history, and a restore function.
- Wikis are good for collaboration, teamwork, and knowledge construction.
- There are three main models of wikiing: (1) the administration wiki, (2) the class wiki, and (3) the individual student wiki (which is less common, but can be used as a student's eportfolio). These last two are learning-focused.
- Special considerations for wikis include engendering trust amongst wiki collaborators, acknowledging issues of control and ownership, edit wars, and scaffolding student wiki contributions.

Resources

Online resources

- Search 'Wikis in education' to find tips and advice on how to start your class wiki.
- WikiMatrix.org will let you compare wiki services.
- Educational Wikis provides a good starting place for examples of wikis in education (search 'Educational Wikis Wikispaces').

- There are wiki handouts, FAQs, and planning materials on the *Using Social Media in the Classroom* companion website. You can find this at www.sagepub.co.uk/poore

Further reading

- Andes, L. and Claggett, E. (2011) Wiki writers: students and teachers making connections across communities, *The Reading Teacher,* 64(5), 345–50.
- Davies, J. (2004) Wiki brainstorming and problems with wiki. MSc Project submitted September 2004. Available at http://www.jonathan-davies.co.uk/portfolio/wiki.php. Accessed 13 October 2011.
- Huvila, I. (2010) Where does the information come from? Information source use patterns in Wikipedia, *Information Research,* 15(3). Available at http://informationr.net/ir/15-3/paper433.html. Accessed 3 November 2011.
- Schillinger, T. (2011) Blurring boundaries: two groups of girls collaborate on a wiki. *Journal of Adolescent and Adult Literacy,* 54(6), 403–13.
- Woo, M., Chu, S., Ho, A. and Li, X. (2011) Using a wiki to scaffold primary-school students' collaborative writing, *Journal of Educational Technology & Society,* 14(1), 43–54.
- Zammit, K. (2010) Working with wikis: collaborative writing in the 21st century. Key competencies in the knowledge society, in N. Reynolds and M. Turcsányi-Szabó (eds), *Advances in Information and Communication Technology,* held as part of WCC 2010, Brisbane, Australia, 20–23 September 2010. Proceedings, vol. 324, pp. 447–55.

CHAPTER 6

SOCIAL NETWORKS

Overview

Social networks are perhaps the most visible form of digital social media today, thanks to the popularity of services such as Facebook and Bebo. Although this chapter touches upon these 'individual-based' social networks, our main focus will be to explore social networks that are more group or topic based and thus more profitable in terms of constructivist approaches to education. We will cover the basics of social networking services, including key functions and characteristics, before looking at the educational benefits and potential problems that the use of social networks in the classroom might generate. In particular, we will discuss some of the issues surrounding privacy, data collection, age of sign-up, and bullying.

What is a social network?

> ### Video clip. Social Networking in Plain English
>
> CommonCraft's video 'Social Networking in Plain English' can be viewed on YouTube (search 'Social networking in Plain English').

Arguably any internet-based site or service that brings people together could be called an online social network, but for our purposes a social network can be said to be any site or service that allows people to connect with each other, to inform others about events and activities, and to share news, photos, videos, and items of interest. Social networks can be divided into two main categories. In the first category, there is the personal social network that centres around the individual. Examples of this kind of social network include Facebook, MySpace, and Bebo. In the second category, the social network centres around a group or a topic. Examples of group- or topic-based social networks include Ning, Edmodo, and Elgg. This chapter deals with group-based social networks, as they are the most suitable for constructivist educational frameworks.

Social networking basics

All social networks – regardless of whether they are group based or personal – share some common attributes: they all feature profiles, friends, groups, member status updates, and 'activity' or news feeds.

Each member of a social network has a profile, which details as much or as little information about a person as they want to share. Profile details may include everything from your birthday, gender, and hometown, to a description of your likes, interests, hobbies, and political views. Once a person has a profile on a social network, they can seek out and make 'friends' (in social network terminology 'friends' are people on the network who you know or who you want to be connected to). Ordinarily, friends will make comments on each other's 'wall' – a space where quick messages or notes to an individual can be left for all to see. Members of a social network can also join groups of people who share similar interests. In the case of a group- or topic-based social network, groups are formed by default, as the network is formed around the group as a matter of course; in a personal social network, however, individuals must actively create or join groups.

Friends and group members on a social network can see each other's 'status', which outlines what a person has recently been doing on the network. For example, a person's status might indicate that they have recently commented on a photo that was posted to the network, or that they have contributed to a discussion, or that they have uploaded a video. All of these status updates get combined into a group's 'activity' or news feed, which aggregates everyone's status into the one spot, usually on the front page, so that others in the group can find out what is going on. Most social networks also support the easy sharing of files, videos, photos, and more.

Group-based social networks in education

When using social networks for constructivist educational purposes, it is best to choose a service that primarily allows communities to form around groups or topics, rather than around individuals. The tools that support such networks are more visibly 'community' focused. For example, services such as Edmodo emphasise discussion forums, announcements, events scheduling, and the creation of sub-groups within the network. Most social network services also support a blogging function, but these are, for the most part, pretty basic; if blogging is a key part of your plan to use social media in the classroom, then students should be provided with proper blogging tools, as per Chapter 4.

Ideas. Social networking ideas

- Ask students to **form groups around class topics**. Get them to post videos, audios, photos, and so on, and to comment on why they have posted them.
- Get students to form sub-groups within the class network. They can then **set up forums for their group and privately discuss upcoming group assessment items**.
- Use social networks to **connect with classes in other schools or other countries**.
- Set up a **reading group** using the discussion forums on a social network.
- Give **group feedback** on assignments using an announcements tool.
- **Manage your entire class** using a social networking site: post latest assignment information, announcements, topics for discussion, useful links and media, and so on.

Setting up a social network

Many readers will already have a Facebook profile but may never have set up their own social network. If you choose to use a social network with your students, then you might explore the following services:

- *Edmodo.com*. A free service specifically designed for classroom environments and very 'Facebook' in appearance and function. Allows you to set and grade assignments, attach files, build libraries, create groups, and send out alerts.
- *Elgg*. A service that has a relatively long history of supplying social network services to educators. Elgg.com provides a paid hosting service with a free trial period, but Elgg.org allows your IT services people at

school to download and instal the Elgg software on your school servers. This latter option bypasses the need to use fee-based external services.

- *Togetherville.com*. A Facebook-like service owned by the Disney company and targeted at children under 10 years of age. There are many 'kid-safe' privacy and security protections built in to the service.
- *Ning.com*. One of the most powerful social network services available on the internet. Ning supplies many useful tools, but their accessibility depends on the pricing option you choose. There is a free education option, but this is usually contingent upon where you live.
- *Groupsite.com*. Very easy to use and contains all the usual social network functions. Different pricing options are available.

All these services should allow you to export your data.

 Activity. Set up your own social network

Create an account with a social network service such as Edmodo.com or Togetherville.com. Once you have created your site by following the step-by-step instructions, start building your network:

- Write a welcome message for new members.
- Create some sub-groups. Once you have some site members, practise managing the sub-groups by adding and removing members (let them know that you're just testing things out!), or by making the sub-groups public or private.
- Explore the file uploads function. Can you attach a file to a discussion post? Is there a central place where you can manage all files?
- Investigate the discussion functions. Start a discussion on the discussion forum. Can you delete or moderate posts or topics? Can you create more than one forum? Can sub-groups create their own forums?
- Add an event to the calendar. Can you invite only select members and sub-groups? Can you schedule the 'release date' of your event?
- Customise the look and feel of your site. Can you shift 'blocks' around? Can you add and delete different functions?

Educational benefits of social networking

Pedagogy

Communication, sharing, and connection are what define social networks, and it is this that makes them perfect for the fluid and dynamic nature of peer learning. With social networking, students can continually share any discoveries they make about class topics, whether via a thread in a discussion forum, a comment on someone's wall, or the posting of a useful video or link. Social networks are thus best suited to whole-of-class projects that require students to consistently interact with each other over a period of time in order to build their knowledge of a topic.

The discussion forum elements of a social network are particularly helpful in eliciting deep and rich conversation from students, which can be useful for exercises requiring critique, reflection, negotiation, and argument-building. At the other end of the spectrum, the easy-to-use sharing tools of social networks enable students to locate and then quickly circulate topic-related resources for use by peers, all of which contributes to the class repository.

Connecting outside the classroom

The success of any social network depends on members being able to make and sustain connections with others, and the networks that flourish best are those that grow organically. As a teacher, you can encourage this process by taking your network *outside* the bounds of your own classroom: why not ask parents or experts to join your class network? Or perhaps you can link up with a class in a different school or even in another country? This not only extends the reach of your social network but also fosters a less 'fabricated' environment that more accurately reflects the types of social networks that students might already be a part of. As we've already seen in Chapter 1, using social media in this way can be highly motivating for students when they feel that they have some kind of control and ownership over their media-based learning environment.

Familiarity

Most children, regardless of their age, are likely to have come across some form of online social networking: youngsters may be members of Togetherville or Club Penguin (which is, technically speaking, a game, but it nevertheless has social network elements to it), and older students may be on Facebook. Thus, it's fair to say that many students are probably more familiar with how social networking operates than with, say, how wikis or blogs work. This makes social networks ripe for exploitation in a social constructivist learning environment – but students still need explicit instruction on how *your* social network will function, lest they become confused about the educational purpose of the network you want to develop.

Ideas. Be inspired!

- *Students Circle Network*. Global network for high school and college-level students. Has resources for teachers and students, study groups, and games (search 'Students Circle Network').
- *Classroom 2.0*. Massive network of teachers using social media in the classroom. Groups, forums, webinars, and more (search 'Classroom 2.0').
- *Art Education 2.0*. Dynamic network that connects art educators worldwide (search 'Art education 2.0').
- *CEET, Community of Expertise in Educational Technology*. Canadian network, but open to all. Includes podcasts, events, groups, and more (search 'CEET Ning').

Special considerations for social networks

Social networks bring with them tremendous opportunities for positively integrating social media into your classroom; however, you will need to attend to a variety of issues, both technical and social, if these tools are to be used competently and safely with your students.

Privacy

One of the most vexed issues surrounding social networking is that of privacy. By their very nature, social networks encourage people to give away information about themselves through mechanisms such as profile and status updates. In most cases, this may not be a problem, but if, for example, you are telling people when your family will be away on holiday, or that you are at the local shops having a coffee with friends, then you are also telling people when you are away from your home; websites such as PleaseRobMe. com and RobMeNow.com attest to how such information can be used for nefarious ends.

A further complication arises when a person on a social network inadvertently or otherwise gives away information about another person without their permission. For example, a student might innocuously post a photo of a group of friends on a kayaking trip that gives away information about how others spend their time, what they do, and where they go.

Of course, most social networks provide privacy controls which let you manage how much and what type of information is available to different people. There are problems with this, however. First, such controls are often notoriously difficult to understand and how they operate may be regularly changed. Further, just because you are 'controlling' how your information is viewed by other members on the network, it does not mean that your information is truly private in that it cannot be accessed by anyone else. For example, your data may be sold on to a third party advertiser (even if sold on anonymously, the potential remains for you to be linked via means other than username or IP address), or it may simply be hacked. Privacy issues are further covered in Chapter 16.

Cyberbullying

The problem of cyberbullying is addressed in more detail in Chapter 15, but it should be noted here that bullying online appears to be more likely to happen on a social network than via, say, a blog or wiki. This is probably because social networks are vehicles for sharing and connecting, whereas blogs primarily support critique and a wiki's focus is on knowledge-building. This is not to say that cyberbullying does not occur on wikis and blogs, but it is simply that the problem appears to be more prevalent on social networks, perhaps due to the dynamics of connection and real-time communication that are fostered by social networks. Further to this, we can say that cyberbullying appears to be more common on social networks that form around the individual, as opposed to those that form around a group or topic. This might go some way towards mitigating the potential for cyberbullying with your class-based network, but you still need to be on the lookout for any signs of bullying behaviour amongst your students.

Data collection

The amount and type of data collected by social networks varies from service to service, but the most that anyone should be required to give away to any social media company is a username, password, email address, and date of birth. Any information beyond this is not required either technically (or, usually, legally) to create an account. However, the nature of online social networks is such that the more information you give out about yourself, the more likely you are to find people you know, connect with others, and generally have a rich and personalised experience on the network. This is where problems can arise.

The more 'kidsafe' networks such as Togetherville have strict controls over how much data they collect about children and how it is used; for example, kids' profiles are not searchable by Google or other search engines and a child's information is not sold to third parties. The same cannot be said, however, for other services, especially those that are geared towards older students and adults. This is where reading and understanding a company's Terms of Service and Privacy Policy becomes essential (see Chapter 16), as some companies collect your data and sell it on to advertising, marketing, and other businesses that profit from the information you have supplied about yourself to the social network.

The information you knowingly give away about yourself might include your likes, interests, political and philosophical views, gender, sexuality, relationship status, religion, and contact details. What you might not know, however, is that everything you view, share, ignore, like, don't like, recommend, link to, embed, comment on, click on, don't click on, vote for, vote against, listen to, and play all contributes to a profile of your online habits. Certain companies collect all this data and sell it on to third parties, all the better to target you for advertising. Although this data may be collected anonymously, the potential still remains for every click you make to be attributed to your computer's unique Internet Protocol address.

As an adult, you can hopefully make educated decisions about what is and is not appropriate to share in this way, and hopefully you realise that any digital information you have sent out about yourself is routinely cached and archived by search engines, and that it cannot be retrieved – only, perhaps, deleted from public view. Young people, however, are often not mature or knowledgeable enough to make informed choices about the amount of detail or the appropriateness of the information they provide to social networking services. They may unwittingly give away information about their family situation, location, preferences, and so on, making them vulnerable to advertisers and online predators, both.

Age of sign-up

Most social networking services set a minimum sign-up age in their Terms of Service. For example, Ning, Elgg.com, and Facebook require that users be at least 13 years of age or older in order to use the service, although there are also many services that are designed with younger users in mind (Togetherville, for example). It is essential that you check the Terms of Service of any social network that you wish children or their parents to sign up for.

Uploading contacts or address books

Social networks (and, indeed, social media as a whole) are based around connecting as many people as possible into and through any particular service at any one time. Thus, most social networks allow members to upload database files (for example, Excel spreadsheets, .csv files, or iCal files) containing your address book or list of contacts so that you can easily add or invite people you know. There are two major problems with this practice. First, the data you are uploading doesn't actually belong to you: it is the property of the person whose details you have in your address book. If you upload someone's phone number or email address, for example, you may be in breach of privacy legislation in your jurisdiction. Secondly, the social networking service that you are using may use the data you upload for advertising, marketing, or other purposes. Again, it is extremely unlikely that you have the express permission of everyone listed in your address book to give away their details like this. Under no circumstances should teachers or students upload address book files to social networking or any other social media service.

Should I use Facebook with students?

Facebook is the world's most popular social networking service, with (at the time of writing and according to Facebook's own statistics), over 800 million active users (search 'Facebook statistics'). Children under the age of 13 are not allowed to join Facebook (although many still do) as per Facebook's Terms of Service, but for those who teach older children, and for teachers who have a Facebook account themselves, the question of whether or not to use Facebook with students will probably arise. In the first instance, you should check to see if your school has a policy surrounding teacher–student 'friend' relationships on Facebook and be sure to comply with any institutional directives surrounding the matter. If, after this, you are still considering using Facebook with your students, then you need to think through some of the following issues before embarking on any Facebook-based classroom project.

First, and perhaps most obviously, you need to consider whether or not to allow students to 'friend' you, and you, them, and in doing this, you need to consider the kind of association that is appropriate in this space. Professional and mentoring relationships are the only kinds of relationships that are appropriate between teachers and students on Facebook: you should never enter into a student's space in order to exchange gossip about other students or teachers, or to engage in inappropriate liaisons. Remember: every single thing you do in any digital space can be found (through hacking and archiving) regardless of privacy settings and regardless of whether or not you have deleted something from public (or even private) view. Further, there is the very real danger of something being taken out of context or misinterpreted; you might find an innocent remark or conversation taken amiss, either deliberately or otherwise, leaving you in a very vulnerable position, both professionally and personally.

> **To think about. Paying for social networking services**
>
> Ning is probably the most popular group-based social network provider on the internet and is used by many educators. However, it is not without its detractors. Initially provided as a free-of-charge service, Ning moved to a full fee-paying business model in 2010, leaving many who had created social networks with the service with only two options: either to pay for continued use of the service, or to have their network shut down. Other services such as Groupsite have followed suit. Be aware that any free online social media service can switch to a fee-paying service at any time.

There is also the question of becoming 'friends' with some students and not with others: students might have legitimate grounds for complaint if they think that you are giving preferential treatment to certain class members simply because you are friends on Facebook. Another consideration is how much you want to expose your own Facebook profile to your students (and, indeed, how much you want to be exposed to your own students' affairs). Many people post quite personal information on Facebook and, as a teacher, you might regularly post information about yourself that you wouldn't want your students to see.

Further, some students and their parents or guardians may not wish their child to be a member of Facebook because they do not agree with the service's business and other practices, do not agree with Facebook's Terms of Service, or because of the potential for cyberbullying, privacy breaches, and the on-selling of data. In other words, it is their right *not* to have their child sign up for these services. And finally, using Facebook with your class will require everyone in your class to become members of Facebook and to agree to Facebook's Terms of Service and Privacy Policy, both of which seem to be the focus of frequent controversy, disgruntlement, and revision, as discussed above.

As with all digital tools and services, informed use is the only acceptable way to apply social media to your classroom environment.

Choosing a social networking service

When choosing a social networking service for use in your classroom, you should evaluate the service's Privacy Policy and Terms of Service to make sure that students' privacy, copyright, and intellectual property are protected. How to do this is covered in detail in Chapter 16. For the moment, however, let's look at some of the functional requirements you will need from your class-based social networking service. In tandem with the general checklist items for choosing a service that are listed in Chapter 2, use the guide below to help you choose a social network for your class or visit the *Using Social Media in the Classroom* companion website for the consolidated list.

- ☐ I can create bulk student accounts without using email addresses.
- ☐ I can make the entire network private if I want to.
- ☐ I can block users if needed.
- ☐ I can monitor and get notifications of changes and additions made to the network.
- ☐ I can delete discussion topics, posts, comments, and similar items if necessary.
- ☐ I can create groups and/or sub-groups.
- ☐ I can make groups either viewable or hidden from the rest of the class network, depending on need.

Using your network for online role plays

As already discussed, obvious pedagogies around communication are well supported by social networks. However, you don't have to limit yourself to sharing, discussions, wall comments, and the like. Social networks can be used in other ways, too. For example, online role plays can unfold quite nicely using the common tools found in a typical social network.

To run a role play using a social network, choose a contentious topic on which several different standpoints can be identified – for example genetically modified foods or climate change. Put students into groups representing different interest groups; in the case of genetically modified foods, you might have groups representing scientists, advocates, farmers, politicians, environmentalists, and sceptics. Once in their groups, students take on the standpoint typically adopted by members of their group in the 'real world'. The groups can discuss issues, strategies, policies, interventions, controversies – anything related to the topic – in their group space on the network. This space should be kept private (if possible), so that their 'strategising', in particular, is kept secret from other groups. Periodically, representatives from each group move into the 'public' space that the whole class can see, and they try to convince other groups of their perspective, negotiate a way through the problem, and so on.

Such role plays need not be limited to contemporary issues: history teachers, for example, could organise role plays where the groups represent various segments of medieval society or the major players in World War II, or art teachers could ask students to form groups around major artistic movements throughout history and then to discuss issues or individual art works from that movement's aesthetic. The trick is to be creative and to customise things to suit your own purposes.

Summary

- Social networks are typically either individual focused or group or topic based. Group- and topic-based networks are most appropriate for educational purposes.
- Communication, sharing, and connection are at the core of social networks, which makes them perfect for peer learning.
- Many students may already be familiar with social networks, but you need to give explicit instruction on how your class-based social network will support student learning.
- Social networks allow students to make connections outside the classroom, which can be very motivating to students as they gain access to present their work to parents, experts and others.
- Before embarking on any social networking project in your classroom, you need to carefully think through issues relating to privacy, cyberbullying, data collection, age of sign-up, and uploading contacts or address books.
- Facebook brings with it its own special set of concerns. Any use of Facebook in the classroom or with students needs to be thought through very carefully indeed.

Resources

Online resources

- Search 'Using social networks in class'. This search will uncover a huge number of websites, resources, and debates that you can use to inform your use of social networking in your classroom.
- Digizen.org has an excellent set of resources devoted to social networking services and young people, including reports, ideas, and activities.
- Mashable.com has a number of articles on social networking and children. Go to Mashable.com and search the site for 'safe social networks'.
- Visit the *Using Social Media in the Classroom* companion website for links, discussions, handouts, and other materials relating to using social networks for teaching and learning. You can find this at www.sagepub.co.uk/poore

Further reading

- Beach, R. and Doerr-Stevens, C. (2011) Using social networking for online role-plays to develop students' argumentative strategies, *Journal of Educational Computing Research*, 45(2), 165–81.
- Collin, P., Rahilly, K., Richardson, I. and Third, A. (2011) Benefits of social networking services. Cooperative Research Centre for Young People, Technology and Wellbeing, Melbourne.

Available at http://www.inspire.org.au/wp-content/uploads/2011/03/FINAL_The_Benefits_of_Social_Networking_Services_Lit_Review.pdf. Accessed 13 October 2011.

- De Zwart, M., Lindsay, D., Henderson, M. and Phillips. M. (2011) Teenagers, legal risks and social networking sites. Faculty of Education, Monash University, Melbourne. Available at http://newmediaresearch.educ.monash.edu.au/moodle/course/view.php?id=37. Accessed 13 October 2011.
- Moayeri, M. (2010) Classroom uses of social network sites: traditional practices or new literacies? *Digital Culture & Education,* 2(1), 25–43. Available at http://www.digitalcultureandeducation.com/uncategorized/dce1029_moayeri_refs_2010/. Accessed 2 September 2011.
- Sieber, D. E. (2010) Teaching with social networks: establishing a social contract. ECAR Research Bulletin 10. Boulder, CO: EDUCAUSE Center for Applied Research. Available at http://www.educause.edu/ecar. Accessed 2 September 2011.
- Waddington, J. (2011) Social networking: the unharnessed educational tool, *Undergraduate Research Journal at UCCS,* 4(1), May. Available at http://ojs.uccs.edu/index.php/urj/article/viewArticle/113. Accessed 2 September 2011.

CHAPTER 7

PODCASTING, MUSIC, AND AUDIO

Overview

Podcasting has become hugely popular amongst internet users, not least because of the rise of personal digital media players such as the iPod. As opposed to broadcasting in the traditional media sense (where large organisations transmit content that is likely to appeal to a mass audience) podcasting allows anyone with a bit of technical know-how and access to the internet to 'narrowcast' material on niche topics. This means that you and your class can set up your own podcast on any topic you like and distribute it to a digital-listening audience.

Podcasting is a large and detailed topic and one that can fill whole books. This chapter, therefore, does not provide you with a technical, step-by-step, how-to guide to podcasting because there are plenty of excellent guides freely available on the web for this (see Resources, this chapter, for suggestions). Instead, the purpose here is to give you an overview of podcasting, its educational merits, and the broad conceptual and technical issues you will need to consider when embarking on a podcasting project with your class.

In particular, we look at precisely what *is* podcasting, the equipment you will need, and the pedagogies that podcasting best supports. Much of the chapter is dedicated to special considerations for podcasting, such as how to conceptualise and develop a format for your podcast, scripting your podcast, conducting interviews, editing and publishing your podcast, and accounting for potential legal issues.

What is a podcast?

The term 'podcast' is used to describe a number of different things, as discussed below.

> ### Video clip. Podcasting in Plain English
>
> CommonCraft's video 'Podcasting in Plain English' can be viewed on YouTube (search 'Podcasting in Plain English').

Clarifying terms

A podcast is commonly understood to mean 'online audio' that can be either streamed (that is, listened to in real time, on your computer), downloaded, or subscribed to via an RSS feed (see Chapter 3). Technically speaking, however, a podcast as properly appreciated really only embraces the last of these forms, that is, a podcast is an ongoing 'radio' show or programme that releases regular 'episodes' that listeners subscribe to via a feed.

Many people subscribe to podcasts using a 'podcatcher' such as iTunes or Juice Receiver, which automatically downloads the latest episodes as soon as they are released. Sites such as PodcatcherMatrix.org will help you compare the functionality of different podcatching software. Once downloaded, you can listen to podcast episodes on your computer or sync them to your MP3 player.

Podcasts can be on any topic – from water politics to ceramic art to gardening – and can be found in podcast directories such as PodcastDirectory. com, PodcastAlley.com, Podbean.com (which will also publish and host your podcast), and, of course, iTunes.

Podcasting equipment

To make a podcast, you will need:

- *Recording equipment*. This might be in the form of a laptop computer or digital voice recorder, or even a smartphone that has voice recording capability. Regardless of the type of device you use, you need to make sure that it has a fairly large recording capacity and/or memory because audio files can be quite large.
- *Microphones*. There may already be a microphone in your laptop or other device; if not, you will have to purchase microphones separately. With microphones you get what you pay for. Most laptops these days have microphones that will be adequate for your purpose, but if your class gets serious about podcasting, then you might want to invest in a condenser microphone, which will improve the sound quality of your podcast considerably. Nothing puts listeners off more than poor quality sound.
- *A computer with audio editing software*. Many, if not most, podcasters edit their audio files using 'Audacity' (search 'Audacity Sourceforge'), which is a free, downloadable sound editor for both Mac and PC. If you are a Mac user, though, you might prefer to use Garageband, which is often pre-loaded onto Macintosh computers. Alternatively, you might want to pay for professional audio editing software such as Adobe Audition or Apple's Final Cut – but these are expensive. Your computer should have a good amount of memory available for editing your project.
- *Headphones*. These are especially used in the editing stage of podcast production. Ideally, you should have headphones that cover the whole ear or that sit on the ear as these types of headphones allow you to listen for irritating background noises that might need to be edited out. Ear buds will work at a pinch, but they are not ideal.
- *A place to host your podcast*. Audio files typically take up a lot of disc space and use a lot of bandwidth (that is, the amount of data that can be transferred through a web server at any one time) so you need to find a site or service that can handle the transfer of large files. Many people host their podcasts on their blog or on a podcast hosting service such as PodBean.com.
- *A way of distributing your podcast*. This may be done either via the blog or podcast hosting service options described above, or in a podcast directory, the most popular of which is iTunes.

Although it might sound as though you need to be a technological whizz to get started with podcasting, that is certainly not the case. All you need is some basic computer competence, a bit of patience, and some problem-solving skills and you can create an informative, fun, and ongoing podcast with your students.

Educational benefits of podcasting

Pedagogy

Although individuals can and do make podcasts on their own, educational podcasting can be highly effective in promoting collaborative, socially con-structivist learning environments where students build and share knowledge and/or opinion. Podcasting also provides exceptional opportunities for peer learning, not least because creating this form of social media invariably throws up technical hitches, especially in the early days of learning how to create, edit, and publish digital audio. Students must work together to identify and solve problems through processes of analysis and negotiation.

Development of a broad range of skills

Podcasting projects are normally large and ongoing, and provide the perfect opportunity for you to teach students a wide variety of skills, including:

- *Technical skills*. Students learn how to record, edit, and distribute digital audio.
- *Project management skills*. This includes developing a project goal; creating an overall plan; and scheduling time for research, technical production, interviews, recording, editing, publication, and legal 'clearances' (see below).
- *Social skills*. Podcasting involves a good deal of teamwork and collabora-tion if the project is to be successful.
- *Communication skills*. Students must learn how best to get their point across to a listening audience.
- *Intellectual skills*. Putting together a coherent, focused digital audio show challenges students to create an engaging experience for listeners.

Research

The amount of research required to put together a successful podcast episode should not be underestimated. Podcasting is perfect for asking students to identify a problem and to find a way of answering it. They might choose to conduct interviews, in which case students need to investigate a topic, find an expert in the field, and develop a list of questions to ask. If students decide to create a mini-documentary, then they need to conduct their background research and work it into an intelligible script that integrates what they've learnt and what they want to communicate.

Podcasting projects for your class

There is really no limit to what you can podcast once you have decided to get a podcasting project going with your class. Below are some suggestions for the kinds of approach you might take to podcasting with your class.

> ### Ideas. Be inspired!
>
> - *Radio WillowWeb*. Radio WillowWeb (search 'Radio WillowWeb Willowdale Elementary'). Produced by the students and teachers at Willowdale Elementary School, featuring classes from K–5.
> - Check out Radiowaves.co.uk for schoolsafe podcasts from around the world.

Informational podcasts

Because podcasting is an excellent medium for distributing information, many teachers ask their students to podcast in key curriculum areas. For example, if your class is learning about the solar system, then different teams of students can be assigned to research and podcast various elements of the solar system as separate podcast episodes. You might have episodes that explore individually each of the planets, an episode on orbits and gravity, an episode on exploration, an episode on the sun, and an episode on asteroids. If you are teaching Roman history, then there is the potential for separate episodes on various aspects of Roman society: the Republic, emperors, democracy, slavery, everyday life, Pompeii, the legions, and so on.

Opinion- or ideas-based podcasts

You class podcast doesn't have to be solely informational, however. The podcasting medium is perfect for exploring opinion and diverse points of view on a topic, especially through interviews and expert panels. A good way to explore such opinions is to develop a framing question for individual episodes. For example, if your class is studying soil science, then you might devote one episode to the question of 'Is compost better than chemical fertiliser?' or 'To what extent is soil salinity caused by humans?' These approaches are still curriculum focused, it's just that the angle into the subject matter is centred on critique and debate as opposed to the construction of a factual knowledge base.

Of course, with opinion-based podcasting, you want to avoid topics that could lead to hateful, defamatory, or otherwise offensive comments, so do think carefully about the direction that any interviews or panel discussions might take.

Special considerations

Entering on a podcasting project with your students is no small matter. First, there are the technical issues you must get across (such as recording, editing, and publishing). But there are also conceptual and legal considerations to take into account.

Conceptualising your podcast

It is important that you spend some time pondering the general approach your podcast will take towards its subject matter. Ask your students to consider some of the following:

- What is the main focus of the podcast? Will you have a broad focus that covers all areas of the curriculum, or will you narrow the focus to more in-depth coverage of a single topic?
- What are the aims of the podcast? To inform? Entertain? Raise awareness? Share discoveries? To create a sense of community? Write down three or four aims – be explicit and use active verbs. You might even consider developing a podcast mission statement.
- Who is your audience? Other students? Parents? Anyone in the world? What sort of audience numbers do you anticipate? How much demand or competition do you expect to encounter? And will that matter?
- What are the ground rules for your podcast? Are there topics that you will avoid? What sort of language is appropriate? What sort of material is out of bounds?

Once you have agreement on your overall concept, it's time to decide upon the best format for realising your ambitions.

Developing a format for your podcast

Podcasting provides you with a wide variety of formats in which to present your content. You may decide to 'mix and match' or choose just one method of presentation. Here are some of the most common:

- Interviews
- Tips and advice segments

- Information segments
- Vox pops
- Hosted panel discussions
- Mini-documentaries
- Musical interludes, intros and outros
- Class report.

The complexity of your format will depend on what you are trying to achieve. For example, you may simply want to present a feature interview that involves a student host, a guest, and some intro and outro music. Alternatively, you might create something more involved, including a feature interview, a vox pop, a tips segment, some music, and a class report all joined together by a couple of student hosts. Regardless, you need to have access to, and regularly publish, fresh content.

You also need to think about the length of your podcast episodes. Although podcasts can be any length (with some even rambling over into the two- and three-hour marks!), this won't be the case for your in-class project. In general, aim for shorter rather than lengthier podcasts. For a 'tips' style podcast, three to four minutes is usually plenty of time to get across your key points; for a feature interview, limit the discussion to 10 to 12 minutes.

A final format decision needs to be made around how regularly to publish your podcast. Will you be able to manage a weekly publication roster over a certain period, or would fortnightly releases be more realistic? Whatever you decide, it's important to keep to schedule and to publish your podcast episodes regularly.

Scripting your podcast

Scripting, planning, or outlining each podcast episode will ensure that you have a clear idea of what will be in the podcast episode. For interviews, it is essential that students develop an interview schedule, that is, a list of questions or key points that they will be presenting to guests. For more complex podcast structures students will need to create a detailed script or running sheet that includes inserts, effects, and cues. See Table 7.1 for an example of how you might script a podcast episode.

As you can see, the format of a podcast episode can be quite complex, but also very exciting. Choose something that works for you.

Doing interviews for your podcast

As part of their chosen podcasting format, many podcasters record interviews with subject experts. Conducting interviews takes time, but it provides you with the opportunity to teach students a variety of skills, techniques, and competencies, including:

Table 7.1   Sample podcast episode script

Item	Hosts	Content
THEME INTRO: Funky track 1		
Welcome and introduction	Alisha	Welcome to Our Brilliant Class Podcast. My name is Alisha and I am your co-host, along with Archie. Hello, Archie. What is today's show about?
Overview	Archie	Hi, Alisha. Today's show is all about the planet Jupiter. We have some tips and advice for viewing the planet Jupiter in the night sky this week and we interview Dr Pat Smith from the Astronomical Society about what it's like to be an astronomer.
INSERT GRAB FROM INTERVIEW WITH DR SMITH		
	Alisha	We've also got our fellow students who tell us what they think is the most interesting thing about Jupiter. It's going to be a great programme, Archie!
Intro to Classroom Report	Archie	It sure is Alisha! But first, here is our regular segment, our Classroom Report from our teacher, Ms Brown.
INSERT CLASSROOM REPORT INTRO THEME MUSIC: Funky track 2		
INSERT CLASSROOM REPORT PRE-RECORD		
INSERT CLASSROOM REPORT BACK-ANNOUNCE MUSIC: Funky track 2		
Back-announce	Alisha	That was our teacher, Ms Brown, with our regular Classroom Report.
	Archie	Thanks, Ms Brown. We have really learnt a lot this week.
Intro to Class Tip	Alisha	And now we will hear from Priya, who has a Class Tip on how to keep track of your timetable.
INSERT CLASS TIP THEME MUSIC: Jazz track 1		
INSERT CLASS TIP PRE-RECORD		
INSERT CLASS TIP BACK-ANNOUNCE MUSIC: Jazz track 1		
Back-announce	Archie	Thanks to Priya for that very useful tip. I'm sure we've learnt a lot from you.
Intro to Vox Pop	Alisha	This week, we asked our classmates what they thought about the new-look Principal's Blog. Here's what they had to say in our regular Vox Pop segment.
INSERT VOX POP MUSIC: Techno track 1		
INSERT VOX POP PRE-RECORD		
INSERT VOX POP BACK-ANNOUNCE MUSIC: Techno track 1		
Back-announce	Alisha	It was really interesting hearing what our class had to say about the Principal's Blog. It seems that they really like it.
Intro to Feature Interview	Archie	Yes, there were some good comments there, Alisha. Well, now we're going to play our feature interview for this episode. This term, our class has been learning about the solar system, so we asked Dr Smith, an astronomer from the Astronomical Society, to talk to us about his work on the planet Jupiter. Here is Dr Smith talking to Michael.
INSERT FEATURE INTERVIEW THEME MUSIC: Classical track 1		
INSERT FEATURE INTERVIEW		
INSERT FEATURE INTERVIEW BACK-ANNOUNCE MUSIC: Classical track 1		
Back-announce	Alisha	That was Dr Smith talking to Michael. I think we all know a lot more about Jupiter now thanks to that interesting interview.
	Archie	Yes, and thank you to Dr Smith for taking the time to talk to our class.
Wrap-up	Alisha	Well, that's all we have time for today. Thank you to everyone who contributed to our podcast, and especially to our production team of Anthea, Hui Yin, and Jonah. You've done a great job!
	Archie	Yes you have, team! Thanks so much. And don't forget to stream or download our next episode in two weeks' time, or subscribe to our podcast by visiting our class blog. Bye for now!
OUTRO MUSIC: Funky track 3 + credits		

- Deciding upon an interview topic
- Researching the topic
- Sourcing a potential interviewee
- Contacting them and requesting an interview
- Explaining the purpose of the interview
- Organising a time and place to conduct the interview
- Writing up an interview schedule
- Conducting the interview
- Sending a note of thanks.

It's important that, when planning an interview and writing up an interview schedule, students think about how much time they've got to conduct the interview and *not* how many questions or points they want to cover. In podcasting, keeping to time is crucial, as there is the potential for the conversation to deviate significantly from the key focus; when this happens, you then have to go back and edit out the unrelated or irrelevant material, which can be very time-consuming. It is always best to record a 'clean' first take, that is, to make a recording without pauses or mistakes, as it means you have much less editing to do later.

It is good form to provide your interviewee with a copy of the interview schedule or the list of questions that you hope to ask them, just so they know what to focus on during the discussion – but you should discourage people from preparing fully scripted answers beforehand, as audiences can always recognise when someone is reading something out. You should also tell your guest a little bit about the recording process (that is, that you can edit out anything they're not happy with), the length of the interview, expectations around sticking to time and any 'wind up' signals that you will use to indicate that you need either to move on or to finish the interview.

 You might also need to consider whether or not you need to get a 'release' from your interviewee, in other words permission to use their contribution on your podcast. See the podcast pages on the *Using Social Media in the Classroom* website for examples of such releases and for forms that you can modify to suit your own situation.

> If you have an ongoing, regularly published podcast, then it is a good idea always to have a few episodes 'in the bag', that is, episodes that are completed and ready for distribution at a moment's notice. If something unforeseen happens and interrupts your recording timetable (for example, an interviewee suddenly becomes unavailable), you can always release an already completed episode, thus maintaining your publishing schedule.

Recording locations

Regardless of how you do your actual recording – for example via a digital voice recorder or straight into your computer – you will need a suitable location for recording your podcast. Of course a quiet location that absorbs noise (so that it doesn't sound like you are recording in a tunnel) is essential. Ambient sound, such as café noises or schoolyard noises, can add to the appeal of your recording but there is a fine line between charming background sound and noise that is distracting for the listener.

In most instances, though, you will have the one, set place for recording, such as a quiet corner of your classroom. The advantages of having such a place are that it is quick and easy to set up and that you can more easily control the ambient noise. If students do 'go into the field' to record, they should find a quiet spot where they can avoid interruptions. They also need to test, re-test, and test again their recording equipment before doing field recordings – they need to know exactly how it works and how to troubleshoot any technical difficulties that might occur.

Finally, and once you have your recording, it is essential that you immediately create a backup of it and place that backup on another device.

Editing your podcast

Once you have made your recording you need to transfer your original audio file to your computer for editing. (Of course, if you have made the recording directly on your computer, you do not need to do that!) I recommend that you keep your original file somewhere safe and that you edit from a copy. Your next step is to open your file copy in your audio editing software – for example,

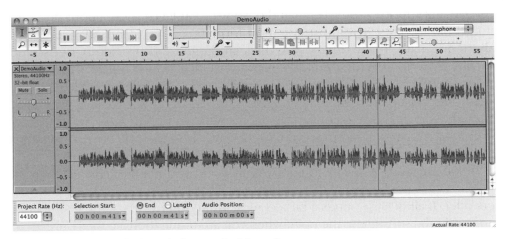

Figure 7.1 Digital audio in Audacity sound editing software

in Audacity. When you do so, you'll see a whole bunch of spiky up-and-down lines; this represents the sound you have recorded (see Figure 7.1).

If you press 'play' in your audio editing software, you will be able to hear the recording you made. You can edit this recording by highlighting certain sections and manipulating them. For example, you can delete whole sections of the audio, amplify quieter bits, insert silences, add effects, fade in or out, and accomplish many other feats of digital modification to your recording. It is prudent to save your work regularly during the editing process.

Dos and Don'ts. Make sure you are using copyright- and royalty-free music

It is easy to assume that all music hosted on a 'podsafe' music network such as Music Alley is copyright free and royalty free by default. It is not. I made exactly this mistake when working on my own educational podcasting project. I had put together three whole, very complicated episodes (as I wanted to be ahead of my publishing schedule and to have a couple of episodes 'in the bag') when on the day before release of the first episode, I realised that I hadn't read the terms of use properly for each individual track I wanted to include – and some tracks required copyright clearance from the owner! I then had to spend many hours scrabbling to find new, copyright- and royalty-free tracks before re-editing all three episodes so that they were not in breach. Don't make this same mistake yourself!

File formats

As you learn more about digital audio, so will you learn more about different audio file formats. The most common formats are WAV and MP3, although there are many, many others. WAV files are larger and provide better sound quality than do MP3 files; but MP3 files are smaller, which means that it is the preferred format for loading on to mobile and other digital devices. Some recording set-ups record straight to MP3; if your recorder records WAV files, though, you will have to convert the larger WAV file to MP3 later on – listeners don't want to download massive files in WAV when the MP3 format provides acceptable-to-good sound quality in a much-reduced file size.

If you are using Audacity to edit WAV files and you need to convert them to MP3, you will not be able to do so unless you download and install the LAME MP3 encoder. If all of this sounds a bit technical, then don't worry – the instructions appear in the software at the point when you are trying to make the conversion.

Choosing music for your podcast

If you want to make your podcast a bit more stimulating for listeners, you will probably want to add some music, as music can break things up a bit, add variety, and contribute to the auditory diversity of your work. But you cannot use just any piece of music you want, for in doing so you might be in breach of copyright. To ensure that you are using copyright- and royalty-free music, select music from 'podsafe' networks such as MusicAlley.com (search 'MusicAlley') or PodsafeAudio.com (search 'PodsafeAudio'). Music uploaded to such services is usually released under some form of Creative Commons licence (see Chapter 16 for more information) which means that artists will allow you to use their music under certain conditions, for example, as long as it's used for non-commercial purposes and as long as you provide attribution for their work. This can be done in a 'back announce' or at the end of the podcast in the credits for the episode. Do not, however, assume that all pieces of music on such networks are released entirely and automatically under Creative Commons – be sure to fully read and comply with any conditions of use associated with each individual track.

Speaking frankly, there is a lot of 'podsafe' music out there that is not very good. Be prepared for you and your class to spend quite some time listening to a lot of poor music before finding the tracks that you consider are good enough for your podcast. Account for this in your project's time management plan.

Publishing your podcast

Once you have an audio file that you have edited, saved, and that is ready to distribute, you will need to publish it somewhere on the web. The key thing is that your podcast (that is, your whole audio series, not just your individual files) has an RSS feed (see Chapter 3 for more on RSS). If you publish your podcast on your class blog, then it will automatically have a feed attached to it (because blogs come automatically with feeds). If you publish your podcast in a podcast directory such as PodBean.com, you will be provided with a feed. It is now a simple case of uploading your latest podcast episode file to your blog or other site. As soon as it is uploaded or 'published', those listeners who have subscribed to your podcast will be able to automatically download the latest episode using their podcatcher. Consider publishing your podcast in various places (such as in iTunes, PodBean, Radiowaves.co.uk, or PodcastPickle) for wide exposure.

Podcasting legal issues

Although it is unlikely that you will encounter legal difficulties because of something someone said in a student interview or because of anything untoward that might happen as a result of material contained in your students' podcast, it is nevertheless prudent to risk manage your project for potential problems in this area. In particular, you should seek indemnities against legal action for any injury, loss, or damage that might be suffered by interviewees or by podcast participants in the course of the podcast's production and distribution. This isn't nearly as awful as it sounds, as all it means is that you ask your participants (or their parents or their legal guardians) to sign a release form that indemnifies your school against legal action. See the podcasting pages of the *Using Social Media in the Classroom* companion website for an example of an indemnity form.

Related to this is the need to get people's permission to be recorded and to have that recording distributed in digital format. As with an indemnity, it is good to get your podcast participants to sign a form giving their permission to be recorded before the actual recording begins. Some podcasters set their recording device going and then ask their interviewees something like, 'Do you give your permission to be recorded and have the recording distributed on the internet?' This provides some 'backup' to a signed form in that you also have a recorded statement from the participants on the original, unedited audio file that can be referred to later, if necessary. So, to this end, always keep your original, unedited file!

Other issues to be aware of – and to discuss with your students *before* podcasting – are those around libel and slander, breaches of privacy and confidentiality, use of copyright materials, and intellectual property. Some of these topics are explored in more detail in Chapter 16.

 ### Activity. Buy lunch for a podcaster

Podcasters love talking about podcasting, so the quickest way to get started with your own project is to find a friend, friend of a friend, colleague, or acquaintance who has experience in the area. Offer to buy them lunch and, over the space of an hour or two, learn everything you can about how they go about their podcasting projects. Ask them things such as:

- Why did you decide to do a podcast?
- How did you get started?
- What is your planning process?
- What is the format of your podcast? Do you host the show yourself entirely, or do you do interviews or something else?

- How often do you publish a new episode?
- What does your audience expect in terms of frequency of publication, sound quality, content, variety, and such like?
- Do you write up and stick to a script, or are things much more free-flowing than that?
- What kind of equipment do you use? For recording? For editing? What about microphones and headphones?
- Where do you record? What problems have you encountered with recording?
- Do you use Audacity, Garageband, or something else for editing?
- How much time does it all take – realistically?
- What do I need to watch out for in the early days?
- How do you publish, advertise and distribute your podcast? Via your blog or website? Via a hosting service such as iTunes, Radiowaves.co.uk, or PodBean?
- What problems did you come up against?
- How do you deal with copyright (your own and others')? How do you find music to use?
- Are there any traps to be aware of (perhaps time, money, technical)?
- What things would you do differently or better if you could?

Make sure to take lots of notes, and don't be afraid of asking for further help and advice as you get your own class podcast underway.

 Activity. Learn by doing ... with your class

Treat podcasting as a whole-of-class learning project: let students guide you as much as you guide them as you learn about the technicalities of creating online audio.

Step 1. Decide upon your podcast concept. Review the points under 'Conceptualising your podcast' and 'Developing a format' in the 'Special considerations' section found earlier in this chapter. Brainstorm the following, either as a class as a whole, or in small groups:

- What should the focus or main concept of our podcast be?
- What is the main aim of our podcast?
- What kind of content would we produce?
- Who will our audience be?
- What are our ground rules?
- What format(s) should we use?
- How often would we publish?

Discuss the ideas that are generated and make some decisions. Write them up.

(Continued)

(Continued)

Step 2. Decide upon some technical basics. Consider your technical resources and expertise and how you will make your podcast happen. Get (older) students to organise themselves into groups to research the best way of achieving the following:

- What recording equipment will we need?
- What editing software should we use?
- How will we get an RSS feed so that people can subscribe to our podcast?
- Where will we publish our podcast?
- What services will we use to further distribute our podcast?
- How and where will we advertise our podcast?

You might use some of the sites and services recommended earlier and in the Resources section of this chapter to get students under way.

Step 3. Make your first podcast episode. Break the work (and the students) up into different areas and get the class working in teams on things such as:

- Outlining and scripting the episode
- Background research
- Logistics (such as organising interviews, booking recording space, scheduling editing time, and so on)
- Hosting the show, conducting interviews
- Recording the show
- Editing the show
- Finding and 'clearing' music (that is, for copyright – older students can certainly do this under your supervision)
- Publication, advertising, and distribution.

Switch the jobs around for the second and subsequent episodes so that students get experience in all areas of podcast production. Whatever you do, just get started.

 Summary

- A podcast is an ongoing digital audio programme that releases regular 'episodes' that listeners subscribe to via a feed.
- To make a podcast, you will need recording equipment, microphones, editing software, a host site, and a way of distributing your podcast (usually via an RSS feed).

- Podcasting helps students develop a wide variety of skills, including technical, social, communication, intellectual, and project management.
- Podcasts can take on a variety of formats. Be sure to think carefully about the format that best suits your class's podcasting aims.
- Podcasting projects are usually long-term and fairly complicated. You and your students will need to conceptualise and develop a format for your podcast; conduct research and interviews; write scripts; record, compile, and edit your podcast; and, publish your podcast on the internet.
- Make sure you have permission from interviewees and music copyright holders to distribute their recordings on the internet.

Resources

People

- Find someone who already has experience with podcasting. Their help and advice will be invaluable.
- Use your students as 'problem-solving assistants'. You are all in this together, so take the time to learn from each other.

Examples of podcasting in education

- Radiowaves.co.uk has lots of examples of educational podcasting across different class levels and provides 'Safe school podcasting, video and blogs for young people to report on their world', according to their website.
- Radio WillowWeb (search 'Radio WillowWeb Willowdale Elementary') is produced by the students and teachers at Willowdale Elementary School, features classes from K–5, and is available on iTunes.

Information on how to podcast

- Search 'How to create a podcast'. You will find numerous step-by-step guides to get you started. Don't neglect some of the older guides such as that published by PeachPit (search 'PeachPit podcasting'), as many of the principles of podcasting (choosing a format, interview basics, and even equipment fundamentals) are the same as they were in 2006.
- PoducateMe.com provides 'practical solutions for podcasting in education' and is one of the most comprehensive 'how to' sites on the web, taking you through everything from the history of podcasting, to system considerations, to show prep, to splicing audio.
- Tony Vincent, of Learning in Hand, has some podcasting resources that are worth looking at, including a podcasting booklet. Search 'Learning in Hand podcasting'.

Technical resources

- Audacity is a free, cross-platform (Windows, Mac, Linux/Unix) audio software for recording, editing, and mixing, and is popular amongst podcasters. Search 'Audacity Sourceforge'.
- Feedburner.com is owned by Google and will generate a free RSS feed for you if you do not already have a feed associated with your podcasting site. There are other RSS generators out there (search 'RSS feed generator'), but some require a fee to be paid.

Legals and podsafe music

- MusicAlley.com and PodsafeAudio.com host music that you can use under certain terms and conditions for your podcast. Just be sure to comply with those terms and conditions, however.
- CreativeCommons.org explains the various 'CC' licences that can be used to distribute creative works on the internet.
- Visit the podcast pages on the *Using Social Media in the Classroom* companion website for sample indemnity forms and releases. You can find this at www.sagepub.co.uk/poore

Publishing and advertising

- Radiowaves.co.uk, PodBean.com, PodcastPickle.com, and PodcastDirectory.com all allow you to publish and advertise your podcast for free.
- iTunes will also distribute your podcast. Search 'iTunes making a podcast' to learn more about how to submit your podcast to iTunes.

Further reading

- Mathison, C. and Billings, E. (2010) The effect of primary language podcasts on third grade English language learners' performance in English-only science education contexts, *Electronic Journal of Literacy Through Science*, 9, 1–30.
- Shamburg, C. (2009) *Student-Powered Podcasting. Teaching for 21st Century Literacy*. Washington, DC: International Society for Technology in Education (ISTE).
- Smythe, S. and Neufeld, P. (2010) 'Podcast Time': negotiating digital literacies and communities of learning in a middle years ELL classroom, *Journal of Adolescent & Adult Literacy*, 53(6), 488 –96.

PART 3

ENRICHING YOUR PRACTICE

This part concentrates on the smaller, more nimble – though no less effective – tools and services that teachers can use in class. Many, though not all, of these tools and services are more suited to short-term learning activities and can give you one or two 'quick wins' when using social media with your students. The chapter structure of this part of the book follows that in Part 2 and covers visual media (Chapter 8); instant messaging, chat, Skype, and Twitter (Chapter 9); bookmarking, clippings, mindmapping, and polls (Chapter 10); educational games and mobile learning (Chapter 11); and productivity tools (Chapter 12).

CHAPTER 8

VISUAL MEDIA

Overview

There are many social media services that allow you to upload and share visual materials, and there are even services that allow you to create and edit such materials directly online without having to install special software on your desktop computer. The focus of this chapter is on how to use social media sites to share and distribute videos, slideshows, and photos, and also on how to create your own comic strips and animations online. We explore story-telling and knowledge-sharing and how they benefit visual learning. Duty of care issues around inappropriate content, comment control, and the posting of images of children are examined, and legal considerations (including those relating to copyright and Terms of Service) are investigated. We also consider more practical issues to do with platform compatibility and bandwidth requirements.

It is important to note, here, that video is treated as 'video sharing' rather than as 'creating video'; however, readers are encouraged to look at some of the many excellent online sites (search 'How to make a video') on how to make a video.

What are visual media?

There are many different types of visual media available to you that can enrich your practice. This section describes some of the most common forms.

Photosharing

Photosharing sites allow you to upload, store, edit, and organise your photos on the internet. Services such as Flickr and Photobucket are probably the most popular and well-known, but there are many others. One of the crucial elements of photosharing is tagging: once you have uploaded your photos to a photosharing service, you can tag them up with keywords that identify the subject matter of the photo and that allow others in the community to locate your images. This, in turn, supports another important feature of such services,

---

Ideas. Photosharing ideas

- Ask students to write, build, and share individual **portfolios** or **creative stories** using photos.
- Break the class up into small groups and ask each to produce a **group album** on a particular class theme. Ask them to present their album to the rest of the class as part of an oral presentation assignment.
- Ask students to edit their photos and **explain their editorial choices**.
- Ask students to find or post a **picture of the week** that encapsulates for them a class topic or theme. Get them to explain their choice in relation to key concepts for the course or topic.
- Get students to create slideshows of photos that reflect particular elements of course or syllabus themes. Ask them to **present their slideshow in class** and to demonstrate the links they've made with course content.
- **Explore issues of intellectual property and copyright** with students. Tell them to research the different Creative Commons licences that images can be distributed under.
- Use photosharing to teach students the importance of copyright **and how to source copyright- and royalty-free images**.
- Photosharing can also be used to **teach students about the assumptions we make about others**. For example, get students to visit photos tagged 'glitter' or 'bmx'. Ask them to reflect on the immediate assumptions they make about the person who posted the photo: their age, gender, ethnicity, other interests, and so on. Use this as a prompt for in-class or discussion group conversations about identity, stereotypes, self-representation, and the like.

and that is sharing. As with most social media, communities develop around the objects that are created or uploaded to the internet and people can then comment on those objects.

You can organise your photos by creating collections, sets, or albums for others to view, writing notes that describe the photo and 'geotagging' (that is, adding your photo to a map) to show people where the photo was taken.

The more advanced services also allow you to edit your photos directly on the web (without having to download and install specialist software on a desktop computer) and you can create cards, books, prints, and even DVDs of your pictures. Further, you can make slideshows and create 'mashups' (a combination of different media) of photos with music, special effects, and captions.

As with most social media, privacy controls allow you to select who can and cannot view your pictures.

Slideshows

Slideshow services such as Slideshare.net and Prezi.com allow you to create a presentation, or to upload a presentation you have already created, and to display it online. This is normally done when the service converts your original PowerPoint, Keynote, PDF, or other file into a flash-type 'movie' that can be clicked through bit by bit. Once you have uploaded your presentation, you can tag it up with keywords, make it public or private, and allow sharing or downloading. People can typically follow you and 'like' or comment on your presentation. Depending on which service you are using, you can create or add an audio voice-over for your presentation, either using the service itself, or by uploading an accompanying MP3 file. You can also generate an embed code for your presentation, allowing you to show your slideshow in your blog, wiki, or other site.

Video and videosharing

Sites such as YouTube, Vimeo, and Blip.tv are all about uploading videos for sharing online (most photosharing sites will also host video). Where the two differ, though, is in the use that members make of the service: some users of photosharing sites merely want to store and organise their photo collections without necessarily sharing them amongst a broader audience; but for users of videosharing services, the distribution of video is the dominant motivation – the more 'views' or hits per video, the better. Videosharing encourages you to vote for, rate or 'like' the videos that you watch, and to comment on them, although you can normally disable these functions if you want to. With the larger services, such as YouTube, you can also create your own channel (which others can subscribe to) to host your videos and your playlists of related content, and you can even edit your video and add music to it directly on the service's website. Most videosharing services will automatically generate an embed code (see Chapter 3) for each video you upload, allowing you and others to display the video in your blog, wiki, or other class site.

There are usually privacy controls on videosharing sites, but these can sometimes be limited, as the whole aim of videosharing is that videos be viewed by as many people as possible.

Animation

You don't need to be a highly trained digital artist to make your own animated videos. Animation services abound on the internet and they vary from providing basic stick-figure and simple cartoon creators such as DoInk to powerful, full-length three-dimensional (3D) movie makers such as Blender, Xtranormal, and Muvizu. In the case of cartoon-type services you create your cartoon by either using stock images or by uploading images or photographs of your own for assembling online.

Digital animation services, however, tend to work in either of two ways. Your first option is to download the animation software to your desktop and create your animation on your computer before uploading it for sharing on the service's main site. Services such as Blender, Muvizu, and Xtranormal's 'State' software all work on this principle. Your second option is to create and publish your animation using the software provided by the service directly on the internet. Generally speaking, this option will produce less sophisticated results than the first, but it has the advantage of not needing to download and install software on your own machine or on computers in a school laboratory – you simply access the service via the web. Services that allow you to create and publish your animations directly on the internet include GoAnimate, Xtranormal, Devolver, and the Zimmer Twins (for younger viewers). Either way, these services allow you to write and animate your own scripts by dragging and dropping stock characters, languages, sets, and music (all of which, when taken together, are called 'assets').

Comic strips

Still (that is, 'not moving') comics can also be made using sites such as MakeBeliefComix, Stripgenerator, the Superhero Squad (from Marvel Comics), Pixton, and ToonDoo. As with the online digital animation services described above, you choose from a stock set of characters and sets, type in your text, and publish your strip directly online – there is no need to download any software.

Educational benefits of visual media

Peer learning and collaboration

Although they can easily undertake individual projects in this area, students can also benefit greatly in working together as peer learners on collaborative project work in which they co-create visual objects for sharing online. The construction and presentation of shared understandings can be a very powerful pedagogy, especially when students publish their work for a wider audience.

Creating narratives and audience awareness

Photosharing, slideshows, and animation all provide creative ways for students to generate narratives and stories around class topics (video *creation* – not covered in this book – serves the same purpose, whereas video*sharing* is rather more didactic in nature). Photographs can be collected and presented as photoessays, especially when students take advantage of a photosharing service's 'slideshow' or 'mashup' capabilities to rearrange images, and to add text, overlays, and music to their creations. In creating an animation, students must develop some form of script to begin with, so the structuring of action and, usually, dialogue to propel a story forwards become central to the task. Aside from structure and design, both formats also require consideration of audience needs and expectations if the narrative is to succeed.

Multiple literacies

Perhaps, most obviously, these forms of rich media support visual learning and provide another format for presenting and sharing materials amongst your class. But these kinds of media also encourage students to create, structure, 'read', interrogate, and critique visual texts in general – all of which helps them develop and strengthen not only their visual, but also their functional, traditional, as well as media, literacies.

Special considerations for visual media

Inappropriate content

Services that support visual digital media can often host – inadvertently or otherwise – material that is inappropriate for younger people to view: pornography and violence are the most obvious offenders. Some services are deliberately marketed at users who fall into the older age-ranges, but others are quite happily directed at smaller children. Be sure to thoroughly research any visual media service you are considering using in your classroom: check it for advertising (soft porn often features in adverts on less reputable services), for the types of videos or images or animations that are published on the site, and for the type of audience that it generally attracts. If you can find a 'kidsafe' service, then so much the better.

Posting images of children

This is not such a problem when dealing with animations and comic strips or when you are simply sourcing and sharing others' photos and videos amongst your class. But it is something that you need to address if you choose to use photos or videos of the children that you teach. Parents should be notified of your intention to use photos or videos that your students have taken or created, they should be told how those images will be used, and they should be informed of your procedures for preventing personal details about their children being posted on the internet (see Chapters 16 and 17). If necessary, seek and receive parental consent for your photo or video project before proceeding. In the end, it should be simple enough to understand that, as a teacher who is using social media in the classroom, your students should *never* be identified or identifiable via work that you ask them to post online. See Chapter 16 for more on understanding risk and Chapter 17 on practical considerations you need to make in this area.

Comments

Sites that host or allow you to create and publish visual media normally encourage users to comment on the objects that have been posted. Smaller services, and those that are pitched at a more specialised audience (such as Vimeo, SchoolTube, and the Zimmer Twins), tend to develop communities that are generally 'well-behaved' when it comes to commenting on others' work. This is not always the case, however, when it comes to the larger or more generic services, such as YouTube. Of course, you can choose to disable comments on many services, but if you choose *not* to do this then you need to be aware that people might make comments that are hurtful, disrespectful, malicious, or just plain vitriolic. You need to monitor comments closely and be able to remove them immediately – but, even then, there is no guarantee that a class member or parent didn't see the comment before you did, leading them to either spread it round or become upset by it.

Copyright

This topic is covered in greater detail in Chapter 16, so if you have concerns about the use of copyright material I suggest you flick ahead to the relevant section. For now, though, it needs to be noted that most content on the internet – including images, videos, stories, articles, music, and other creative works – is subject to copyright. Details vary from jurisdiction to jurisdiction, but generally speaking the owner or creator of an original work is said to have 'all rights reserved' in that work, meaning that they alone have the right to reproduce, modify, adapt, distribute (and so on) that work. If you take the copyright owner's work and do something to it, then you are likely to be in breach of copyright. (There are exceptions, of course, but see Chapter 16 for more information.) *Just because the work is on the internet, it doesn't mean that you have permission to do whatever you want with it.*

Here are some points to bear in mind when using internet content with your class:

1 Uploading content: only use material that you are *certain you hold copyright in*, for example, photographs that you have taken yourself.
2 Downloading or 'repurposing' others' work for adaptation or distribution or similar: you need to have the copyright owner's permission.
3 Embedding content that a copyright owner has posted elsewhere, for example, on YouTube: this is normally acceptable, as the copyright owner has given permission to the service to generate an embed code on the understanding that their work may be embedded in people's blogs, wikis, social networks, and the like.

Creative Commons

Creative Commons (CC) has developed in response to the tricky copyright issues that have arisen along with the internet. Under CC, people choose a free licence that allows their creative work to be distributed in a more open manner and in a way that suits them best. CC gets around the '*all* rights reserved' strictures of regular copyright by allowing the copyright owner to give up some of their rights voluntarily under a '*some* rights reserved' licence. For example, a photographer may decide to release photos under a CC licence that allows their work to be used and distributed as long as it is attributed to them and as long as it is only ever used for non-commercial purposes. This is known as an 'Attribution-Non-Commercial licence' and it means that people don't need to get in touch with the copyright owner to ask permission to use or distribute their work under these conditions.

Creative Commons, like copyright, is also covered in Chapter 16, but, for the moment, if you are asking students to 're-purpose' internet content that they don't own copyright in, or don't have express permission to use, then you should try to find material that is released under a CC licence. This will make your obligations for classroom use clearer. Further, you should teach students about Creative Commons and show them how to source, identify, and acknowledge CC material. This isn't always as easy as it sounds, but many sites – Flickr included – explicitly provide information on how each individual object appearing on the site should be distributed, that is, whether it's full copyright or CC; you can even do an advanced Flickr search and search 'The Commons' for material that is only distributed under CC.

If you have any concerns about copyright or Creative Commons, then I suggest you read the relevant sections in Chapter 16 before going much further.

Terms of Service

Most reputable services do not require that you give up your copyright in order to upload and distribute your original materials on their site. Most will, however, require from you a licence to your 'intellectual property' (IP, that is, the 'intangible' property of your mind or intellect, such as corporate and proprietary knowledge, designs, music, and so on) in order to display or host your work. Usually speaking, this is an acceptable state of affairs that allows the service to operate in a practical sense: if you don't agree to this licence, then the service cannot host your content, pure and simple. However, a growing number of services are extending the conditions to include a *sub-licensable* licence to your IP, which is rather less satisfactory. If you give a company a licence to your IP that they can then sublicense, it means that they can sell on your work to a third party which may then use and modify your content and make money from it. This may or may not be acceptable to you, personally (if you have a Facebook account, then you have already agreed to this provision), but when it comes to giving away such a licence to student work, you may need to think twice. See Chapter 16 for more information on Terms of Service.

Ideas. Be inspired!

- Visit Radiowaves.co.uk and FilmsForLearning.org to view examples of high-quality videos from students of all ages.

Platform compatibility and bandwidth

Photosharing, videosharing, and comic strip sites are normally compatible with both Windows and Macintosh operating systems and with the major internet browsers (Explorer and Firefox) and some of the smaller ones (such as Safari and Opera). However, once you get into the more complex environment of animation creation and video editing (whether it's done directly online or via software that you have installed on your desktop), you can encounter compatibility problems. For example, some software downloads (such as Xtranormal's 'State' animation software and Muvizu) will only work on Windows; if you are a Mac user you might have to investigate running Windows on your Mac, which might be a bit complicated for some. In other instances, if you are creating animations or editing videos directly online, then you might find the service to be a little 'buggy', meaning that things might not work exactly as you'd hoped, dialogue might drop out or not be entirely editable, or your animation might not play back as you expected. Such problems are most often encountered either when you are dealing with a large project or when there are many users visiting the site at the same time, causing pressure on the site's bandwidth. Finally, many videos and animations made in this way are done so using the 'Flash' format, and Flash does not display on all devices (especially Apple devices such as the iPad).

Limited free usage

Because digital visual media use up a lot of bandwidth and server space there are often limits applied to how much you can do for free with an online service. This is especially the case for online animation creators. (Note that in the case of software downloads such as Blender, Muvizu, and Xtranormal's 'State' software, these limits do not apply as you are creating your object on your own computer before uploading it elsewhere.) Some services might limit how much you can do for free per month, whilst others might allow you to use only the most basic of functions before you are required to 'upgrade' your account or buy 'points'. Many, however, will provide account upgrades specially for educators. This can often be done by contacting the service provider using your .edu, .sch.uk, or .ac.uk email address, so always check to see if there are special accounts available for educators.

 Activity. Investigate copyright issues relating to the use of visual media

Look at the Terms of Service and Frequently Asked Questions of some of the videosharing, photosharing, or animation sites and services discussed in this chapter (or use others that you know of). Find out the following:

(Continued)

(Continued)

- Does the service own copyright in anything you create, share, or post on the site?
- How does the service say it will deal with 'infringeing' material? Will you be asked to take it down? Will your account automatically be suspended?
- Is there material provided already on the site (for example, photographs, animation objects, soundtracks, sound effects) that you have permission to use in any 'mashups' or remixes you might create?
- Is your work automatically distributed under a Creative Commons licence? If so, can you opt out of this or change the licence in your settings?

Make a start on understanding some of the copyright issues you might face when using social media in the classroom. If you are unsure about how things work, ask a colleague to look at the Terms of Service with you and to provide their interpretation. The Wikipedia entries on copyright and Creative Commons are also worth looking at, as are CreativeCommons.org and the sites of any regulatory copyright councils or services in your country. You don't have to become a copyright expert, but you should at least have a working knowledge of how copyright operates in your jurisdiction. See Chapter 16 for more information.

 Summary

- There are many rich media tools and services available that allow you to share photos and videos, and that allow you to create animations and cartoons.
- Producing and/or sharing visual media is excellent for building multiple literacies and helping students work collaboratively on peer learning projects.
- Photosharing and animation both provide creative ways for students to generate narratives and stories.
- Sharing inappropriate content, uploading images of children, and posting offensive comments are all risks that need to be managed when using visual media with students.
- You need to understand how copyright, Creative Commons, and Terms of Service all work as regards the creation, sharing, and distribution of visual media on the internet.
- You may need to account for technicalities such as bandwidth quotas, platform compatibility, and storage limits when using rich visual media online.

Resources

Online resources

- Search 'Flickr in the classroom' for articles and websites relating to photosharing in schools.
  ... relating to classroom photosharing.
  ... to access resources and information
  ... ntry.
  ... s on using YouTube and video in the ... ideo'.
  ... nce to distribute your or your class's

... anion website for links, discussions, ... with your class. You can find this at

... ools animation project: Using anima-
... ls, *Journal of Assistive Technologies,*

... lf-presentation through online image
... 28(4), 549–64.
... pyright and media literacy through
... 8(4), 52–5.
... cipatory media discourse on school
... 36.
... l abyss: getting started in the class-
... *g House: A Journal of Educational*

... icipation in an online photo-sharing
... *nal of the American Society for*

... lling been so easy or so powerful,

CHAPTER 9

INSTANT MESSAGING, CHAT, SKYPE, AND TWITTER

Overview

This chapter begins by outlining the characteristics of, and differences between, instant messaging (IM) and chat (both of which you may already be quite familiar with) and explores the related social media of Skype and Twitter. All these tools are considered for their ability to promote free-flowing, real-time conversation, which can support peer learning, brainstorming, and creativity. We will also look at issues relating to invisible audiences, 'following' students online, and institutional policies and hardware. With a little organisation and careful selection and use of services, your class could experience the benefits of being involved in real-time collaborative work with students and experts the world over.

What are IM, chat, Skype, and Twitter?

Instant messaging (IM) and chat

'IM' stands for 'instant messaging' and is a way of using digital text to 'talk' one on one with other people in real time. It is similar to SMS text messaging in that the messages sent are usually brief (a few dozen characters or so) and can include shorthand symbols and abbreviations in the form of 'text speak'. Mobile instant messaging (MIM) allows IM services to be accessed via a mobile device, such as a mobile phone. Instant messaging conversations can usually be saved for retrieval later on.

> ### Ideas. IM and chat ideas
>
> - Use group text chat to **discuss** or **brainstorm** class topics.
> - Connect via a chat room with similar **learning communities** in other cities or countries.
> - Set up a **language exchange** via IM or chat with a class in another country.
> - Use IM and/or chat in a computer laboratory: students who don't speak up in class will sometimes take part more readily in a chat environment.
> - Conduct **meetings** via IM or chat with staff or colleagues who are in different places.

Chat is a form of instant messaging but the key difference is in their participants: 'chat' usually refers to discussions that take place in 'chat rooms' amongst many people who may or may not know each other. Instant messaging, on the other hand, can be thought of as a 'personal' form of chat, and usually takes place between people who know each other in 'real life'.

With IM, you can 'fire off' messages quickly without having to wait for a direct response, meaning that IM is much less structured than, for example, email. Instant messaging is further different from email in that IM allows for more free-flowing conversation, and this is what makes it especially popular amongst young people who want to communicate directly with school friends after hours. Email, on the other hand, is akin to traditional mail in that it is very 'linear': you send a message, wait for a reply, then respond to the reply.

Instant messaging and chat can be delivered either via software (such as Windows Live Messenger or Skype) that you download and install on your computer, or via a web-based service (such as Google Chat or the IM services that come with many social networks including Facebook, Togetherville, Club Penguin, and Meebo). Many chat services, such as Windows Live, Google Chat, and Skype, also have video capabilities.

Skype and VOIP (Voice Over Internet Protocol)

> ### Ideas. Skype (VOIP) ideas
>
> - Language teachers can set up a multi-user video chat with a class in another country as part of a **language exchange**.
>
> *(Continued)*

(Continued)

- Set up regular **meetings** with colleagues from different schools and keep in touch using VOIP.
- Arrange a **debate** with a class from another school or country.
- Set up an **expert interview** and get students to prepare and ask questions on a class topic. Students can take notes, add material on what they've learnt to a class wiki, or contribute their reflections to a class blog.
- Give **feedback** or **study advice** to students using VOIP.
- Use VOIP to teach **oral communication and oral presentation skills**.

Skype is generally recognised as the standard-bearer for VOIP and can best be described as 'internet telephony': VOIP allows you to make telephone calls over the internet using your computer or internet-connected digital device. Most VOIP services support both voice and video calls – video if you have a camera accompanying your device. Unlike IM conversations, not all VOIP conversations, especially video conversations, can be directly recorded. Moreover, some VOIP services and/or calls are free, others you have to pay for – check the pricing arrangements before embarking on a VOIP project with your class.

As with IM, you can either download and install VOIP software (for example, Skype) or you can directly access the service on the web by creating a 'room' with a specific URL. This latter option is not always the most secure, however, as there is the potential for uninvited guests to find your URL and to enter your room without permission. See 'Special considerations' later in this chapter for more information.

Twitter

Twitter is a special case when it comes to social media: it is neither a proper blogging service (although it can be thought of, perhaps, as 'micro-blogging') nor a proper social network, and it can't really be described as chat or instant messaging. Instead, it is a service that allows people to compose (either via computer or mobile device) short, frequent messages or 'tweets' of up to 140 characters that are distributed via the Twitter network on the internet. People on Twitter can follow and invite others, set up lists, send photos, and, of course, tweet privately.

Video clip. Twitter in Plain English

CommonCraft's video 'Twitter in Plain English' can be viewed on YouTube (search 'Twitter in Plain English').

Because there are millions and millions of tweets made each day on Twitter, it would be easy for tweets to get lost. To help people cut through the 'noise', Twitter users have developed ways of making sure that their tweets connect with, and can be found by, others. In particular, Twitter members use 'hashtags' (a tag that is preceded by a hash '#' symbol) to tag up their tweets so that others can find messages on topics of mutual interest. Hashtags are also used to map 'trends' on the site: if many tweets on a topic suddenly receive the same hashtag, then the topic can be said to be 'trending'.

Ideas. Twitter ideas

- Use Twitter to **continue class discussions outside of school** hours.
- Post **advice and generic feedback** for students in the form of tweets.
- **Share links and resources** via Twitter. Encourage students to share, also.
- Send out **announcements and reminders** via Twitter.
- Ask students to **tweet their thoughts, questions, observations**, and so on during class. Make sure you use a dedicated hashtag so that you can follow the class's Twitter stream.
- Use Twitter for **'Q&A's on class topics**.

Twitter users can also direct message each other by adding an '@' symbol to the main recipient's username in the message they are sending. So, if I wanted to send a message to my friend 'jsmith36' about an upcoming lunar eclipse, I would write something like: '@jsmith36 Check out the sky tonight at 1130 pm for a brilliant #lunareclipse'. Although intended for jsmith36, my message can be viewed by anyone, so it is essential that you do not share any personal, controversial, or sensitive information in such a public forum (see 'Special considerations', this chapter for more).

Educational benefits of IM, chat, Skype, and Twitter

Pedagogy

Instant messaging, chat, Skype/VOIP, and Twitter are based on real-time communication, so it seems logical that socially constructivist, dialogical, and peer learning pedagogies would be well supported by these kinds of social media; and, indeed, collaboration, teamwork, networking, negotiation, and community-building are all important skills that can be nurtured by the effective use of such tools. But so, too, can processes of creativity and evaluation be encouraged, especially if a brainstorming session via, say, chat or Twitter leads to the merging of analysis and synthesis into a class-based task.

Integration of diverse perspectives

The immediacy of the communication that occurs in such 'chat-type' environments (and that includes Skype and Twitter) allows for a diverse range of perspectives to be generated, and, under the guidance of a facilitator, considered and hopefully integrated. This advances what Dewey (2004 [1916]) would recognise as a 'democratic' classroom, that is, one in which free interaction and mutual interests come together to build common values from numerous and varied points of contact.

Connection outside the classroom

All these tools can be used effectively within a single class; however, they are perhaps at their most potent when used to connect your students to people or organisations outside of your specific classroom. Language teachers, especially, should be able to see the benefit of linking up with students and teachers in other countries for the purposes of a language exchange. But other exchanges – cultural, study, research – can also be arranged, whether it be across town or across nations. All it takes is a little organisation and the synchronising of schedules and suddenly your students' work gains value in a much larger domain and amongst a much larger audience. This, in turn, should inspire your class to greater efforts through increased motivation and a stronger sense of control and ownership over their work and ideas.

Special considerations for IM, Skype, and Twitter

Knowing who you are talking to

As with any and all social media, knowing who you are talking to is critical to keeping safe online. Open chat rooms are notorious for harbouring 'weird' or 'dodgy' individuals with ill intentions. Further, some chat rooms might display unsuitable advertisements or encourage inappropriate link-ups. The same applies for Twitter: it can be very easy to start up a conversation with '@anothertwitteruser' without knowing who is on the end of the '@' symbol. Instant messaging conversations, however, are generally regarded as less risky, as such conversations usually occur between people who know each other 'face to face' and who can verify that the person on the other end of the conversation is indeed who they say they are.

> ## Key point. Don't these tools just encourage a lot of 'surface' or 'rubbish' communication?
>
> The fact that services such as chat and IM take a written form arguably gives us a false sense that the conversation should, somehow, be elevated above the natural flow of face-to-face chitchat. In this instance, we need to be careful not to conflate writing with thinking and to remember that, like most things, it's the use to which a tool is put that determines its value and place in any kind of communications 'hierarchy'.

Institutional policies regarding the use of VOIP

Some institutions have strict policies governing the use of Skype and VOIP services – policies that you may not even currently be aware of. Such policies may have been implemented due to bandwidth usage concerns or because the use of a particular VOIP service will compromise the contract your organisation has with a different (that is, non-Skype) telephony provider. In either case, you need to check to see if your use of VOIP services will put you in breach of local rules and guidelines.

Need for working audio and video hardware for VOIP

Although audio and video are becoming more and more common in our personal digital environments, there is no guarantee that your school will have access to reliable, working audio and video internet technology. To use Skype and similar services, you need at least a microphone and speakers (inbuilt or external), and maybe a headset. Of course, if you are videoconferencing via the web, you will need either a webcam or inbuilt camera. All of this can cost money, so student equity issues also need to be considered.

'Following' students on Twitter

Before you 'follow' any of your students on Twitter, you should carefully think through the implications of doing so. If you are using Twitter for a class project, then there might be very good reasons for having everyone in the class follow everyone else. But even if this is the case, you should still take into account the fact that you might appear to be 'playing favourites' if you followed some students and not others: even if you *thought* you had followed them all, you might still have missed a couple.

Outside of this situation, bear in mind that it could also seem a bit 'creepy' if you, as a teacher, followed your students and you weren't actually using Twitter for any class-based reason. Whatever you decide to do, be sure to make an informed (preferably pedagogy-based) decision around the whole 'following' issue.

Invisible audiences on Twitter

If your Twitter stream is public, then be very careful about the types of tweets you make, the tone you adopt, and any names or personal information you might use. danah boyd (2011, *sic*) uses the term 'invisible audiences' to describe one of the elements of 'networked publics', and it is these such audiences that you need to be aware of. You never know who might be reading your public Twitter feed, and you can never account for how you might be misinterpreted or taken out of context and misrepresented by those who are unfamiliar with your particular classroom environment. For example, you might have certain 'running jokes' or offbeat subjects of discussion within your class that could appear odd to those who aren't privy to the idiosyncrasies of your class's culture. If someone misreads what your tweets are about, and doesn't have the context to interpret them correctly, you may find yourself the subject of unwarranted scrutiny and attack.

 Activity. Explore the 'culture' of different instantaneous communication methods.

Spend some time exploring different means of instantaneous communication. Figure out how each works in a 'functional' sense, but mainly get a feel for the 'culture' of this mode of correspondence. Consider things such as:

- Who takes part in such conversations?
- How do people connect via social chatting – and why?
- How do people express themselves?
- What kinds of topics are discussed?
- Who is the target audience for comments, posts, tweets, or messages?
- How is dialogue encouraged or discouraged?
- Do people 'take turns' or do they simply post messages without expecting a response?
- What meanings, beliefs, and values do participants share as regards the tone, style, and content of conversation?

Once you have identified some of the key characteristics of these cultures, you should be in a position to decide whether or not this form of communication would be a good 'fit' for your class.

Summary

- Instant messaging, chat, Skype, and Twitter all provide real-time, digital communication services.
- These tools can be used to build and support socially constructivist, dialogic, and democratic classrooms that integrate a variety of perspectives.
- When using public, 'chat-type' services (including IM and Twitter), you should be especially conscious of the 'invisible audiences' that might be following your class. Your messages, tweets, and other communiqués could invite inappropriate contact or be misinterpreted or be taken out of context.
- You may need to account for technical (hardware) or institutional (contractual and policy) considerations when using VOIP services such as Skype.

Resources

Online resources

- Search 'Twitter in education' and 'Instant Messaging in education' to find tips and advice on how to use these tools in your classroom.
- 'Skype in the Classroom' is Skype's own teacher network where you can connect and share ideas. Search 'Skype in the Classroom'.
- Visit the *Using Social Media in the Classroom* companion website for links, discussions, and other materials relating to the use of IM, chat, Skype, and Twitter for teaching and learning. You can find this at www.sagepub.co.uk/poore

Further reading

- Bowman, L. L., Levine, L. E., Waite, B. M. and Gendron, M. (2010) Can students really multitask? An experimental study of instant messaging while reading, *Computers & Education,* 54(4), 927–31.
- Eaton, S. E. (2010) Using Skype in the second and foreign language classroom. Paper presented at the Social Media Workshop 'Get Your ACT(FL) Together Online: Standards Based Language Instruction via Social Media', San Diego, CA, 4 August 2010. Available at http://eric.ed.gov/ERICWebPortal/search/detailmini.jsp?_nfpb=true&_&ERICExtSearch_SearchValue_0=ED511316&ERICExtSearch_SearchType_0=no&accno=ED511316. Accessed 1 November 2011.
- McCarty, C., Prawitz, A. D., Derscheid, L. E. and Montgomery, B. (2011) Perceived safety and teen risk taking in online chat sites, *Cyberpsychology, Behavior, and Social Networking,* 14(3), 169–74.
- Murthy, D. (2011) Twitter: microphone for the masses? *Media, Culture & Society,* 33(5), 779–89.

- Schwarz, O. (2011) Who moved my conversation? Instant messaging, intertextuality and new regimes of intimacy and truth, *Media, Culture & Society,* 33(1), 71–87.
- Varnhagen, C. K., McFall, G. P., Pugh, N., Routledge, L., Sumida-MacDonald, H. and Kwong, T. E. (2010) lol: new language and spelling in instant messaging, *Reading and Writing,* 23(6), 719–33.
- Weaver, A. (2010) Twitter for teachers, librarians and teacher librarians, *Access,* 24(2), 16–20.

CHAPTER 10

BOOKMARKING, CLIPPINGS, MINDMAPPING, AND POLLS

Overview

This chapter rolls together some of the smaller, but no less effective, social media tools that have as their educational focus the skills of analysis, synthesis, and evaluation. First we look at the basics of bookmarking, mindmapping, clippings, and polls, before moving on to the benefits they entail for collating, organising, visualising, evaluating, critiquing, and presenting information. The chief considerations for the use of these tools are similar to those that apply for many other social media, that is, ensuring that students don't generate or share inappropriate content. But more than this, students may well need guidance on how to best use these tools and techniques in enhancing their cognitive skills.

What are bookmarking, mindmapping, clippings, and polls?

Bookmarking

Bookmarking services (also known as 'social bookmarking services') enable you to save and share your bookmarks (or 'favourites') on the web instead of solely on your computer's hard drive. This saves you the hassle (and frustration) of having different sets of 'favourites' on each machine or device you use. When you find a website or online resource that you want to 'favourite' or save, you simply add it to a bookmarking service such as Delicious.com, Diigo.com, or Connotea.org and tag it with appropriate keywords so that you can retrieve it later by linking directly to it. Some services allow you to organise your bookmarks in 'batches' or 'bundles', which more or less act as folders. Both batching and tagging your bookmarks gives you dual pathways to accessing your bookmarks. A final component of bookmarking is being able to keep a note on each of your bookmarks, which records perhaps why you decided to save it, how it is relevant, or how it relates to the other sites you've bookmarked.

Ideas. Bookmarking ideas

- Ask students to start up their own bookmarking account. Use a unique tag that identifies your class and aggregate the group's links on a certain topic. Tell students to **find and save links and resources and to justify their choices** by using the **'Notes'** field for the link they have tagged.
- Use your own bookmarking account to **create bundles of tags based around class topics**. Post links to your account and use the 'Notes' function to give students instructions. For example, tell students to visit the websites found under 'Topic A'. Then ask them **to comment on the three most important things** they learnt from the site.
- Send students to your own bookmarks collection. It's a good way for you to **model how you work** and for students to see what resources you are compiling **for your own research or teaching**.
- **Create annotated resources lists** for group projects.

By default, your bookmarks will normally be made public; however, most services allow you to make your bookmarks private if you wish. The advantage of having public bookmarks is that you can let others see what sites you have discovered and saved. At first glance, this might not seem a huge bonus. But when you consider *the value of searching other people's bookmarks*, the benefits of this kind of social media use should become clear: you no longer have to treat Google as your only port of call for search – instead, you can search tags, identify users with similar interests, and explore the web this way. This kind of searching will likely yield all manner of useful and interesting results that a traditional search engine will not – this is not least because the resources you will stumble upon are assembled by humans rather than by an algorithm (no matter how sophisticated the algorithm may be).

Bookmarking services automatically generate an RSS feed (see Chapter 3) for your account, allowing people to subscribe to your public bookmarks. Similarly, each and every tag in a bookmarking service also has its own RSS feed, meaning that if you don't want to subscribe to any particular user's account, you can, instead, subscribe to a tag or tags. If, for example, you are looking at wind power in class, you can subscribe to tags such as 'wind power', 'wind energy', and 'wind power generators'; each time a new resource is added using one of those tags, you will see it in your RSS feed reader and you can check it out.

Clippings

Ideas. Clippings ideas

- Get students to create a clipcast on a class topic. Ask them to use the comments section to **justify their choice of clippings**.
- Ask students to use the comments section to **give feedback to others' clipcasts**.
- Keep a library of **interesting finds**.
- Ask students to contribute their clipcasts to a class blog. Get them to **discuss the clipcasts and rate them**.
- Introduce students to **clippings as a way of managing the research** they do for a class topic. Get them to make a series of clippings and to share them with the class.
- Clippings are a great way to **keep a track of the best bits of web resources** you've found during your research.

Sometimes you don't want to save a whole web page or resource as a bookmark; you just want to save a sentence or two or perhaps an image or video. Clipping services such as Clipmarks and Evernote allow you to highlight, clip, and save bits of websites in one spot, a bit like a scrapbook. To do this, just highlight the material you want to clip and then save it in 'clip mode' or via a 'clipper' or 'amplify' button that you have added to your browser (you will need to follow the clipping service's instructions to do this). Your clippings will be saved to your clipping account where you can access them, tag them up, make them public or private, turn them into 'clipcasts' for others to view, embed them in your wiki, blog, or similar site, and print out customised versions of your clips. As with bookmarks, searching other people's public clips can be a great way to find resources that a Google search won't always turn up on the first couple of pages.

Mindmapping

Ideas. Mindmapping ideas

- Brainstorming: Ask students to **collaborate on building a mindmap or debate map of a class topic**. Get them to explain their map to the rest of the class.
- Use Bubbl.us to **map out your class topics for students**. This is a great way of showing how material in your syllabus connects and can be a great conceptual aid or advance organiser for students. Embed your map in your class website.

Mindmapping tools allow you to create, share – and even collaborate on – concept diagrams online. To start mindmapping you simply add, drag, and drop 'bubbles' or 'branches' around an onscreen diagram, and link them together to help you visualise your ideas and the relationships between them. Once complete, your diagram can be exported to your desktop as an image file (such as a jpeg or png), printed out, embedded in your blog, wiki or other website, or shared via a direct link. Popular mindmapping tools include Bubbl.us, Exploratree.org.uk (which has been built specifically with teaching and learning in mind), and Cacoo.com. Each offers a slightly different set of tools, so it is best to explore a few before settling on which service would best suit your class.

Polls and surveys

Ideas. Polls and surveys ideas

- Ask students to **create polls on class topics** and insert them into their wiki, blog, or other site.
- Ask students to create a poll for a class investigation. Get them to **collate their results and present a report**.

- Use polls to **demonstrate to students how survey questions can be used to manipulate opinion**. Ask students to construct a poll that deliberately biases each side of an argument.
- Create your own poll and use it as a **quiz to check student understanding** of a topic.
- Use a poll to **gather student feedback** on your teaching or on class topics.
- Teach students how to **create meaningful poll questions** around class topics.

You can gather opinions and information quite easily via online polls and surveys. Polls tend to be constructed in simple 'yes/no' or limited-choice format, whilst surveys are generally more complex and might seek qualitative (in the form of open-ended questions) as well as quantitative data. Once you have created your account, you can begin to construct your poll or survey question by question, so it is a good idea to have something mapped out beforehand. You can usually publish your poll or survey via a direct link (which the service will generate for you), which you add to your website, or via a widget (which you also add to your website). Polldaddy. com and Vizu (search 'Create Vizu web polls', and note that there is a marketing and advertising site that needs to be distinguished from the web polls site) are well-known poll services, but there are others. In terms of surveys, SurveyMonkey.com and Zoomerang have proven both widely adopted and reliable in the past.

 Activity. Compare bookmarking services

Create an account with one or more bookmarking services (perhaps start with Diigo.com, Delicious.com, and/or Connotea.org). Add some bookmarks, tag them up, and begin exploring the functionality of the service:

- How easy is it to bookmark or save a site?
- How are tags organised? Alphabetically? By most recent? Other?
- Can you change how tags are displayed? Can you create bundles, lists, or folders of tags around particular topics?
- How easy is it to sort or filter your bookmarks – by tag or bundle?
- How many characters are allowed in the 'notes' area?
- Are bookmarks automatically made public or private? Can you change these settings?
- Can you share individual bookmarks with others?

Activity. Create a mindmap

Sign up with Bubbl.us after having read, understood, and agreed to the Bubbl.us Terms of Service.

Step 1. Think of a syllabus topic that your class will be studying in the next few weeks. Map out the topic, showing key concepts or ideas as 'parent' bubbles and use 'child' bubbles to draw out subsidiary or secondary concepts. Use links and arrows to show how ideas relate to each other, or how you will progress through the topic (as you would with an advance organiser to help orient students). Experiment with changing bubble colours, positions, and relationships to other bubbles.

Step 2. Run your mindmap or 'bubble map' past a trusted colleague for feedback. Can they easily follow your logic? Are there too many connections being made between bubbles (in other words, have you created a 'spaghetti map')? Do you need to 'slim' things down a bit to communicate your information more clearly? Is there a better way of organising your map?

Once you are happy with your map, embed it in your site either as an image or get the embed code and embed it as a widget or similar object.

Educational benefits of bookmarking, clippings, mindmapping, and polls

Bookmarking: Collating, organising, and sharing information

Saving and organising online sources using bookmarking is a valuable technique for collating and organising web-based materials. When bookmarking a site, students should be encouraged to evaluate the source material for suitability, to tag their bookmark with useful keywords, and to also record a note that justifies their selection of the bookmarked source. In doing this last task, students are not simply finding and saving 'stuff', they are also asked to qualify their choices and therefore evidence skills of evaluation and judgement.

Mindmapping: Visualising ideas and problems

Mindmapping tools help students to conceptualise and visualise the relationships between ideas and things and are thus excellent supports for higher-order cognitive skills such as analysis, synthesis, and evaluation. A mindmapping tool can be used first as a collaborative instrument for brainstorming, in which students quickly (and without concern for 'accuracy' or whether or not the idea seems 'silly') generate ideas and topics, which are recorded in bubbles or branches on the mindmap. Having done that, students can then evaluate their material for relevance and usefulness before structuring it. Problem-solving and decision-making are also readily supported by mindmapping techniques, especially if students present their mindmaps in the form of 'decision trees' where the consequences of different actions are mapped out. See Figure 10.1 for an example of a mindmap made using Bubbl.us.

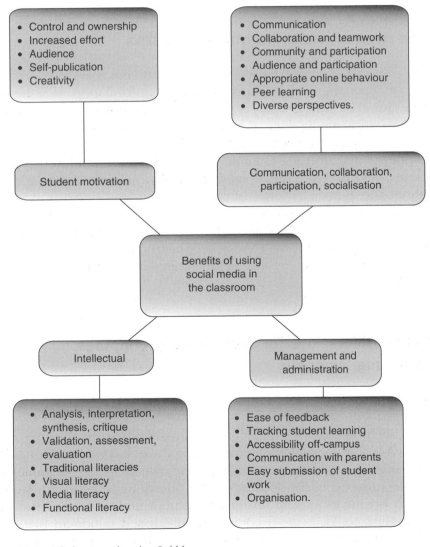

Figure 10.1   Mindmap made using Bubbl.us

Clippings: Evaluating and synthesising online materials

In making a 'clipcast' or scrapbook of online materials, students should be encouraged to heavily scrutinise source items and select only the best for sharing. Some clipping services allow you to share clippings of no more than 1,000 characters, meaning that appraisal skills are built into the system almost by default. Clippings also provide a way for students to keep and manage notes of important or relevant information that they have found on the web, again encouraging skills of evaluation, validation, and synthesis.

Polls and surveys: Research and critical media skills

The most obvious educational use for polls and surveys is in the collection of opinion or feedback, and in the gathering of information as a basis for research. However, polls and surveys also help to underline the importance of developing critical media skills, as students learn how information and statistics can be manipulated to attain certain ends.

A wonderful and amusing example of how this can be achieved appeared in a scene from the classic BBC comedy *Yes, Prime Minister*. In the scene, Sir Humphrey asks Bernard a series of questions that lead Bernard to be both for and against national service – depending on how the questions are framed. The clip from the show can be viewed on YouTube (search 'Truth behind opinion polls minister') and is very instructive if you want your own students to develop a survey that demonstrates how easily opinion can be tampered with.

Special considerations for bookmarking, clippings, mindmapping, and polls

Inappropriate content

As always, the potential for students to generate, find, or share inappropriate content is a major consideration when using these kinds of social media in the classroom. If students are creating their own polls, for example, then there is the prospect of frivolous or puerile questions being asked. Students might also bookmark or clip unsuitable content and distribute it to classmates, or they could create a completely ill-advised mindmap that needs immediate deletion. To avoid situations such as these, you can either create a general class account over which you have access and control, and which allows you to remove improper materials, or you can remind students before the start of their social media project of the consequences for poor online behaviour and your readiness to enforce those consequences. As always, you need to consider your own level of skill with the social media you want to use in your classroom, as well as the amount of trust you have built up with your students, before you decide on whether to take a 'carrot' or a 'stick' approach.

Mindmapping skills

Although some people find mindmapping an easy and, indeed, logical way to develop ideas and to discover linkages between concepts, others can become quite lost when asked to 'map an idea' or 'demonstrate the flow of a decision-making process'. They can become even further confused if instructed to 'brainstorm first'. If you are going to use mindmapping tools with your class, then you need to be clear in your own mind about what makes an effective mindmap to begin with. A good map should be simple, have clear linkages between bubbles and branches, be logical, use a minimum of words, include pictures (if appropriate), use colour to 'group' ideas or levels of ideas, and so on. A bad mindmap is a 'spaghetti map', that is, one in which each bubble seems to link to every other bubble. Similarly, if you are going to ask students to brainstorm a topic or problem before they begin mindmapping, you will need to lay out some ground rules (such as 'all ideas are accepted, no criticism, no judging of ideas until the evaluation phase begins', and so forth). To learn more, google terms such as 'brainstorming rules' and 'how to mindmap'.

Summary

- Websites and other online resources can be saved, tagged, and shared via bookmarking and clippings services. Collating and organising such resources fosters analytical and evaluative skills.
- Mindmapping services encourage students to visualise, organise, and present information such that the relationships between ideas become clear to the viewer. This engages skills of synthesis and evaluation, as well as those of problem-solving and decision-making.
- Polls and surveys can be used to gather data or feedback on an issue, but they can also be fun tools for teaching students critical media literacy, as they learn how questions can be manipulated to achieve certain responses.

Resources

Online resources

- Search 'Bookmarking in the classroom' for tips and advice on how to use social bookmarking in education.
- Search 'Mindmapping for students' and 'Mindmapping in education' for relevant tips and advice.

- Visit the *Using Social Media in the Classroom* companion website for links, discussions, resources, and other materials relating to using bookmarking and mindmapping for teaching and learning. You can find this at www.sagepub.co.uk/poore

Further reading

- Burton, R., Barlow, N. and Barker, C. (2010) Using visual tools for analysis and learning. University of Huddersfield. Available at http://eprints.hud.ac.uk/7843/. Accessed 1 September 2011.
- Edwards, G. and Mosley, B. F. (2011) Technology integration can be delicious: social bookmarking as a technology integration tool, in C. Wankel (ed.), *Educating Educators with Social Media* (Cutting-edge Technologies in Higher Education, Vol. 1), Bradford: Emerald Group, pp. 207–25.
- Harrison, C. (2011) Literacy, technology and the internet: what are the challenges and opportunities for learners with reading difficulties, and how do we support them in meeting those challenges and grasping those opportunities? in C. Wyatt-Smith, J. Elkins and S. Gunn (eds), *Multiple Perspectives on Difficulties in Learning Literacy and Numeracy*. Springer Netherlands, pp. 111–31.
- Wang, W-C., Lee, C-C. and Chu, Y-C. (2010) A brief review on developing creative thinking in young children by mind mapping, *International Business Research*, 3(3), 233–8.

CHAPTER 11

EDUCATIONAL GAMES AND MOBILE LEARNING

Overview

The present chapter covers two quite large topics in the field of educational technology: educational games and mobile learning. Educational games are explored as excellent tools for building problem-solving and strategic thinking skills, and the benefits that games have for collaboration and competition are also examined. We look at the problem of variation in the quality of educational games, as well as specific issues related to the virtual world Second Life.

The basics of mobile learning are described, but a comment on its coverage is in order: unlike everything else that has been covered in the early parts of this book, mobile learning is obviously not a tool or service but is rather a 'form' of learning. Mobile learning is covered here as it is a major digital 'genre' that supports all kinds of educational purpose and outcome: how you choose to engage with it will be up to you.

The coverage of each topic is not designed to be all-encompassing, but instead should be used as a 'launching point' for further study. If you are interested in pursuing either subject further I recommend you seek advice from experienced colleagues and some of the many, many online resources available.

What are educational games and mobile learning?

Educational games

Ideas. Ideas for educational games

Unlike other social media tools, a simple list of potential 'activities' cannot be provided for educational games – for the games themselves are the 'activity'. However, you can think of games as supporting different kinds of skills you want from your students: problem-solving, factual recall, strategic thinking, collaboration, and so on. Choose games that suit your purpose and that support the learning outcomes you desire.

Educational games can either take the form of traditional 'computer games', in which you install software and play the game from your hard drive, or, more commonly these days, they can be played online. Educational games (also known as 'serious games') are developed for particular ages or level of learner and designed to meet the learning outcomes of a syllabus topic or topics and typically incorporate social media elements, such as sharing resources, collaboration, and networking.

Games vary greatly in complexity, depending on the purpose of the game and its format. For example, a simple game might be a calculation or spelling game that comes as part of your interactive white board (IWB) software package at school; a more complex game might compose a 3D (three-dimensional) or virtual world that players can wander around in as they complete challenges or tasks. Players in these larger gaming environments often create an avatar of themselves, which represents them in the game. In fact, avatars can be great ways of having students share an online picture of themselves without the need to upload a personal photo. Students can use one of the many avatar creator sites to build their own avatar (search 'Avatar creator' and check to see if it is appropriate for use in your classroom).

Other games are available as 'apps' for smartphones and tablet devices, or may take the form of simulations that allow students to model real-world processes. Again, these vary in complexity.

Key points. Game or interactive content?

These terms are often used interchangeably, although there is a technical difference between the two. A game generally requires decision-making and strategising on behalf of the player in order to move on to a higher level; interactive content, on the other hand, might eschew strategy in favour of more straightforward knowledge construction. But as with many social media, there is often a lot of overlap.

Interactive content also falls under the rubric of 'educational games' and can be found easily across the internet. Many reputable organisations produce such content for use in schools. For instance, an entire part of the NobelPrize.org website is devoted to education and includes games on topics such as immunology, literature, physics, democracy, and much more. Similarly, the BBC has a wide variety of games for students of all ages (search 'BBC games' to find games for school-age pupils, as well as games produced by CBBC for younger children). The BBC also provides games as part of their regular websites for history, science, nature, and so on (search 'BBC interactive'). The National Aeronautics and Space Administration (NASA) also provides masses of interactive content, simulations, games, and apps (search 'NASA interactive games').

Private companies, too, develop games that can be used for educational purposes, but which may also have commercial motives behind them. Club Penguin and Moshi Monsters are prime examples that are directed at younger users.

 Activity. Make your own game

You don't have to rely on proprietary or commercial companies, or even your own education authority, to supply your class with educational games: you can make your own game.

Conduct a search for 'online game creator' and find something that suits your purposes (that is, something that matches your own skill level, the age of your students, and so on). Sites such as Sploder.com and CartoonNetwork.com are based on simple creators (just follow the instructions), whilst Blender.org is a rather more complex platform that supports 3D game and content creation. Don't let that put you off, though: remember, social media tools are designed to be as easy to use as possible.

So, set yourself an hour or two, or a whole afternoon (depending on your skills and level of enthusiasm), to create a game. It doesn't have to be for use with your students at this stage – the key thing is to learn how these systems function and to identify the potential for use in your own classroom. If the idea of making a smash-up derby game currently has more appeal than does making a game about the national coinage, then that's OK for now.

Mobile learning

Sometimes referred to simply as 'mlearning', mobile learning can be described as 'anywhere, anytime' learning that is not fixed by time (by schedule) or space (by location) and that is supported by digital technologies. Mobile learning has two main elements: (1) the learner, and (2) a portable digital device (or devices) through which they can access content. Such devices include mobile phones (both 'smart' and 'dumb'), digital cameras, voice recorders, tablet devices (such as iPads), laptops and netbooks, video cameras, and MP3 players.

Ideas. Ideas for mobile learning

- Ask students to investigate a topic and **create information resources** (websites, simple files, whatever) that can be accessed by a mobile device whilst on a school excursion.
- Create a **digital storytelling project** using photographs taken on digital cameras or mobile phones.
- Use internet-connected devices to encourage **just-in-time and *in situ* learning**.
- Use **geotagging** to classify data collected on mobile devices outside of the classroom.
- **Recommend apps to students** for loading onto their smartphones or tablet devices. Use the apps in class and/or to support external learning activities.

Portable digital devices can support a variety of files and functions, including audio, video, and text files and recording; wireless internet; news content; RSS feeds; email; social media and other apps; and, GPS and geolocation – all of which can be used for 'learning on the go'. Internet connectivity is not essential for mobile learning although such connectivity is fast becoming the norm. Nevertheless, much effective mobile learning can still be achieved with devices that simply record or 'play back' content and information.

 Activity. Conduct a mobile digital device inventory of your house or classroom

This is a fun activity that can be done either solely amongst your own household or with your entire class. Conduct an inventory of all the mobile digital devices that you and/or your class own or have ever owned. Make it comprehensive and don't overlook anything. You will find all sorts of devices that can be used to support mobile learning projects including:

- Mobile phones (both 'smart' and 'dumb')
- Digital cameras
- Voice recorders
- Tablet devices (such as iPads)
- Laptops and netbooks
- Video cameras
- MP3 players.

Once you have finished, brainstorm possibilities for in-class use and lay out the groundwork for potential mobile learning projects. If you happen to find devices that are no longer usable or that are obsolete, find out how and where you can recycle them.

Educational benefits of educational games and mobile learning

Pedagogy of educational games

Although some games are used to support the recall of facts, games are at their most effective when designed to support strategic thinking and problem-solving. Steven Johnson, in *Everything Bad is Good For You* (2006), states that all good games – not just educational games – share common characteristics. In particular, they should be hard, be about exploration, teamwork and reward, and they should force you to prioritise and choose between options, which involves weighing evidence, analysing situations, referring to long-term goals, and making decisions. Games, he argues, should encourage players to use a 'scientific, probing method' approach in which they (1) probe the environment, (2) form an hypothesis, (3) reprobe and check the effect, and (4) rethink based on feedback (Johnson, 2006 [2005], p. 41). And, finally, Johnson says that games should force players to 'telescope', that is participants should look to their ultimate objectives and co-ordinate a plan to meet them, usually through creating order and constructing proper hierarchies (Johnson, 2006 [2005], p, 45).

Games are motivational

If educational games exhibit the above characteristics – that is, if they are well designed and manage to balance challenge and reward – they can be very motivational for students. The reason that many young people will spend hours playing non-school games is that they become caught up in the game's 'narrative' and feel a part of it; they feel an element of control over the environment. Good educational games share these factors and can be used to provide incentives for study.

Collaboration and competition in educational games

Although many teachers might shy away from the more 'competitive' elements of gaming, it should nevertheless be recognised that *healthy* competition can be central to the improvement of an individual's comprehension of a topic, and, in a flourishing classroom, can contribute to the group's conceptualisation of class topics. In this manner, both competition and collaboration go hand in hand.

Mobile learning pedagogies

Mobile learning supports a myriad of pedagogies, many of them constructivist in nature. Depending on how they're set up, mobile learning projects promote problem-based learning, peer learning, just-in-time learning, and active learning. For younger students, game-based learning is also evident in mobile pedagogies, whilst, for older students, research- and inquiry-based learning are obvious benefactors. Suffice it to say that the benefits of mobile learning are manifold, and will depend on how mobile devices are used in your classroom, and to what purpose.

In general, however, mobile learning brings with it a host of other advantages, most of which are based on the portability and pervasiveness of mobile devices. In the first instance, mobile learning can be personalised and made relevant to the learner and their specific context or environment. For example, if students are on a field trip to the British Museum, they might use an internet-connected mobile device to search the web for more information about one of the displays. In this sense, mobile learning is also often spontaneous and informal and allows for immediate engagement with the current environment, making self-directed, student-centred learning experiences truly possible.

Activities supported by mobile learning

Although we can catalogue the variety of mobile devices available to students for use in education, perhaps what is more important are not 'tech specs' and functionality (both of which are in a constant state of change, anyway), but, rather, the *types of activities that mobile devices can support*. From this perspective, we can see that mobile learning supports relevant educational undertakings such as:

- Data gathering
- Information processing
- Voice recording
- Video recording
- Image/photograph recording
- Access to content
- Podcasting, vodcasting, photosharing
- Other collaborative and knowledge-construction activities.

If we take this kind of 'meta-focus' then we can avoid an emphasis on particular devices and instead explore how important educational activities and outcomes might be best achieved.

Administrative advantages of mobile learning

Mobile devices provide many administrative advantages for teachers, the most basic of which include being able to access calendars, clocks, and reminders from any location. This can be extended if you have a device that supports apps that allow you to keep attendance records, create class lists, and develop contact registers for parents and guardians. Mobile devices also enable the easy delivery of content to students and can even be used for your own professional learning as you make connections with colleagues, explore the viability of mlearning for your own classroom, or access development materials yourself via your portable device.

Special considerations for educational games and mobile learning

Variations in quality and suitability of educational games

Although there have been improvements in the quality of educational games in the recent past, there is no denying the fact that many of the games developed for educational purposes (often by education departments or authorities) simply aren't very good. In particular they often lack the spontaneity and interest factor that students find in the 'real' games they play on the internet or on their PlayStation. This is becoming less of an issue with the rise of game-based apps that are placing more emphasis on 'playability' and interaction, but you should still be careful to choose games that motivate and challenge students at their particular level.

A further consideration in this area is the suitability or otherwise of commercial games. Although some games might fit the learning outcomes for a particular topic and might seem a good way to get students engaged in the subject matter, you should nevertheless check the content of the game for its acceptability for use in your classroom. Many commercial games – especially those with more socially based narratives – inadvertently or otherwise perpetuate or contribute to stereotypes based on race, gender, ethnicity, religion, and more. Alternatively, such games may promote business interests or encourage unsuitable consumerist and materialist habits. You need to carefully check the content of each game (commercial or otherwise) you want to expose your students to before introducing it into the classroom.

Should I use Second Life with students?

Second Life is probably the world's most popular virtual world. Users create an avatar for free and, after signing up, they move around the world (known as 'the grid') visiting different 'islands' where they participate in activities, chat with others, and generally interact via their avatars. Many businesses and organisations, including tertiary educational institutions, have islands in Second Life and many teachers are firm advocates for the use of Second Life in education. Whilst virtual worlds undoubtedly have huge educational potential, you should think carefully before asking students to sign up for Second Life. In the first instance, the minimum age of sign-up is 16, which puts most school-age students out of the running to begin with. Next, Second Life is a highly commercial enterprise and requires payment if you want to develop your own island. And, finally, a good deal of Second Life's 'content' is adult in nature and not at all suitable for minors.

Despite this, there are other virtual worlds that you can explore with students, such as Jumpstart.com (ages 3–8) and Wiglington and Wenks (ages 7–14).

Visibility of students' online profiles

As soon as students embark on any form of online gaming that takes them into a virtual world or game space, there is the danger of inappropriate contact from adults posing as minors. As with all forms of social media, student profile information should be kept to a minimum, with only the basics of a username, password, and email address (if a bulk email account cannot be created) being provided. Nevertheless, many online games and virtual worlds require that participants have an avatar; this is actually a good thing, as an avatar avoids students having to upload photographs of themselves and the avatar can thus be used to protect student identity.

Technical issues relating to mobile learning

Device functionality and specification can be a limiting factor in mobile learning. For example, if a mobile device has an LCD display, it might be difficult to see in full sunlight; older devices might not have the amount of storage needed for students to complete a task set for them, especially if they are using video or audio functions; or a device might not allow direct transfer of data via USB or other connection (some tablet devices do not have a USB port, meaning that a wireless connection is essential if files are to be stored 'in the cloud').

Loan systems, data plans, firewalls, and insurance

If your school is providing devices for student loan, you will need to establish a loan system that tracks items and their use. You also need to consider, if necessary, what kind of data plan your devices should be covered by: How much data will you need to pay for? Will you set limits? If a device is school-supplied, will you need to set firewalls to prevent students accessing inappropriate content? If the device is the student's own, how can you 'control' access to such content? You also need to consider issues of insurance: What happens if a school-owned device is damaged, destroyed, or lost?

'It's just another school aid'

Doug Vass (2011, online) found in the MLC's City Experience iPad project that some students felt that school-supplied mobile devices were 'just another school aid'. Although using mobile technology for learning might seem exciting to us as teachers, it's always smart to keep some perspective on things.

Access to devices

A common consideration of any social media use in the classroom is accessibility to technology. This is a big topic (and is covered in more detail in Chapter 14 when we discuss the 'digital divide') but it should be enough here to alert you to the fact that not all students will have private access to the mobile devices you want them to use in the classroom. If the school cannot or will not supply the mobile learning tools you need, then you might have to organise some kind of 'buddy-up' system that allows for peer sharing.

Summary

- Educational games be accessed online or via apps on 'smart' devices. They might also be provided as part of a broader IT package that your school hosts.
- Educational games can be used to develop different skills in students, from basic factual recall to problem-solving, strategic thinking, and collaboration.
- There are wide variations in quality in educational games, many of which lack the spontaneity and challenge associated with games that students play in their own time.
- Mobile learning is learning that can occur anywhere, anytime, and that is supported by portable digital devices such as digital cameras, MP3 players, mobile phones, tablets, and video cameras.
- Mobile learning can be used to support a variety of pedagogies, including peer learning, problem-based learning, just-in-time learning, active learning, and research- and inquiry-based learning.
- There can be technical, data, insurance, and access issues associated with the portable devices used for mobile learning.

Resources

Online resources

- iSocial is '3D Virtual Learning: Helping youth with Autism Spectrum Disorders develop social competence'. Search 'iSocial 3D'.
- MLC School's City Experience iPad project. Search 'MLC school city experience' for a case study of using iPads in class.
- M-learning.org provides advice, information, resources, and case studies on mobile learning.

- Visit the *Using Social Media in the Classroom* companion website for links, discussions, and resources relating to using games and mobile devices in teaching and learning. You can find this at www.sagepub.co.uk/poore

Further reading

- Chiong, C. and Shuler, C. (2010) *Learning: is there an app for that? Investigations of young children's usage and learning with mobile devices and apps.* New York: The Joan Ganz Cooney Center at Sesame Workshop. Available at http://www.joanganzcooneycenter.org/Reports-27.html. Accessed 13 October 2011.

- DEECD (2011) In their hands. Getting started. Classroom ideas for learning with the iPad resource booklet for schools. Department of Education and Early Childhood Development, State of Victoria. Available at http://www.ipadsforeducation.vic.edu.au/userfiles/files/ipads_for_learning_21Steps.pdf. Accessed 13 October 2011.
- Habgood, M. P. J. and Ainsworth, S. E. (2011) Motivating children to learn effectively: exploring the value of intrinsic integration in educational games, *Journal of the Learning Sciences,* 20(2), 169–206.
- Hew, K. F. and Cheung, W. S. (2010) Use of three-dimensional (3-D) immersive virtual worlds in K-12 and higher education settings: a review of the research, *British Journal of Educational Technology,* 41(1), 33–55.
- Mallan, K. M., Foth, M., Greenaway, R. and Young, G. T. (2010) Serious playground: using Second Life to engage high school students in urban planning, *Journal of Learning, Media and Technology,* 35(2), 203–25.
- Ulicsak, M. and Williamson, B. (2010) *Computer games and learning*. A Futurelab handbook. Available at http://www.futurelab.org.uk/resources/computer-games-and-learning-handbook. Accessed 1 November 2011.

CHAPTER 12

PRODUCTIVITY TOOLS

Overview

Digital productivity tools extend beyond proprietary 'office' software such as Word and Excel – and by the same token it can be said that social media tools extend beyond services used primarily for entertainment and social connection. This chapter covers online tools that blend these two 'formats'. These tools use the sharing elements of social media to improve the productivity emphases of office software. Not only can such tools be useful in the management of your own workflow, but they can also be used with students to encourage object sharing, which, in turn, can improve students' skills for storing and managing information. Online documents, calendars, file repositories, note-taking services, and to-do lists are all described before moving on to benefits for efficiency, productivity, and collaboration. Issues around backup and editing, as well as privacy and copyright considerations, are covered in the last part of the chapter.

What are productivity tools?

A variety of online productivity tools is available. This section explores some of the most common.

Ideas. Productivity tools ideas

- Use these tools to **teach students information management**.
- Set up a group account and **share files** easily between students or research team members.
- Use Google docs for **group writing activities**.
- **Track students' document development** and assess weekly.
- Ask students to set up their Google Docs or Zoho space as an **information management task**.
- Ask students to share the school or class parts of their calendars within the class. Get them to use their calendar for **time management** purposes, and ask them to share their calendars with a buddy in the class to keep them on track.
- Give students access to the class parts of your calendar (but keep your other stuff private, obviously!).
- Explore various research management tools with your students. Ask them to **consider how they would use the tools for their study** or research assignments.
- Use Evernote, Connotea, Zotero, or Mendeley to **keep track of your academic bibliography and research notes**. Use them to add links, keep notes, tag resources, and compile bibliographies.
- Get class members **to subscribe (using RSS) to fellow students' online book-shelves** and to comment on the resources others are finding.

Online documents

Online documents provide a way of writing, storing, sharing, and managing text documents and other similar 'office' software (such as spreadsheets and slideshows) via the internet. Tools such as Google Docs and Zoho.com allow you to create documents and other common file types online without the need for downloading and installing separate, proprietary software. Because your documents are created and stored online, all you need to do is to log in to your account to access your files from any internet-connected device. Most services also allow you to create your document on a local drive, using software such as Microsoft Word, and then have them converted to Google Docs or Zoho format when you upload them to your online space. You can choose to keep your documents private, to share them with selected others who you invite to view or edit your file, or you can share them with the world – as with most social media, it depends on how you set it up and what your preferences are. If you have different users contributing to the same document, you can track their contributions both in real time and through a document or revision history, and you can add comments to a page or page section, just as you can with a wiki.

Dropboxes

Other online productivity services, such as Dropbox.com and Box.net, provide you with a repository space for 'dropping' files. Once you have put files into your 'dropbox' you can organise them into folders, share them, make them private or public, and edit and save as you want. These services synchronise your files across all your digital devices, enabling you to access your documents regardless of your location; if, for example, you use a desktop computer at home, but a laptop at school, then you can use a dropbox service to open a file at school, work on it, save it, and then access the same version of the document at home – this allows you to keep all your documents organised.

To-do lists

Instead of scribbling a list of important tasks on a ratty piece of paper that you are likely to lose, you can keep your to-do list on the web and access it from anywhere. To-do lists are supported by quite a number of different services, so make sure to do a comparison, as some services offer a very basic set of functions (add, 'complete', and remove items, only), whilst others include the ability to add due dates, schedule reminders, set up checklists, create folders and sub-folders, and much more.

Calendars

With internet-based calendar services such as Google Calendar you can keep your diary or calendar on the internet instead of in a paper diary or on software on your local harddrive. This allows you to add events and synchronise them across your various digital devices, which is especially handy if you are fairly 'mobile' and you need access to an up-to-date calendar at all times. You can easily shift between various views in a calendar (daily, weekly, monthly, yearly), and you can run several different, colour-coded calendars alongside each other.

Your web-based calendars can also be made public or private; if public, you can control how much information about your timetable people can see by simply displaying a 'busy' message in a timeslot instead of giving out the details of your schedule. Online calendars will give you notifications of upcoming events and will allow you to subscribe to other people's public calendars, so that you can keep track of the latest changes to their schedule, or you can make your own calendar open for subscription.

Note and research management

There are various ways to keep track of and share resources that you have found – and found useful – on the internet. Bookmarking was discussed in Chapter 10, and dropboxes discussed above, but there are other methods. Some services, such as Evernote.com, Zotero.org, and Mendeley.com are dedicated singly to helping you manage your research collections, bibliographies, and notes online and to synchronise them across your various digital devices. With these tools you can keep bookmarks, write and save notes, tag resources, upload and share documents and collections, and generally manage everything to do with a research (or other) project you might have under way. These services, although they all offer excellent functionality, have different target markets: Zotero and Mendeley are aimed at scholars and students wanting to organise their study and research materials in the one library, whilst Evernote tends to target a general audience and then relies on people to define how they want to use the service themselves. In any case, you should explore each of the services on your own, noting pluses and minuses for your context before deciding upon which would be best suited to your intended use.

Online bookshelves

A number of social media services allow you to create an 'online bookshelf', that is, a catalogue or virtual collection either of real books that you own or of books that you wish were sitting on your shelves at home. Online bookshelves such as Shelfari.com, Goodreads.com, and LibraryThing.com provide space for you to build reference lists and bibliographies, write book reviews, get recommendations, and, of course, share your collection and reading interests with others. You can browse others' lists, search tags for topics you wish to explore, or find authors you wish to read. As with almost all social media tools, online bookshelves also support RSS, so you can subscribe to different lists and collections.

Educational benefits of productivity tools

Improved workflow and efficiency

By their very nature, productivity tools are meant to improve workflow and efficiency. Although this can be useful for students, it is likely that such gains will be of more value to your own classroom administration processes.

Collaboration, group work, and editing

Productivity tools have clear benefits for group work: if you can create, edit, share, and access materials, then whole groups can collaborate in building documents online. This applies to teachers as much – perhaps even more so – as it does to students. As a teacher, you can work with colleagues on shared lesson plans, curriculum documents, school policies and guidelines, and the like. Students can work in teams to build documents, slideshows, and spreadsheets around class topics, and each student's contribution can be tracked. Perhaps the greatest educational benefit in this area is that students learn that writing is an ongoing process of revision and refinement.

Key point. Should I use a wiki or a collaborative document?

As with all social media, it depends on your purpose. Although the functionality of both would seem very similar, each is best used for different *types* of collaborative exercise. You should use a wiki if you want to create an ongoing information resource that can be updated as new or more relevant information becomes available. On the other hand, if you needed to work on just a handful of documents more for productivity purposes than for knowledge-construction and dissemination, then you might find a collaborative document of more use.

There is obviously some overlap, and in some cases one can easily be substituted for the other, but at least give it some thought before you start.

Class resource repositories

Both dropbox and shared document services can act as class resource repositories. Unlike wikis, where you aim to build a series of web pages around class topics, dropboxes allow you to simply deposit files for access by others or yourself. In a class context, you, as the teacher, could be the main curator of the repository, or you could ask students to curate different parts of the repository themselves. In the latter case, you could use the exercise as a way of teaching students about file management, especially as regards the value of consistency in file naming protocols.

Online bookshelves are ideal 'repositories' for library collections, whether the collection is real or virtual. Students can learn the art of writing book reviews by publishing their work on the bookshelf site. Alternatively, you might wish to teach information management and cataloguing by getting students to input the metadata for a book (such as tags, ISBN, publication date, language, summary) as part of an assignment.

Document version control and single storage location

We have all sent documents to our own email account so that we can collect them on another computer. This is a common, but not very elegant, solution to document version control and access. Using an online document avoids this inferior practice by allowing you to keep all your documents in the one place – either, say, in a folder in your dropbox, or in your Google Docs account. Moreover, having your files in an online space such as those just mentioned allows you to more easily share and collaborate on documents. This allows for easier document version control than it would if you were emailing a document around to your group and trying to keep track of who made which changes and when, and what version of the document you are up to. I have known workplaces that have emailed up to *27 versions* of a document within a group. Suffice it to say that there was much confusion as regards just about everything to do with the workflow involved.

Access across devices

A final advantage of using online productivity tools to organise your workflow is that your documents, to-do lists, calendars, and files can all be accessed across your electronic devices. Although many people still prefer to carry notebooks and such like, for those who are, perhaps, more 'mobile', this is a huge advantage: even if you have for some reason left your smartphone at home, you can always log on to your calendar on someone else's computer to check your availability for a meeting.

Special considerations for productivity tools

Conflicting edits on shared items

Collaborative online environments, such as those that support shared documents, always bring with them the potential for conflicting edits and changes. Although this is rare (often people are *not* working on a document at the same time), it nevertheless can cause problems if concurrent editing leads one version to be saved at the expense of another. Most services have systems in place to deal with these situations, however: for example, both versions might be saved, allowing you to make decisions about what material to combine later, or both versions might be 'merged' in real time.

Back-ups of online documents

If you set them up correctly, dropboxes will typically store a version of your files on each local hard drive you set up to receive dropped documents. Thus, if you lose your files on one computer or device, they should be stored on another that you have a dropbox on. This is not always the case with documents that are stored only online, however. In the event of a system-wide internet crash, any files that you have saved solely in the one online service could possibly be lost. The likelihood of this is remote, however, if you are using a large, reputable service, as such companies have multiple backup strategies in place for your data. That said, it is always prudent to export and keep safe (see Chapter 17) any essential documents that you simply cannot afford to lose.

Ideas. Be inspired!

- *Global warming speakout.* This project ran several years ago, but you can see how the group shared and documented their brainstorming processes for developing strategies to fight global warming (search 'Global warming speakout').

Public calendars

Although there are workflow benefits to allowing others to see your 'availability' in your public calendar, there are also obvious privacy and safety issues to consider if you share parts of your schedule. If people know that you will be, say, at a meeting or at lunch at a certain time and place, then it means that you are not at another location that an ill-intentioned person might desire access to.

The same applies to all forms of social networking: do not tweet or blog or write on Facebook messages such as, 'At Lady Gaga concert in London. Having a great time'. Similarly, you should never give away information about others' locations or interests: 'At Lady Gaga's London concert with Ella and Will'. In the first instance the information isn't yours to give away, and, in the second, all information can be used to construct a profile about you and your friends: people now know that you like Lady Gaga and are likely to attend any of her concerts next time she is in your home town.

The bottom line is that you need to be particularly careful about any information you publish to the wider world regarding your location. To give away such information is to telegraph your movements and compromise your security or that of your friends and students.

Although it is probably good advice to say that you should only share calendars with people you trust and know personally, you can still never account for the fact that trusted others might inadvertently share information about you that you would rather not have made public.

Copyright

Although dropboxes and similar online document repository services allow for the convenient storing and sharing of documents and files, they also allow for the easy breach of copyright. This can happen quite innocently if you share (or, in some cases, even just upload), for instance, a journal article or other item that you do not own copyright in. Be sure to understand the Terms of Service of your dropbox or similar service as they relate to the posting of materials that are not under your own copyright and to make informed judgements about the legality and suitability or otherwise of your sharing (or even hosting) such materials via your dropbox or other online repository. See Chapter 16 for more information.

 Summary

- Online productivity tools use social networking features such as sharing, collaboration, and synchronising to support efficient workplace and time management practices in online environments.
- Productivity tools can be used to access documents, calendars, notes, to-do lists, and similar items from any internet-connected device.
- Students can be taught file management and time management skills through the use of productivity tools.
- When using online document repositories, be sure to back up essential documents to a local drive or drives, just in case.
- Do not share specific location information – either yours or others' – when using social media. Such information can easily compromise your security.
- You may be in breach of copyright if you upload and/or share copyrighted documents via an online repository.

Resources

Online resources

- Google Docs for educators. Provides advice, examples, tips, and tricks. Search 'Google Docs for educators.'
- Search: 'Google docs school project' to find many interesting examples of and ideas for online document sharing in your classroom.
- Visit the *Using Social Media in the Classroom* companion website for links, discussions, and other materials relating to using productivity tools in teaching and learning. You can find this at www.sagepub.co.uk/poore

Further reading

- Benz, A. (2010) Writing a book with students, using Google Docs as shared learning environment: an experience, *International Journal of Innovation in Education,* 1(2), 139–47.
- Blau, I. and Caspi, A. (2009) What type of collaboration helps? Psychological ownership, perceived learning and outcome quality of collaboration using Google Docs, in Y. Eshet-Alkalai, A. Caspi, S. Eden, N. Geri, and Y. Yair (eds), *Proceedings of the Chais Conference on Instructional Technologies Research 2009: Learning in the Technological Era*. Raanana: The Open University of Israel. Available at http://telem-pub.openu.ac.il/users/chais/2009/noon/1_1.pdf. Accessed 13 October 2011.
- Kaimuloa Bates, B. (2011) Using Google Apps in professional learning communities. PowerPoint presented at the Technology, Colleges and Community Worldwide Online Conference, 14 April 2011. Available at http://scholarspace.manoa.hawaii.edu/bitstream/handle/10125/19960/etec_kaimuloabates.pdf?sequence=1. Accessed 13 October 2011.
- Leshed, G. and Sengers, P. (2011) 'I lie to myself that i have freedom in my own schedule': productivity tools and experiences of busyness, in *Proceedings of the 2011 Annual Conference on Human Factors in Computing Systems*. Available at http://leshed.comm.cornell.edu/pubs/p905-leshed.pdf. Accessed 13 October 2011.

PART 4

SOCIAL
CONTEXTS

Part 4 deals with issues of central concern to anyone who uses social media with their students, regardless of the age or experience levels of those students. Chapter 13 addresses debates around 'digital natives' and explores the need for 'new learning' approaches and for teachers to address digital literacy deficits amongst their students. Chapter 14 examines the digital divide and digital participation, whilst Chapter 15 focuses on the tricky topic of cyberbullying. The last two chapters look in depth at some of the more difficult legal, policy, and service issues you need to account for in your use of social media (Chapter 16), as well as the practical and in-class considerations that you may be confronted with (Chapter 17).

CHAPTER 13

'DIGITAL NATIVES', NEW LEARNING, AND DIGITAL LITERACY

Overview

This chapter begins by addressing the idea of the 'digital native' and argues that although young people today certainly don't come to us 'hard wired for the web' many of them nevertheless have certain expectations and needs that are a result of the considerable amounts of time they spend online. From this, we move on to discuss the need for 'new learning' through an examination of the current historical and techno-social moment in which we find ourselves. This entails an exploration of the technological revolutions that humans have undergone, as well as a critique of the industrial model of schooling and why it is failing us at the start of the 'digital revolution'. Curriculum issues are also covered as a way of interrogating the rationales for including information and communication technologies in education.

The discussion of digital literacy that follows next is an important one, not least because I identify three core components that provide a useful framework for building students' (and our own) all-round abilities in digital environments: functional, network, and critical digital literacy. The chapter ends by investigating just how digitally literate our students are and identifies some of the key challenges we face in building students' online literacy for new learning.

The 'digital natives' debate

In 2001 Marc Prensky coined the term 'digital native' in a now-famous paper called 'Digital natives, digital immigrants'. In the paper, Prensky argued that, because of their immersion in digital environments, today's students 'think and process information fundamentally differently from their predecessors' (Prensky, 2001a, p. 1, emphasis removed) and that 'it is very likely that our students' brains have physically changed – and are different from ours [older generations'] – *as a result of how they grew up.*' (Prensky, 2001a, p. 1, emphasis added). Prensky followed this paper with another that investigated the role of neuroplasticity in the brain structures of 'digital natives' (as he called them), showing that neuroscientists were discovering the amazing ability of the brain to 'rewire' itself and to create new neural pathways, even into adulthood. This malleability, said Prensky, meant that digital natives were laying down cognitive structures that supported quick-fire parallel processing rather than sequential thinking 'as a result of repeated experiences' (Prensky, 2001b, p. 4).

Both papers sparked a huge amount of debate and discussion in education circles – debate and discussion that is still going on. On the one hand, there were educators who instinctively 'knew' that their students were different from the kids they'd taught over previous generations and for whom Prensky's arguments made intuitive sense. On the other hand, there were those who criticised Prensky as a biological and technological determinist (cf Kennedy et al., 2006; Oliver, 2011) (although it should be made clear that Prensky was by no means arguing for some kind of spontaneous evolutionary shift in the brain structures of people born after a certain date, as some seem to have inferred).

Regardless of these debates, we need to be very wary about what Eric Hoover (2009) calls 'generational thinking', which, he says, displays two underlying assumptions: (1) That millions of people born after a certain date are 'fundamentally different' from other age groups, and (2) that 'those people are similar to each other in meaningful ways' (Hoover, 2009, online). Hoover further notes that the Millennial (or 'digital native') label has really only been applied to affluent, white teenagers with good life opportunities, rather than the 'poor and black'. A further problem is that there is no agreed-upon 'start date' for the generation that is also variously labelled the 'Net Gen', the 'iGen', and the 'Google Gen', amongst other things.

Bearing these cautions in mind, there should, however, be little argument that socialisation and environment each have a large impact on how one thinks about, interacts with, and views the world. This simple fact of culture requires us, as educators, to respond to the current techno-social conditions that our students experience, whilst at the same time recognising that (1) not all students grow up with digital technology at their fingertips, (2) that there is nothing 'innate' about any group of people, but (3) that we should use any positive features furnished by digital technology for the benefit of our teaching and learning.

So, what can we say about the historical techno-social moment in which we find ourselves? And how might this demand a shift in our approach to teaching and learning? The next section examines these questions in light of 'new learning', that is, learning that adjusts our focus from industrial models of schooling to more personalised, digital ones.

New learning

In order to grasp some of the broader societal processes that are presently putting pressure on formal, western education systems, we need to briefly examine the history of technological revolutions as they apply to industrialised nations. This should help us gain an appreciation for the uniqueness of the historical moment that confronts both our students and ourselves as educators. The point is that if we understand the history and complexity of the situation – and not just the technical elements of digital technologies – then we can bring that understanding to bear on the informed and effective use of social media in the classroom.

The Digital Revolution

Every so often, humanity experiences a technological revolution, that is, a rapid and dramatic change in how we use tools and techniques to structure our systems of production, our culture and civilisation, our social and political relations, and our everyday lives more generally. Even more than these impacts, though, technological revolutions typically lead to shifts in consciousness, that is, to shifts in how we understand the world, and how we understand ourselves and others: *revolutions change how we think and what we think about*. Today, we are arguably undergoing a 'digital revolution' (more on this, shortly) – but this is not the first such revolution that humanity has faced: there have been technological revolutions in the past.

Perhaps the earliest example of such a phenomenon is the Agricultural (or 'Neolithic') Revolution which began around 10,000 years ago. This revolution was characterised by the cultivation of crops and the domestication of animals, but also, conceptually speaking, by notions of sedentarism and boundedness (as we started to 'put down roots' in the one spot and mark off our own territory to distinguish it from that of others'), all of which led to social, cultural, political, and economic transformation. The Industrial Revolution, which began in the late eighteenth century, is another identifiable technological revolution. In this instance, we see the introduction of manufacturing and machinery that support processes of mass production, the introduction of large-scale markets, changes in the concept of labour, the emergence of commodities, and the development of ideas of economic rationalism, capitalism, and socialism. Again, these changes went hand in glove with shifts in consciousness at a societal level.

Presently, we are seeing another set of technological impacts that are compelling us to adjust our systems of production, our sociocultural structures, and the ways in which we think about our world and our relation to it; digital technologies are arguably forcing us into another revolutionary period, this time characterised by the internet, digital computing, unprecedented access to data and information, and new modes of communication. This revolution might be viewed as the 'Digital', 'Information', or 'Knowledge' Revolution, as what is driving the transformation of industrial modes of socio-economic operation is not mass production, but rather processes of customisation, data generation, and information expansion.

It is important to understand these changes because, through the Industrial Revolution, we have developed systems and structures that suit the schooling of children under conditions of mass production, continuous flow, and proprietary ownership. However, such structures might not be so acceptable under circumstances that favour the growth and sharing of knowledge in a connected social media network that functions on creativity, personalisation, and openness.

Industrial-model schooling

The type of schooling that currently characterises our approach to education is often described as the 'industrial model of schooling', which, as signalled above, emerged alongside processes of mass production, standardisation, and continuous flow that characterise factory work. Churches (n.d.) describes classrooms based on this model as being represented by inflexibility, passivity, one-to-many instruction, competition, memorisation, separation. This comes about through a system that emphasises standardisation, homogeneity, uniformity, regimentation, and sequencing as a form of hidden curriculum that prepares students to be useful contributors to industry-based economies.

It is easy to criticise this industrial model as being out of date, repressive of human creativity, and unduly driven by economic concerns. However, we must bear in mind that the Industrial Revolution also led to improved standards of living, better health care, increased life expectancy, and – because of, not despite, the industrial model of schooling – a more literate and educated populace. Nevertheless, there is no denying that little has changed in schooling since the nineteenth century, and the end results are:

- *A mostly unchanged curriculum* that emphasises facts and memorisation for tests. The problems that are taught are taught for the test and to quantify 'learning', and are not necessarily those problems that might be 'best' for the student.
- *Over-use of 'old' technologies* and little to no use of social media and other digital technologies at all. Effective interactive whiteboard use is a rarity, not the norm.
- *Transmission practices and pedagogies* where 'I speak, you listen', which perpetuates 'old' knowledge and things we already know, rather than 'new knowledges' that are developed co-operatively.
- *Teacher-centric classrooms in which the teacher is the main repository of information in the room*. This method of classroom operation is unsustainable when the whole internet is available to students as a research tool.

> '[w]ith good discipline, it is always possible to pump into the minds of a class a certain quantity of inert knowledge.' Alfred North Whitehead, *The Aims of Education* (1967 [1929]).

The broader social, cultural, and economic processes at play today are rendering these approaches to schooling obsolete and demand that we revisit our model of education and make it more relevant for a twenty-first-century learner living in a milieu permeated by social media. To this end, we need 'new learning' that accommodates both the learner and the environment. But what, exactly, has changed? What is 'new'?

Why do we need 'new learning'?

At the turn of the century, the Australian Council of Deans of Education (ACDE, 2001) drew up a charter for Australian education and called it 'New learning'. In it, they identified three areas of society that are changing and that require a response from the education sector if we are to provide relevant schooling for twenty-first-century learners. These areas were:

- Technology
- Commerce
- Culture.

The ACDE argued that we cannot continue to teach 'old subjects' (science, maths, business studies, English, history, and such) across these areas, and, instead, we need to teach 'new basics' for the 'new worker', the 'new citizen', and the 'new person' (ACDE, 2001, p. 92). These new basics are described as being competencies in discovery, navigation, negotiation, mediation, communication, reflection, investigation, and discernment, amongst other things (ACDE, 2001, p. 92). In other words, the skills needed to succeed in a knowledge society are different from those needed in an industrial one. Although the basic literacies and numeracies remain the same, in an information-rich environment students also need to have skills for discovering, accessing, evaluating, applying, and creating new knowledge, and for 'learning how to learn'. This entire notion of 'new learning' is important in the current context because the use of social media in the classroom so obviously provides us with the opportunity to force a break with industrial models of schooling and to embrace models that are more personalised, customised, and flexible.

> '[t]he capacity to learn something new has become more critical than knowing what is currently known.' David Loader, *Jousting for the New Generation* (2007).

In fact, there are numerous calls for new approaches to teaching and learning, and most of them recognise the centrality of ICTs in education (see, for example, Bruns, 2008; Carrington and Robinson, 2009; Loader, 2007; Yelland, 2007). Again, we can look to ideas posited at the turn of the century – this time around curricula – to help us understand the current context and how it impacts on our use of social media in classroom activities.

Curriculum issues

Toni Downes et al. (2001, p. 23) identify four main 'types' of rationale that are usually given when arguments for integrating ICT into the curriculum arise. They are:

Type A: encouraging the acquisition of ICT skills as an end in itself;

Type B: using ICTs to enhance students' abilities within the existing curriculum;

Type C: introducing ICTs as an integral component of broader curricular reforms that are changing not only how learning occurs but what is learned;

Type D: introducing ICTs as an integral component of the reforms that alter the organisation and structure of schooling itself.

Nicola Yelland (2007, pp. 1–2) allies herself with the Type C rationale when she says, 'we should not be mapping the use of new technologies onto old curricula; rather, we need to rethink our curricula and pedagogies in light of the impact that we know new technologies can have on learning and meaning making in contemporary times'. So, on this view, new technologies demand a fundamental shift in how we conceptualise curricula and pedagogies and how we respond to the sociocultural context – and social media are central to that context.

We are now in a position to compare 'old learning' with what I call 'new learning *potential*' (see Table 13.1). I say 'potential' because simply having access to and using digital technology in the classroom does not immediately secure effective use and positive learning outcomes (see Chapters 1 and 2). Further, many of the items that appear in the 'new learning' column, below, are already indicative of the best classrooms (and, arguably, have always been) and do not need technology to make them happen.

Table 13.1   Old learning vs new learning potential

Old learning	New learning potential
Teacher-centric	Learner-centric
Passive	Active and interactive
One-to-many	Individualised learning
Lack of flexibility	Flexible
Monolithic learner	Learning communities
Competition	Sharing and networking
Memorisation	Creativity, discovery, exploration
Separation	Participation and collaboration

In any case, there can be no doubt that digital technology in general, and social media in particular, are central to twenty-first-century life and culture in the west. As teachers, we have a moral obligation to respond to the socio-technological moment in which we find ourselves, and, as teachers, that means that we must prepare young people to participate usefully and ethically in a social media world. In the first instance, that means understanding, and addressing, students' digital literacy.

> It is no longer sustainable to approach the educational enterprise as if the teacher is the sole repository of information and knowledge in the room. The internet has changed all that.

Digital literacy

The notion of literacy has expanded in recent years. No longer is it confined to the ability to read and write; as Julia Davies (2009, p. 29) points out, '[l]iteracy is not just about decoding marks on a page; it is also about performing social acts of meaning, where meanings and practices vary according to context'. Thus, we now talk of 'financial literacy' (the ability to understand money and finance), 'scientific literacy' (the ability to understand and apply scientific concepts), 'cultural literacy' (the ability to understand and take part in particular cultural practices), 'visual literacy' (the ability to understand and interpret symbols and images), and so on. 'Digital literacy' is a term that can be added to this list, and it is one that concerns us as users of digital social media.

Before we explore digital literacy in more detail, though, it should be noted that 'digital literacy' is sometimes referred to as 'ICT literacy', 'media literacy', 'new media literacy', and even 'information literacy'. Here, I endorse the term '*digital* literacy' for two main reasons: first, it does not limit us to devices, tools, and their functionality (as could be inferred from the term 'ICT'), and, second, it does not invite confusion around the term 'media', which can be taken to mean both (or either) digital products and the social processes that constitute their use. 'Digital' is a term that allows us to describe a spectrum of skills and knowledges that characterise literacy in this area.

What is digital literacy?

There is no single, agreed-upon definition of 'digital literacy', although there is a good deal of cross-over in the discussions around the topic.

David Buckingham (2006, p. 267) demonstrates that 'digital literacy' is more than simply knowing how to point and click:

> The skills that children need in relation to digital media are not confined to those of information retrieval. As with print, they also need to be able to evaluate and use information critically if they are to transform it into knowledge. This means asking questions about the sources of that information, the interests of its producers, and the ways in which it represents the world; and understanding how these technological developments are related to broader social, political and economic forces.

Payton and Hague (2010, p. 4) of Futurelab.co.uk point to a similar set of issues when they describe digital literacy as:

> the ability to make, represent and share meaning in different modes and formats; to create, collaborate and communicate effectively; and to understand how and when digital technologies can best be used to support these processes. Digital literacy involves critically engaging with technology and developing a social awareness of how a number of factors, including commercial agendas and cultural understandings, can shape the ways in which technology is used to convey information and meaning.

And similar qualities can be found in MCEECDYA's (Australia's Ministerial Council for Education, Early Childhood Development and Youth Affairs) definition, which describes digital literacy (MCEECDYA uses the term 'ICT literacy') as 'the ability of individuals to use ICT appropriately to access, manage, integrate and evaluate information, develop new understandings, and communicate with others in order to participate effectively in society' (2010, p. viii). All of this points to the fact that rather than see literacy simply as a set of functional or cognitive skills, we need to understand it as a set of social practices (Grant, 2007, p. 5.).

Functional, network, and critical digital literacy: towards a holistic understanding of digital literacy

From all of the above, we can see that there is a good deal of definitional crossover and conceptual alignment as regards the notion of digital literacy. To help tidy things up a bit, though, it might help to think of digital literacy as being separated into three literacy 'sub-divisions':

1   *Functional digital literacy*. In the age of Web 2.0, this does not mean knowing how to hard code, or how to program, or how to write javascript, as it might once have done. With new social media all the 'technical' work is done behind the scenes, allowing 'non-techies' to have a web presence without knowing how to create a website from scratch (see Chapter 1). Rather, *functional* digital literacy refers to the ability to operate in a digital environment from a practical standpoint: it means knowing how to sign up for a service and how to activate your account; it means knowing how to find, add, and invite friends; knowing how to upload a profile photo; knowing where to sign in and how to log out, and so on. Many younger users of the internet develop this kind of literacy through simply being online, and they have a facility with some social media – especially social networks – in which they know where to click.

2   *Network digital literacy*. This entails understanding what it means to be a networked citizen, which in turn means knowing how to manage your

various online profiles and identities; knowing what happens to the material you upload; knowing about data management; understanding online risk management; knowing how to read and interpret Terms of Service and Privacy Policies; understanding the privacy implications of posting photos and other information, and so on. At base, we are referring, here, to an understanding of boyd's (*sic*) four properties of networked publics. They are (1) persistence, (2) searchability, (3) replicability, and (4) invisible audiences (boyd, 2011). When exploring network digital literacy, we would ask questions such as, 'Do you know what it means when Facebook asks for a "non-exclusive, transferable, sub-licensable, royalty-free, worldwide license to use any IP content that you post on or in connection with Facebook"?' Many people lack this digital literacy.

3 *Critical digital literacy*. This element of digital literacy links into the ability to use social media and ICT to further cognition and to critique the world around us. Critical digital literacy is about using skills to find, validate, interpret, analyse, critique, evaluate, synthesise, and communicate information, and then to use those skills to transform old meanings or to create new ones. Critical digital literacy is about higher-level thinking and engagement with cultural, social, political, and intellectual life more generally in a networked world. It could be argued that you can have a critical digital literacy without knowing how to use a computer, or how to manage online risk. In fact, I know one professor who has written well-regarded and critically informed books about 'digital schooling' but who simultaneously has little idea about how to tag a photo and whether it is appropriate or not to do so.

How digitally literate are our students?

Independent authorities that regulate communications in developed nations frequently conduct studies into the take-up and knowledge of, attitudes towards, and concerns about, digital and social media amongst parents and children. The UK regulator, Ofcom, conducts ongoing interview-based surveys into children's media literacy, as does ACMA, the equivalent Australian authority. These studies provide valuable insights into questions such as, What kinds of devices are being used for what purposes and by whom? Where do children access the internet? How many children play online games? and, How many children have an online profile? Such surveys also tell us about children's attitudes and behaviours as they apply to accessing, evaluating, and trusting the information they obtain from websites and other media sources. That said, such surveys do not seek to measure digital literacy proficiency levels – they merely report on current attitudes, usage, concerns, and knowledge. Australia's National Assessment Program for ICT Literacy, however, does strive to provide us with just such a measure.

In 2010, the National Assessment Program published the results of its second study of Australian school students' 'ICT literacy' levels at Years 6 and 10. Using a scale of proficiency that measured students' abilities across three 'strands' (specifically, working with information, creating and sharing information, and using ICT responsibly), it was found that:

- 57 per cent of Year 6 students met the proficiency standard (up from 49 per cent in 2005), and
- 66 per cent of Year 10 students met the proficiency standard (up from 61 per cent in 2005).

In discussing these results with teachers and parents, the comment is often made that these results seem 'low'. This is especially the case if we entertain the image of the 'digital native' described earlier. However, such results remind us that today's students do not come to us as fully formed 'tech-heads' who somehow instinctively know how to use computers. Instead, today's students are just like anyone else involved in a complex undertaking: their skills and knowledge must be advanced over time and appropriately scaffolded if higher-order thinking skills and digital literacy are to be developed.

 Activity: What are young people doing online in your country?

Visit the website of the communications regulatory authority in your country. Here is a starting list:

- Australia: Australian Communications and Media Authority (ACMA).
- Canada: Canadian Radio-television and Telecommunications Commission (CRTC).
- New Zealand: Commerce Commission of New Zealand (ComCom).
- South Africa: Independent Communications Authority of South Africa (ICASA).
- UK: Office of Communications (Ofcom).
- USA: Federal Communications Commission (FCC).

If your country is not listed, search Wikipedia for 'List of telecommunications regulatory bodies' and try to locate it there. Otherwise, conduct a web search.

(Continued)

(Continued)

Find a study that investigates and reports upon young people's media use in your country. Look for patterns as well as specific data on:

- Television viewing routines
- Internet behaviour
- Video and game playing habits
- Mobile phone usage
- Music downloading practices
- Media literacy and awareness.

Ask yourself questions such as, Are there patterns associated with gender? Age group? Socio-economic background? What do you think students will expect and need from you in terms of digital literacy? What will you need to account for in your classroom? How developed are their media literacy skills?

Students' experiences with using digital technologies in formal learning

In the past decade, various studies have examined the student experience of technology use in schools, colleges, and in universities (CIBER, 2008; Green and Hannon, 2007; JISC, 2008; Oblinger and Hawkins, 2006; Salway et al. 2009). If we consolidate the findings of this research, we can identify some key themes as they apply to formal learning across a range of ages.

- Students see digital technology primarily as a platform for delivery or administration.
- Convenience and control, not learning, are often the main reasons cited by students for using digital technology at school or college.
- Students are frequently uncertain about how their current use of technology might be transferred to their study – they often cannot see how technology and formal learning can work together. They expect teachers to show them.
- Belief in proficiency is often over-rated: confidence does not equal competence. Young people often have quite under-developed media and digital literacy skills.
- There has been an increase in full-phrase searching and students often use only the most basic forms of search, looking only at the first page of 'hits' returned by a search engine.
- Little time is spent evaluating sources for accuracy, relevance, validity, or authority and students have difficulty in prioritising search results.
- Young people are concerned about the 'unmanageable scale' (Green and Hannon, 2007, p. 68) of the web and often feel overwhelmed by the amount of information available.

- There is sometimes a gap between knowing how to create content (say, videos, images, and so on) and how to create *meaningful* content.

At this point, it should be stressed that there is no evidence that young people's information literacy is worse than it was before the growth of social media in particular and the web in general. Rather, we need to remember that youngsters do not come online fully formed as expert searchers, that they have always had trouble evaluating information, and that their intellectual practices are now more visible and public than they have ever been. Just as they always have, young people need guidance on how to think and how to think well. In the digital environment this still holds: students often require guidance – not so much on how to use the technology itself in a functional sense – but more on how to *think with the technology* and how to *think with information*.

The implication of all this is that facility with and confidence around digital technology does not equate to digital literacy: we need to be careful about the assumptions we make regarding the skills, competencies, and knowledge that young people bring with them to online environments and, perhaps most importantly, we need to build digital literacy through 'systematic teaching rather than incidental use' (MCEETYA, 2007, p. 93).

 Summary

- There is a danger in 'generational thinking' in that it can label entire groups of people as being essentially different from others, and that it can imply that those people are 'similar to each other in meaningful ways' (Hoover, 2009, online). This danger applies to labels such as 'digital natives', 'net gen', 'millennials', 'iGen', and 'Google gen'.
- Nevertheless, there is no doubt that socialisation and environment each have a large impact on how one thinks about, interacts with, and views the world. This simple fact of culture requires us, as educators, to respond to the current techno-social conditions that our students experience.
- We need to take advantage of the digital technologies available to us for 'new learning' as we experience a 'digital revolution'.
- Being digitally literate is essential to success in modern life and work. There are three main elements of digital literacy: functional, network, and critical digital literacy.
- Students may appear confident around digital technology and social media, but confidence should not be mistaken for competence. Students are often looking for guidance on how to think *with and about* the technology.

Resources

Online resources

- Futurelab.org.uk hosts many excellent digital literacy resources. Go to their website and search for 'digital literacy' in the search box.
- Digital media literacy is a focus of the Australian Communications and Media Authority. Go to Acma.gov.au and search for 'digital literacy' in the search box.

- Visit the *Using Social Media in the Classroom* companion website for links, discussions, and other materials relating to using digital literacy and 'new learning' issues. You can find this at www.sagepub.co.uk/poore

Further reading

- Bostrom, N. (2007) Technological revolutions: ethics and policy in the dark, in N. M. de S. Cameron and M. E. Mitchell (eds) *Nanoscale: Issues and Perspectives for the Nano Century*. Hoboken, NJ: John Wiley, pp. 129–52.
- CIBER (2008) Information behaviour of the researcher of the future. Centre for Information Behaviour and the Evaluation of Research. Available at http://www.ucl.ac.uk/infostudies/research/ciber/downloads/. Accessed 13 October 2011.
- Grant, L. (2010) Connecting digital literacy between home and school. Futurelab. Available at http://www.futurelab.org.uk/resources/connecting-digital-literacy-between-home-and-school. Accessed 13 October 2011.
- Hague, C. (2010) 'It's not chalk and talk anymore'. School approaches to developing students' digital literacy. Futurelab report. Available at http://www.futurelab.org.uk/resources/%E2%80%9Cit%E2%80%99s-not-chalk-and-talk-anymore%E2%80%9D-school-approaches-developing-students%E2%80%99-digital-literacy. Accessed 13 October 2011.
- Hague, C. and Payton, S. (2010) Digital literacy across the curriculum. A Futurelab handbook. Available at http://archive.futurelab.org.uk/resources/publications-reports-articles/handbooks/Handbook1706. Accessed 13 October 2011.
- Hoover, E. (2009) The Millennial muddle: how stereotyping students became a thriving industry and a bundle of contradictions, *The Chronicle of Higher Education*, 11 October 2009. Available at http://chronicle.com/article/The-Millennial-Muddle-How/48772/. Accessed 25 January 2010.
- Payton, S. and Hague, C. (2010) Digital literacy professional development resource. Futurelab. Available at http://www.futurelab.org.uk/resources/digital-literacy-professional-development-resource. Accessed 13 October 2011.

CHAPTER 14

THE DIGITAL DIVIDE AND DIGITAL PARTICIPATION

Overview

This chapter explores the development of the idea of the 'digital divide' and describes current understandings of how the digital divide is affecting our lives, that is, that the divide today is often described more in terms of access to networks and knowledge than it is simply in terms of access to hardware. The chapter then goes on to discuss the differences between a 'participation' approach and an 'inclusion' approach to bridging this divide, meaning that, although social inclusion agendas may have a noble end in mind, they nevertheless cannot help but present those 'being included' as passive objects of policy rather than as active participants in a society. A participation approach is preferred because its starting point assumes not that students need to have things done to them (that is, to 'be included'), but that young people have something valuable and worthwhile to contribute to begin with. The chapter demonstrates the importance of building the digital capital of all students.

The digital divide

What is the digital divide?

The term 'digital divide' has been around since the mid-1990s and is generally understood to describe the gap between those who have access to digital technology and those who do not (Green and Hannon, 2007, pp. 59–60). In the early days of home computing this problem of 'access' was explained almost solely in terms of access to the hardware systems that supported it – meaning, access to PCs, printers, laptops, the internet, servers, email, and the like.

Today, however, the nature of the divide has shifted. No longer is simple access to equipment as big a problem as previously: hardware has become cheaper, allowing more and more people to have a computer or similar device, and even if you don't have a desktop computer at home, you are likely to have a computer in your pocket (namely, your smartphone), or you might own a netbook or laptop. If this is so – that *most* people have *some sort* of access to computing hardware – then we might be forgiven for thinking that the digital divide is no longer an issue in contemporary society. But this is not the case. Rather, we are seeing the clear emergence of other forms of divide as regards digital technologies, only this time in relation to patterns of *use*, as opposed to patterns of ownership.

What we are seeing now is a divide that is becoming more and more about *access to knowledge and networks*, and *the ways in which people use technologies to participate* in daily social life, rather than a divide that is only about access to PCs (Green and Hannon, 2007, pp. 59–60). As we saw in Chapter 13 in relation to digital literacy, this is all tied up with *knowing how to think with and about the technology*: it is not just about knowing how to point and click, because simply having a computer at home does not automatically guarantee its effective use for learning or for constructive social participation. This situation has no doubt been exacerbated by the rise in collaborative social media technologies since 2005.

Digital capital

Lyndsay Grant (2007) describes this problem in terms of the 'capital' that people use to negotiate their daily lives. 'Capital' is a term used by social scientists to describe people's 'wealth' as it relates not to money but to the resources, knowledge, skills, networks, and connections that are valued by, and valuable in, a society. In terms of access to digital technology, 'economic capital' refers to the financial resources to purchase hardware; 'social capital' refers to having the social connections to access networks of expertise, to being able to ask the right people for advice or help, and to getting recommendations and suggestions; and 'cultural capital' refers to how to perform and operate in culturally appropriate ways, that is, how to use the technology for communication and engagement. Without the appropriate capital, people find it difficult to take part in society. In particular, Grant says that:

> [s]tudents who do not have the economic, cultural and social capital to achieve meaningful and effective engagement with ICTs out of school ... may find themselves disadvantaged as a new literacies paradigm becomes increasingly important for participation in social routines. (Grant, 2007, p. 6)

In other words, students can have all the latest devices and gizmos that are out there, but can still be left behind in terms of the type of 'digital capital' they generate or have access to. For example, one student might be using their netbook's internet connection to spread gossip about a classmate via Facebook, whilst another might be using it to take part in a biodiversity action group discussion and arrange a meeting with a Member of Parliament about the encroachment of urban areas on local wildlife habitat. Each student is using digital technology (both hardware and collaborative social media tools and services) but they are using it in ways that will affect their life opportunities quite differently.

All of this is more about the ability to participate in meaningful social – and societal – relations than it is about just accessing hardware. However, there is one final element of this complex situation that we need to consider, and that is the difference between theoretical and effective access to digital technologies, also discussed by Grant (2007, pp. 1–2).

Theoretical access versus effective access

'Theoretical' access refers to the access to technology that a student has, or would have, under ideal conditions. For example, the student's family has a desktop computer at home, therefore the student has theoretical access to it. However, the student's 'effective' access might be limited to the times when it is not in use by another family member: perhaps mum has priority because of a report she's finishing for work, or maybe an elder sibling needs the machine to complete an assignment for a university course. Similarly, a student might have theoretical access to a computer at the local library, or in a school computer laboratory, but their practical or effective access is limited to opening hours, the times that they can get to the library, the times that the laboratory is not booked by teachers, time limits on usage for public computers, and so on.

None of this is to deny, however, that there are, indeed, groups within our society that simply do not have access to either digital technology or to *working* digital technology outside the school environment (and even then the 'working' elements of the equation can sometimes be called into question). Students from low socio-economic backgrounds might fall into this category, especially if their families cannot afford to pay for an internet connection, as might students who live in rural or remote areas where internet connectivity is intermittent or non-existent, or students whose families simply do not hold with the use of social media or online technologies in the home. It is essential to remember that although many young people today appear to 'always be connected' things might not be as they seem.

To summarise, the digital divide was originally described largely in terms of access to hardware and its supporting technologies. Today, however, a second 'passage' in the divide has opened up, and it is one that affects the ability to use digital technologies to develop the knowledge, skills, connections, and resources used to participate in social life and build digital capital in a networked society. Nevertheless, it should not be forgotten that some students have limited effective access to digital technology both inside and outside the home, and some have none at all.

 Activity. Survey your class

Step 1. Build a survey (using an online survey tool such as SurveyMonkey or Zoomerang – see Chapter 10) that measures your students' levels of digital participation and digital literacy. Consider asking questions along the lines of:

- Do you have a computer at home? If so, what kind (PC, Mac, laptop, desktop, other)?
- Do you have an internet connection at home?
- Do you own or have access to a mobile phone? Tablet device (such as an iPad)?
- How many hours a day do you/can you access the internet at home? Where else do you access the internet (school, library, friend's house, elsewhere)?
- How many hours a week do you spend on Facebook? Club Penguin? Moshi Monsters? YouTube? Twitter? Discussion forums? Blogging? Podcasting? Online gaming? (Or whatever else you think might be relevant to the age and level of your class.)
- Do you create rich media objects or mashups?
- How would you rate your own digital literacy?
- How would you describe the kinds of activities that you participate in online (such as social, political, educational, school-based activities, and so on)?

These questions are just to give you an idea of the types of data you might want to collect. You will have to spend some time refining your own questions to suit your classroom context. Some questions will require simple 'yes/no/don't know' answers, whilst others will need a 'Likert scale' that ranges from 'strongly agree' to 'strongly disagree', or answers that are along the lines of 'often, sometimes, rarely, never'. You might also consider asking some open-ended questions so that students can provide more personalised responses.

The Annenberg School for Communication and Journalism at the University of Southern California has an excellent media literacy quiz that you could base your class survey on (search 'USC media literacy quiz'). Alternatively, search for other quizzes to give you some ideas for questions you should include in your own survey.

Step 2. Once you have collected your data and analysed it, consider the special needs of your class. Are there students or groups of students who have greater or less access than others? What is the general skill level like? Are there strengths in the class (for example, a preference for gaming or rich media) that you can work to in terms of developing useful learning activities that are likely to suit students' learning preferences? Are there areas that need improvement? Are there certain kinds of activities that you simply cannot ask students to undertake because they do not have effective access to the right kinds of tools? How can you develop in students the skills and knowledge they will need to build digital capital in an online world?

Digital participation

If, then, the problem of the digital divide is rather more complex than simply having access to hardware, how can we conceive of a culture in which students use digital technologies and social media to build digital capital? What sort of social and school policy frameworks do we need if we are to encourage young people to use social media in active, meaningful, and responsible ways? How can we bridge the digital divide? To answer this question, we must first make a brief examination of social inclusion policies that seek to rectify imbalances in other areas of society. We then need to identify where these policies fall short so that we can avoid such pitfalls in the development of a more 'participatory' – not merely 'inclusive' – digital culture.

Social inclusion

The current social policy settings in western democracies favour what is known as 'social inclusion'. Social inclusion policies recognise that there are people in society who are disenfranchised and/or being left behind in employment, housing, health, transport, finance, and other important areas. The UK, in contrast to most other jurisdictions (for example, France, the European

Union, Australia, Canada, and New Zealand), takes a 'deficit' approach and focuses on 'exclusion' rather than 'inclusion', but the intended policy outcomes are the same across nations in that they seek to redress imbalances and to improve outcomes for the socially disadvantaged.

Whilst the sentiments behind inclusion are surely well-meaning, the concept is not without its problems, most notably in that the notion of 'inclusion' presents those 'being included' as passive objects of policy rather than as active participants in a society (Buckmaster and Thomas, 2009). Indeed, inclusion could be seen to imply the need to conform to dominant social discourses as opposed to the right to engage in the building of mutual interests through the free interaction of numerous and varied points of contact. This latter – the building of mutual interests through free interaction – is how John Dewey (2004 [1916]) describes true democracy in *Democracy and Education*, but it is also similar to Buckmaster and Thomas's concept of 'participation' (2009), where participation assumes not that people need to have things done to them (that is, 'be included'), but that people have something valuable and worthwhile to contribute to begin with.

Henry Jenkins (2006) is also a proponent of 'participation', especially as it pertains to young people and their use of digital social media. In his influential White Paper 'Confronting the challenges of participatory culture: media education for the 21st century', Jenkins described a participatory culture as:

> a culture with relatively low barriers to artistic expression and civic engagement, strong support for creating and sharing one's creations, and some type of informal mentorship whereby what is known by the most experienced is passed along to novices. A participatory culture is also one in which members believe their contributions matter, and feel some degree of social connection with one another. (Jenkins, 2006, p. 3)

Jenkins locates this culture in the digital realm by identifying several 'forms' of participatory culture (2006, p. 3) that include memberships to online communities (such as social networks, discussion forums); creation of new digital products (via mashups, digital sampling and the like); collaborative problem-solving (via Wikipedia, cheat manuals, and similar); and shaping the flow of media (for example, through blogging, Twitter, and podcasting). Through participation in these areas, young people, says Jenkins, are engaging in peer learning, developing skills for the modern workplace, assimilating diverse forms of cultural expression, and generating 'a more empowered conception of citizenship' (p. 3).

Digital participation on this view, therefore, is from the ground up (not imposed from above, as we have seen that inclusion is), and, because it is generated by the users of digital media themselves, it is a far more active concept than is inclusion – because although participation is a right and entitlement it also comes with civic responsibilities. Participation, here, means giving all the opportunity to develop skills and capital for meaningful, active, and responsible involvement in society, culture, and politics.

But Jenkins, as does Grant above, sounds a warning. He clearly states that:

> [a]ccess to this participatory culture functions as a new form of the hidden curriculum, shaping which youth will succeed and which will be left behind. (Jenkins, 2006, p. 3)

Again, we are reminded that the digital divide is about the ability to build capital through digital networks and knowledge, and not only about the ability to access a computer.

Finally, Jenkins identifies three main challenges for 'pedagogical interventions' (p. 3) as they relate to the digital divide and participatory culture. The first is what he calls the 'participation gap', that is, 'unequal access to the opportunities, experiences, skills, and knowledge that will prepare youth' for full participation in twenty-first-century life and work (Jenkins 2006, p. 3). Next is the 'transparency problem', that is, challenges in grasping how media shape our knowledge of the world. And finally is the 'ethics challenge', that is the task we face in preparing young people for their 'increasingly public roles as media makers and community participants'(p. 3).

In meeting these challenges teachers will increasingly need to focus on those skills that will help young people to meaningfully and responsibly contribute to public online spaces and that will provide them with the digital capital necessary for successful participation in modern life. Jenkins says we need to 'rethink literacy' and develop amongst young people participatory skills that encourage play, experimentation, performance, improvisation, multitasking, modelling of real-world processes, creative appropriation, judgement, networking, negotiation, and transmedia navigation (Jenkins 2006, p. 4). Note that these skills are almost all social skills – they are multimodal and quite different from traditional literacy and numeracy skills. As a teacher, your role in this participatory environment thus becomes one in which you:

- Facilitate discovery
- Stimulate community
- Demand critique
- Encourage collaboration
- Inspire experimentation
- Foster creativity
- Model problem-solving
- Promote respect.

Activity. Encouraging participation

Two resources will be of particular use to you in this exercise:

- Walker and Logan's Futurelab handbook 'Using digital technologies to promote inclusive practices in education.' Available at http://archive.futurelab.org.uk/resources/publications-reports-articles/handbooks/Handbook1248, and
- Hague and Williamson's 'Digital participation, digital literacy, and school subjects'. Available at http://archive.futurelab.org.uk/projects/digital-participation, also from Futurelab.

Step 1. Think about the demographic, social, and ethnic composition of your classroom. Can you identify any students who might have 'special needs' in these areas as regards their digital participation? Such students might include those from minority faith and/or ethnic backgrounds, asylum seekers and refugees, those whose schooling has been interrupted for one reason or another, gifted and talented students, children in care of one form or another, students who work long hours in a family business, young carers, students who spend several hours in travelling to school, teenage mothers, and so on.

Ask yourself, In what ways does their life situation preclude them in their ability to participate in social and cultural life online? For example, a student whose family is seeking asylum might be anxious about their housing situation; a gifted and talented student might feel bored by the work set in class; or a teenage mother might have to suddenly make a trip to the hospital because her baby has a temperature. In other words, what social, cultural, political, ethnic, religious, or other barriers might stand in the way of their full and meaningful digital participation, as described above?

Step 2. How can you support these students? What is your role in helping them to participate as responsible digital citizens? Do they need to be taught baseline collaboration, communication, or thinking skills? Do they need basic functional digital literacy skills (see Chapter 13)? Are they at risk of being victims of cyberbullying, grooming, or similar (see Chapter 15)? If so, what is your role in educating them about safe online behaviour?

Step 3. Interrogate whether or not you might be approaching this activity from an 'inclusion' standpoint as opposed to a 'participation' standpoint. Is there a danger of focusing too much on the 'deficits' that students with special needs bring to the participatory realm, as opposed to what they might introduce to it? How can you encourage their contributions and what do they need from you in order to make those contributions? Are there peculiarities in your own classroom's culture that prevent students from contributing equally and having their contributions valued equally?

Step 4. What kinds of digital and/or social media can promote digital participation in your classroom? For example, can visual and auditory material be used to help students whose traditional literacy levels might be low? Can wikis, blogs, or social networks be used to engage students with people outside the classroom? Can you provide more creative options for students who prefer to express themselves through music, art, or video? Can mobile devices be used to help students take part in classroom activities even when they cannot be at school? In other words, how can you expand your pedagogical and digital repertoires so that all students have a chance to get involved in your daily classroom activities?

 Summary

- The term 'digital divide' describes not only the gap between those who have access to digital hardware and related systems and those who do not, but also the gap between those who use digital technology to access knowledge, networks, and resources to build digital capital and those who do not.
- Digital capital refers to the resources, knowledge, skills, networks, and connections that are valued by, and valuable in, a society, and that can be built using digital technologies.
- There is a difference between 'theoretical' and 'effective' access to digital and online technology. Whilst some might have theoretical access, in that there is a computer with an internet connection in their house, they may not be able to access that technology in practice.
- Participatory cultures are those that acknowledge that everyone has something to contribute and that build connections with others as equals. Participation is preferred over 'inclusion' as participation is a more active concept and does not imply that people need to have something 'done' to them (that is, to 'be included') in order for them to provide something of value to the group.
- Digital participation can be found in online communities, in the creation of new digital products, in collaborative problem-solving, and through shaping the flow of media.
- Challenges for participation include the 'participation gap', the 'transparency problem', and the 'ethics challenge'. There is a danger that access to participatory frameworks will simply contribute to the digital divide, and will influence who succeeds and who does not in the online environment.

Resources

Online resources

- Digizen.org (Search 'Digizen'). The aim of this site is to build awareness and understanding of responsible digital citizenship. Advice and resources are available for users of all ages.
- Search 'Digital divide' and 'digital participation' to find articles, sites, and resources that engage with debates in these areas.
- The Annenberg School for Communication and Journalism at the University of Southern California has an excellent media literacy quiz that you could base your class survey on (search 'USC media literacy quiz').

- Visit the *Using Social Media in the Classroom* companion website for links, discussions, and other materials relating to using digital divide and participation issues. You can find this at www.sagepub.co.uk/poore

Further reading

- Davies, J. and Merchant, G. (2009) Web 2.0 as social practice (Chapter 2). *Web 2.0 for Schools. Learning and social participation*. New York: Peter Lang, pp. 11–22.
- Grant, L. (2007) Learning to be part of the knowledge economy: digital divides and media literacy. Available at http://www2.futurelab.org.uk/resources/publications-reports-articles/discussion-papers/Discussion-Paper816. Accessed 13 October 2011.
- Green, H. and Hannon, C. (2007) Their space. Education for a digital generation. pp. 59–60. Available at http://www.demos.co.uk/publications/theirspace. Accessed 21 October 2008.
- Hague, C. and Williamson, B. (2009) Digital participation, digital literacy, and school subjects. A review of the policies, literature and evidence. Available at http://archive.futurelab.org.uk/projects/digital-participation. Accessed 13 October 2011.
- Jenkins, H. (2006) Confronting the challenges of participatory culture. Media education for the 21st Century. Available at http://www.nwp.org/cs/public/print/resource/2713. Accessed 13 October 2011.
- Walker, L. and Logan, A. (2009) Using digital technologies to promote inclusive practices in education. Futurelab handbook. Available at http://archive.futurelab.org.uk/resources/publications-reports-articles/handbooks/Handbook1248. Accessed 13 October 2011.

CHAPTER 15

CYBERBULLYING

Overview

This chapter begins by describing the nature of all forms of bullying before exploring the questions of why and how cyberbullying is different from 'traditional' (or 'schoolyard') bullying. Although there are similarities between the two, especially as regards power imbalances and exclusionary practices, cyberbullying is shown to be a slightly different, or extended, phenomenon particularly in terms of pervasiveness, the potential for infinite audiences, and the permanence of the communication. Gender (as it relates to cyberbullying) and the phenomenon of 'sexting' are both examined before we look at some of the problems relating to the research on cyberbullying. The final section of the chapter provides basic advice on identifying and responding to cyberbullying and urges you to 'keep up' with young people's online behaviour and 'fads'. In conclusion, the chapter argues that education and prevention is the key to keeping young people safe online.

It is important to note that the current chapter does not address cybersafety measures per se – as stated in the Preface, the entire textbook is essentially about keeping safe online, and thus a special section on cybersafety would draw attention away from the notion that cybersafety awareness should infuse all your online activities.

What is bullying?

In her landmark book on cyberbullying, Shaheen Shariff (2008) describes bullying as 'a form of abuse that is based on an imbalance of power' (p. 11). Even though there are some differences between 'traditional' (for want of a better term) bullying and 'cyberbullying', this definition serves us well if we are to understand the underlying characteristics of all forms of bullying.

All bullying

Shariff (2008) describes both the physical (hitting, spitting, punching) and verbal (teasing, ridicule, sarcasm, scapegoating) attributes of 'school' bullying, noting that hostile, bullying behaviours normally occur in areas with minimal adult supervision, for example, in bathrooms and hallways (pp. 10–11). Bullying can occur solely between two individuals or there may be a large number of people who are indirectly involved, such as bystanders and witnesses who do nothing to intervene for fear of becoming the next victim if they get involved (pp. 10–11). There are also others who might take on the role of 'assistants' (that is, those who join in) or 'reinforcers' (those who observe and laugh), or those who simply are unaware of the situation altogether (Shariff, 2008, p. 24). In any case, Shariff identifies a number of elements that generally characterise bullying, no matter what:

- There is always a power imbalance that favours the perpetrator(s) over the victim.
- The perpetrators are often supported by a group of peers, some of whom actively encourage the bully and others who watch, but do nothing to help peers who are targeted.
- Targeted students draw the negative attention of their peers and are actively pushed out of the group and isolated […].
- Exclusion and isolation of the victim from the larger peer group fortify the power of the perpetrator(s).
- The perpetrators' behaviour is uninvited and unwanted by the victim.
- The perpetrators' actions are deliberate, repeated, and often relentless. (Shariff, 2008, p. 16)

How teachers respond to bullying is often determined by their attitudes to bullying. Shariff points to various studies that show that teachers often prioritise physical injury over verbal bullying, that many see 'teasing' as normal or harmless, and that children should 'toughen up' and learn to deal with verbal bullying on their own (2008, pp. 14–15). But cyberbullying is largely verbal (Shariff, 2008, pp. 15, 22), and it is this exact characteristic that makes it different from schoolyard bullying, as we shall see presently. It is also why it should be taken just as seriously.

 ## Activity. Who fits the bullying profile?

Step 1. Do a quick internet hunt for materials relating to the term 'bully profile' or similar. Jot down a few of the key characteristics listed in the research about the psychology of bullies – spend about 30 minutes on this, and, as you go, compare your list with a friend.

    Step 2. Using the material you've found, as well as the information provided in the bullet points above, identify some hard-core bullies from literature, TV, film, or other media. I'll give you a start with some 'classic' bullies such as Nelson from *The Simpsons*, Vicky Pollard from *Little Britain*, and maybe even Sauron from *Lord of the Rings*. If you're having trouble, simply search for 'TV bullies' and you'll find various lists and commentaries.

    Step 3. Next, run a 'character analysis' to see where they fit into the bullying profile. The idea of the activity is to have some fun with it, but at the same time to grasp what makes bullies 'tick', all the better for you to identify and understand this kind of behaviour when you encounter it in the school environment.

What is cyberbullying?

There are many definitions of cyberbullying that could be provided here – a quick internet search will pull up thousands of websites, all offering variations on a theme. In the interests of keeping things as uncomplicated as possible, I simply define cyberbullying as

> *any hostile act directed towards another person that occurs using digital technology.*

This definition eschews terms such as 'intentional' or 'deliberate' (which are often included in definitions of cyberbullying), as it could be argued that young people of a certain age may not yet exhibit the cognitive development required to make informed distinctions between morally right and wrong acts. Similarly, the definition avoids the terms 'repeated' and 'ongoing', also often included in cyberbullying definitions, for reasons that will be outlined shortly.

    Cyberbullying can occur as hateful, hurtful, and harassing messages sent or posted via SMS/text messages, wall comments on social networking sites, chat rooms, blog posts, and the like. But it can also take the form of uploading or distributing embarrassing videos or images or other media: it need not be limited to 'written' or 'verbal' communications.

Cyberbullying: Why it's different

Although bullying behaviours and discriminatory attitudes have always existed, the ways in which they are made manifest have changed somewhat in the digital era. It is true that all bullying involves a power imbalance between perpetrator(s) and victim, but there are also certain characteristics that make cyberbullying a slightly different phenomenon from schoolyard bullying. In particular:

- *Cyberbullying does not stop at the front door*. Children can now be bullied wherever they go, as mobile phones and internet access become almost ubiquitous. Young people can access their Facebook page or text messages in their bedrooms and away from the notice of their parents. Further, it can be very difficult to ignore what others might be saying about you, no matter how spiteful or untrue (as the victim of malicious digital conduct myself, I can attest to this).
- *A single instance of digital harrassment can be replicated infinitely*. Although most definitions of bullying (and many of cyberbullying) point to the repeated or ongoing elements of bullying behaviours, a single nasty message, post, or comment can be forwarded and reproduced over and over again and spread widely amongst 'invisible audiences' (boyd, 2011). Of course, this can be regarded as 'repeated', but it must be remembered that the initial offence was a one-off instance that 'went viral'.
- *Cyberspace contains millions of onlookers*. Again, the 'invisible audience' (boyd, 2011) factor is at play here and people who are completely unknown to either victim or perpetrator can become implicated in acts of bullying or be lending a form of 'peer support' to the tormentors.
- *Instances of digital harrassment and bullying can be saved, replicated, and distributed without being limited to time and space*. Whereas school-yard bullying is confined to the physical world of atoms, cyberbullying occurs in the world of bytes. The very nature of digital media supports the easy spread of acts of hostility and humiliation.
- *Once posted, hurtful or embarrassing information is virtually impossible to delete*. Once something is 'out there' you should assume that it cannot be removed (even if you posted it yourself). Even if you delete offensive material, there is a very strong possibility that Google or another search engine has already found and 'cached' the material, allowing it to be accessed at any stage in the future. This means it is permanent almost as soon as you post it.

- *There is a greater potential for anonymity on the part of the perpetrator*. Cyberbullies can hide behind false names or identities: whereas victims of schoolyard bullying come face to face with their tormentors, victims of cyberbullying do not always know who it is who is persecuting them.
- *Cyberbullying is mainly written and verbal, not physical*. This means that its effects can be less obvious to spot. If many teachers believe that verbal bullying is less harmful than physical bullying (see above), then there is a danger that cyberbullying will not be treated as seriously as more 'traditional' forms of bullying.

Gender and bullying

There are identifiable differences in the types of bullying behaviours that boys and girls engage in, and it is these differences that could explain why girls are becoming more and more 'active instigators' (Shariff, 2008, p. 40) of cyberbullying. Typically, boys are involved in more physical and outwardly aggressive forms of bullying, whereas girls are more likely to take part in more 'psychological and covert' types of bullying and more likely to do it in groups (Shariff, 2008, p. 93). This arguably provides girls with a 'preferred mode' (written and verbal) for bullying – one that furnishes them with ample opportunity to gossip and spread malicious rumours about others they have marginalised or targeted for victimisation.

Sexting

'Sexting' is the sending of sexually explicit photographs, messages, or other media via digital devices, usually mobile phones, although it can occur by way of social media sites and apps. Most times such messages or photographs are sent privately to a boyfriend or girlfriend, but, as with any digital object, there is the possibility of things being forwarded to unintended recipients and to go viral from there. Aside from the obvious potential for humiliation and hurt, and the fact that it is almost impossible to be able to forever retrieve or delete something once it is 'out there' in digital form, there is also a serious legal implication of this behaviour: *in many jurisdictions this kind of conduct can be prosecuted under child pornography laws*. Offenders, regardless of age, can find themselves charged with production, possession, and/or distribution of child pornography. A quick internet search will provide dozens of examples of cases where youngsters have been brought before the law on child pornography charges. Although there are moves under way in various territories to revise legislation as it relates to minors engaged in sexting practices, you and your students need to be aware of the potential legal and criminal repercussions of this form of digital communication.

Activity. Some moral questions

Case study 1
Chris Webster (2004) on the site Cyberbullying.info recounts the story of Ghyslain Razaa, aka 'the Star Wars Kid':

> Ghyslain became an internet sensation in May 2003 when four classmates discovered a private video of him pretending to be a Jedi Knight. Rather than laughing at the video in the privacy of their homes, the classmates decided to upload the video to the internet. Within weeks it had been seen by millions.
>
> ... While the world laughs, and spin-offs are created at an average of one per day, Ghyslain and his parents don't find the situation very funny. The parents have filed a lawsuit against the classmates that uploaded the video.
>
> The lawsuit is accompanied by instant messaging transcripts, in which the classmates gloat over their success.
>
> Ghyslain was forced to drop out of high school, and finished the year at a faculty specialising in child psychiatry. (Webster, 2004, online)

Consider the ethical and moral questions raised by this case. Some of the questions below are phrased in a deliberately provocative or ambiguous manner.

- Is this a case of cyberbullying? If so, why? If not, why not?
- In making the video should Razaa have realised that it might 'get out' there and just accept the consequences?
- Does his age matter?
- Does Razaa just need to 'toughen up'?
- What about the role of his parents?
- Where do a person's feelings come into it?
- Do you think Razaa's classmates knew what they were doing? If not, does this make them 'less responsible' for what happened?
- Do you think Razaa might have already been the target of bullying at school?
- Should Razaa be grateful for his internet fame and try to make money out of it?
- What role should the school and its teachers have played (if any) in this situation?
- In viewing the Star Wars Kid video are you contributing to his humiliation? Are you a bully, too, if you watch it? What if you watch it but don't laugh?

I leave it up to you to decide whether or not you want to track down and view the video for yourself.

Case study 2
Visit Wikipedia and read the entry on Rebecca Black. In 2011, 13-year-old Black's music video 'Friday' was uploaded to YouTube. Black's parents paid ARK Music Factory to write the song and produce the video. The video went viral as 'the worst song ever recorded' and attracted tens of millions of views and comments. Most comments were negative and many were vitriolic, hostile, and even threatening (along the lines of 'If I saw you, I would cross the street and kill you', and 'I want to bash you for making this song'). Black has also reportedly received death threats via email and phone and was bullied at school after the release of the video (see the Wikipedia entry). Black has gone on to achieve a moderate level of mainstream success.

Consider the ethical and moral questions raised by this case. Some of the questions below are phrased in a deliberately provocative or ambiguous manner.

- Why the huge backlash? Was it 'just' about the song, or is it because people think Black is a spoilt rich kid?
- If you put yourself 'out there' should you expect this kind of reaction?
- Does Black deserve her public pillorying?
- What was the role of Black's parents in all of this?
- Did she 'have it coming' to her?
- Does Black's age matter?
- Does her subsequent celebrity, success, fame/infamy impact on how you see this case?
- What role should the school and its teachers have played (if any) in this situation?

Problems with research into cyberbullying

Before moving on to what can be done about cyberbullying, and how we can promote anti-bullying practices amongst our students, we should take a quick look at some of the problems that arise when considering the research into cyberbullying. This is important because there are widely differing claims made for how widespread and serious the problem of cyberbullying actually is. Whenever we explore cyberbullying research, we should be attentive to the following:

- *Lack of definitional clarity*. We have already seen that, due to the very nature of digital technology, problems arise when we try to define cyberbullying as 'ongoing' or 'repeated', or when we use terms such as 'intentional' or 'deliberate'. But further definitional issues surface when we examine the question, What 'counts' as bullying? Are teasing and name-calling included, regardless of context? Am I a victim of bullying if I feel sad because of what others say about me? Who decides? The researcher on some kind of 'objective' measure, or self-identified victims?

- *Methodological inconsistencies*. Each study on cyberbullying uses a different method for collecting data and analysing it. One study might rely entirely on multiple-choice or Likert-scale-type questions, another might run a series of focus groups, and yet another could be based on ethnographic observation. Whilst it is undeniably important to draw on a full range of methodological approaches in examining cyberbullying as a phenomenon, we should nevertheless be sure to account for differences in method whenever analysing a body of literature relating to a single topic.

- *Varying sample sizes*. Many research studies into cyberbullying have quite small sample sizes (under 100 participants). Whilst smaller samples might be acceptable for dense, ethnographic studies of particular bullying instances or episodes, they cannot tell us much about the more generic phenomena attached to cyberbullying (unless we are examining a particular class or year-level in a specific school). To make claims for how prevalent cyberbullying is or is not within a particular country, large surveys that investigate the experiences of all children (not just those from more privileged backgrounds) need to be conducted.

- *Claims made for the long-term effects of cyberbullying*. If cyberbullying is a phenomenon that has really only come about since the turn of the twenty-first century, then it is temporally impossible for any longitudinal study to yet definitively state what the long-term effects of cyberbullying are on its victims. Although we might intuitively 'feel' that cyberbullying is more psychologically damaging than 'traditional' bullying, it is simply impossible for us to say at the current historical moment with any certainty that this is the case.

One final thing to bear in mind is the problem identified by Juvonen and Gross: 'these data do not tell us whether youth experience cyberbullying mainly through these particular communications tools or whether their usage pattern merely reflects risky online behaviour' (2008, p. 497). Again, context counts for much in this area.

Identifying and responding to cyberbullying

There is a huge amount of advice available to teachers, parents, and students about how to identify and respond to cyberbullying. This section provides only a 'bare bones' outline: you are encouraged to search the net for more detailed information and to discuss any cyberbullying-related matters with both colleagues and senior staff in your school.

Identifying cyberbullying

Both perpetrators and victims of cyberbullying exhibit behaviours that can help teachers and parents identify whether or not cyberbullying is occurring. Hinduja and Patchin (2010, p. 3) point to the following as markers of cyberbullying:

The victim may

- Withdraw or become isolated from peers, family, or friends.
- Complain of physical symptoms such as headaches, stomachaches, or feeling unwell.
- Become anxious when a new message is received.
- Exhibit mood swings or changes in behaviour or regular patterns (for example, changes in general temperament, appetite, or sleep).
- Become distressed after using the internet, or display emotional anguish (such as depression, anger, or irritation).
- Suddenly shut down a computer screen or mobile phone when someone else draws near.
- Be reluctant to answer questions about computer or phone use or about what is happening on the internet (or similar).

The perpetrator may

- Spend long periods at the computer, especially late at night.
- Become agitated or angry when computer or mobile phone use is restricted.
- Suddenly laugh or snicker (and do so frequently) when using the computer or mobile phone.
- Suddenly shut down a computer screen or mobile phone when someone else draws near.
- Be reluctant to answer questions about computer or phone use or about what is happening on the internet (or similar).

As Hinduja and Patchin say, '[i]n general, if a youth acts in ways that are inconsistent with their usual behavior when using these communication devices, it's time to find out why' (2010, p. 3).

Basic cyberbullying advice

Your school should already have a policy on how to deal with cyberbullying. If not, it is time for you to either suggest it at a staff meeting, or to take the lead on developing such a policy yourself. There are numerous websites, books, leaflets, organisations, and other resources that you can draw on to help you build your policy and to inform your own and your school's approach to this problem; in the mean time, here is some advice from LifeSkills4Kids.com

(2009, online) that you can use with students to help them respond to claims of cyberbullying:

- Do not engage the bully. Do not reply to abusive messages, comments and the like.
- Identify the perpetrator if possible.
- Advise the victim to keep all abusive communications as potential evidence. This can be difficult, however, when all the victim wants to do is to erase upsetting messages.
- Try to block contact from the bully. This may prove difficult if the bully uses different accounts or phone numbers to continue the bullying.
- Tell an adult and tell the school. Either or both may be able to address the problem.

LifeSkills4Kids.com (2009, online) also advises that you, as a teacher, should:

- Educate students and staff about cyberbullying.
- Monitor students' internet behaviour for signs of bullying or being bullied.
- Talk regularly to students about their online activities.
- Investigate reports of cyberbullying immediately.
- Talk regularly with students about bullying and cyberbullying.
- Explain that all bullying is unacceptable and give reasons.
- Outline your expectations for responsible online behaviour and make the consequences for poor behaviour clear.
- Remind students that many acts of bullying are also criminal offences for which there can be legal consequences (for example, threats, extortion, harassment, and discrimination).

If a case of cyberbullying comes to light in your classroom or amongst your students, it is advisable that you discuss the matter with a senior colleague to work out how best to handle the situation. In some instances, the matter can be put to rest by talking directly to the parties involved; in others, parents might have to be brought in. In more serious cases you may need to consider whether or not to contact the police, especially if threats of violence are made, if there is evidence of extortion, if the communications involve obscenities, harrassment, stalking, hate crimes, or if there is child pornography going on. But do not act without first consulting a senior staff member and getting agreement on a course of action.

Keeping up

It is quite possible that you will never be able to keep up with all the latest and greatest websites, apps, online fads, and digital devices that your students are 'into'. Nevertheless, you need to be knowledgeable about social media formats and how they work in a generic sense (that is what Parts 2 and 3 of this book are all about) and be able to quickly figure out the specific details of the functionality and online 'culture' of a format if you need to. Say, for example, masses of students suddenly leave Facebook (or Moshi Monsters, or Club Penguin, or whatever) for another service (as they deserted MySpace in 2008–09). As a teacher, you should be able to enter the new space, explore how it works, get a sense of how people interact in it, and what its culture is (see Chapter 9). *Keeping track of these things is not a frivolous distraction from your 'real' teaching work: it is part of your ongoing professional development*. Sites such as Techcrunch.com, Cnet.com, and Mashable.com provide the latest news about social media and can be good places to start. In any case, you should have a working knowledge of:

- *Social networking sites* such as Facebook, or Club Penguin for younger users.
- *Video sites, especially YouTube* (YouTube often exhibits a quite large number of inflammatory and abusive comments).
- *'Underground' websites* such as those promoting self-harm, fascism, racism, misogyny, anorexia, violence, and the like.
- *Twitter*. Many people unwittingly give away information about their location (or other personal details) via tweets (for example, 'enjoying a coffee on my own in Kingston' or 'Taking our dog Ptolemy for a walk along Taupo shore. Back in an hour').
- *Sexting* and its criminal implications (see above).
- *Internet scams*, which extend beyond the infamous 'Nigerian' scams to include bogus contests, diet scams, lottery scams, bank account/PayPal/Visa impersonation scams, requests for donations, and many more. Search 'Types of internet scams'.

Concluding remark: Education is the key

Cyberbullying can be a serious problem in schools but we should be careful to not blow it out of proportion simply because the mainstream media chooses to run stories about the more extreme cases, tragic though such cases may be. It is a mistake to start from the belief that the internet is an inherently risky place. But it is also a mistake to believe that without supervision children and young people (and, indeed, anyone who uses social media) will be able to surf the net with impunity. Instead, we need to acknowledge that the internet and mobile digital technologies are here to stay, that they are a key part of young people's lives, and that we are responsible for helping them to safely navigate digital environments. Denial is no longer an option.

In our culture we teach children how to cross the road because cars are an unavoidable technology that we encounter on a daily basis. We also teach children about pool and fire safety in the home, and about stranger danger.

Cyberspace is no different: it is an inescapable part of twenty-first-century life and children need to be taught how to navigate it unharmed. To do that, we need to educate our youngsters into safe online behaviour and to scaffold that education just as we do any other. For ourselves, we need to understand and control the risks.

The next chapter explores understanding online risk in more detail.

Summary

- All bullying involves a power imbalance between perpetrator and victim as well as exclusion and isolation from the peer group. Bullying is repeated, unwanted, and uninvited.
- Cyberbullying is any hostile act directed towards another person that occurs using digital technology. It is different from schoolyard bullying in that hostile digital communication can be pervasive, replicated, viewed by invisible audiences, widely distributed, sent anonymously, and is mainly verbal.
- There has been an increase in bullying behaviour on the part of girls, who are becoming 'active instigators' of cyberbullying.
- 'Sexting' puts young people at risk of prosecution for the production, possession, and distribution of child pornography.
- The research into cyberbullying is at an early stage, and needs to be considered carefully before any sweeping statements about cyberbullying can be made.
- You need to be able to identify the behaviours exhibited by both victims and perpetrators of cyberbullying, you need to know how to advise victims, and you need to keep up with current trends in children's online activities.
- Education is the key to preventing and responding to cyberbullying.

Resources

Online resources

- Bullying.co.uk provides information and resources for parents, students, and teachers on all forms of bullying.
- The Cyberbullying Research Centre at Cyberbullying.us brings together tips, advice, research, publications, and case studies.
- Cybersmart.gov.au is hosted by the Australian Communications and Media Authority and provides resources, activities, advice, and training for children, parents, and teachers.
- Visit the *Using Social Media in the Classroom* companion website for links, discussions and other materials relating to cyberbullying and cybersafety. You can find this at www.sagepub.co.uk/poore

Further reading

- Byron, T. (2008) *Safer children in a digital world*. The report of the Byron Review. Available at http://www.education.gov.uk/ukccis/about/a0076277/the-byron-reviews. Accessed 1 November 2011.
- Hinduja, S. and Patchin, J. (2010) *Cyberbullying prevention, and response*. Cyberbullying Research Centre. Available at http://www.cyberbullying.us/resources.php. Accessed 18 October 2011.
- Juvonen, J. and Gross, E. F. (2008) Extending the school grounds? Bullying experiences in cyberspace, *The Journal of School Health,* 78(9), 496–505.
- Shariff, S. (2008) *Cyber-bullying. Issues and Solutions for the School, the Classroom and the Home*. London: Routledge.

CHAPTER 16

UNDERSTANDING RISK ONLINE

Overview

This chapter explores some of the issues surrounding keeping safe online by helping you to identify areas of risk. In particular, we examine legal and policy considerations relating to the use of social media in the classroom, including school (or institutional) regulations – topics such as copyright and intellectual property, privacy, confidentiality, and jurisdiction are covered here. Next, we move on to specific considerations you might encounter under the Terms of Service you sign up for when creating an account with a social media company, such as (again) copyright and IP, content distribution, data security, and changes to the Terms of Service. Finally, we consider the nature of the service itself, such as business robustness, longevity, and reliability, software version control, and advertising.

The chapter is based on the premise that *if we are serious about education, then we must embrace the best tools that are available to us*, and if that means accessing tools that are hosted by social media services that are not supported by our organisation, then we must find ways of making that access happen safely and responsibly. The main sections of the chapter provide an overview of the issue at hand, some points for consideration, and finally some suggestions for what to do if it all goes wrong, that is, some suggestions for your 'risk response'.

It should be noted here that nothing in this chapter constitutes legal advice. If you wish to use social media in your classroom, then you should seek the requisite approvals, comply with the law, and make informed, risk-managed decisions about what is legal, acceptable, and appropriate in your situation.

Risk management

The choice to use an externally hosted social media service for teaching and learning purposes should not be taken lightly. Blindly stepping into the world of Web 2.0 can expose your school, staff, and students to a number of risks, including risks to reputation, privacy, confidentiality, copyright, data security, and intellectual property ownership.

As with any risk, though, the response should not be to launch a blanket ban on activities, but, rather, to manage the risk and to educate staff and students about what, exactly, they are embarking upon – for education about the risks involved in using social media services (and how to mitigate against those risks) is fundamental to raising the online and digital literacies of both teachers and students (see Chapter 13). As Fitzgerald and Steele remind us:

> … all teaching and learning involves risk and … we must develop strategies to manage risk in ways that still enable students to become knowledge producers and creators. (Fitzgerald and Steele, 2008, p. 34)

In making decisions about risk, you need to weigh up the pedagogical and educational benefits of using social media with your students with the level of risk involved and the potential for negative outcomes. I strongly urge you to do your own research into how to conduct a risk analysis (also known as 'risk assessment') – there are many excellent online sources that can guide you through this (search, 'How to write a risk analysis'). Having done that, you can then use the information contained in these final two chapters to inform your own risk assessment for your intended social media use in your classroom.

The information below describes a variety of issues that will affect your analysis of, and responses to, the risks of using social media in the classroom. Please note that this is only a starting point and provides suggestions only; as always, you will need to choose what works best for you. Visit the *Using Social Media in the Classroom* companion website for risk management templates that you can adapt to your situation.

Legal and policy considerations

This section outlines some of the general legal and policy considerations and obligations you might encounter when wishing to use social media in the classroom. Your legal obligations may apply to the country you are living in and/or the country out of which the social media service provider operates; policy obligations will likely apply to your school, institution, and/or education authority.

Some of the points discussed below deal with subtle and nuanced elements of law and policy: you may need to read some things twice and to think about them before they make sense. Note, also, that a lot of what is covered is not yet 'fixed' and is still being negotiated in the courts, in schools, and in the community. This is a difficult area, and it may take you some time to get across it.

Copyright and intellectual property (IP)

Copyright is the ownership of the exclusive legal right to reproduce, publish, perform, or otherwise distribute an original, tangible work. Intellectual property is very similar to copyright, the main difference being that IP protects rights to *intangible* works, such as inventions, ideas, symbols, and designs, rather than rights to tangible or fixed forms of expression (such as text, pictures, and music recordings). Copyright and IP are important because they recognise that creative works need to be protected from theft every bit as much as cars, handbags, household items, and other pieces of personal property.

In normal circumstances, the creator of a work is automatically granted copyright and/or IP rights to that work – they can sell the work, license it out to others to use, or reproduce it in any way they please. Frequently, however, the copyright or IP holder is *not* the creator of the work. This is the case, for example, when a band sells its rights over music it has created to a music company, or when an architect gets paid by a corporation to produce designs for a building or shopping complex. More importantly for you as a teacher, though, it might be the case that your school or institution claims (that is, owns) exclusive rights over any work you have produced for, or inventions you have contributed to, your organisation whilst in their employ. Check your employment contract or your institution's policies if you are unsure whether or not you own copyright or IP rights to material you produce at work.

Note that copyright and IP laws differ from jurisdiction to jurisdiction (that is, from country to country), and that institutions will have different policies relating to how copyright and IP are handled within the organisation. It is your responsibility to do the additional research you need to come to a proper understanding of how legal and policy issues impact upon your particular situation and your particular use of social media in the classroom. Following is some guidance for dealing with copyright as it relates to legal and policy considerations in your institution.

Institutional copyright and IP ownership

Your institution (that is, your school, university, or education department) may hold copyright and/or IP rights over material that you produce whilst in their employ – they have paid you to produce it, so they claim ownership over it. In some cases, the institution might allow you to retain copyright or your IP rights but might insist that you grant them an exclusive right to use them. Or it may work the other way around: the institution might own copyright to materials you produce whilst working for them but they might grant *you* a non-exclusive licence to use it (that is, the institution might give others the right to also use your work).

When you sign up for a Terms of Service with a social media site, for example, you can expect to agree that you will not infringe another party's copyright by posting material in which copyright is not held by you. So, if you sign up for a Terms of Service and you post materials that you *thought* were yours but are actually owned by your school (for example, syllabus or study materials you have written), then you could technically be in breach of your contract and in breach of the law.

Points for consideration:

- Do you know what content, exactly, you hold rights in, in terms of copyright and intellectual property, and under what conditions? You may be unwittingly giving away institutional copyright or intellectual property when you publish your syllabus, study lists, or other materials to a service.
- Do you understand the Terms of Service that you are signing up for and its implications for your institution's policy and your employment contract?
- Do you have approval for posting content over which the institution holds copyright or in which it has intellectual property rights?
- Have you spoken to a member of your school executive or a legal expert from your relevant education authority regarding any uncertainties you have?

If it all goes wrong ... (risk response):

- Strip or neutralise infringing content from the site.

Institutional copyright bottom line: You may be unwittingly giving away institutional copyright or intellectual property when you publish material you have produced to an external social media service. Know the terms of your contract and your institution's copyright and IP policies.

Student copyright and IP ownership

Students at any level (primary, secondary, tertiary) are not normally required to give over any of their copyright or intellectual property to the institution they are studying at. But even if this is the case for your institution, and if you go ahead and decide to use an externally hosted social media service with your class course, then you should nevertheless be careful to *choose a service that does not require students to hand over their copyright or IP to that service* when they sign up.

One thing to note, though, is that while social media services might allow users to retain ownership of their IP, the licences to their IP that they are required to provide (so that the service can display their work) can be so all-encompassing that there could be little value left in such ownership. Whether students are prepared to give such a broad licence is a matter for them and/or their parents.

A related issue is whether or not students can freely decide to accept these Terms of Service if signing up to these sites is a requirement to undertake their studies (it shouldn't be). Of course, if students are given an alternative option for completing an assignment that doesn't involve them signing up to these sites, then this isn't such an issue.

Points for consideration:

- Does the service allow users to retain copyright over creative content?
- Is it a requirement for students to sign up for this service in order to undertake their studies or to complete an assignment? It shouldn't be.
- How broad is the copyright and/or IP licence that the service is asking for? If the Terms of Service do not include a phrase to the effect that the licence will only be used for the *sole purpose* of displaying, distributing, or promoting the users' content on the service, then the chances are that the licence is too broad and the service should not be used.
- Do students and/or their parents understand the terms of the copyright and/or IP licence that the service is asking them to assign? Students should be advised to *not* sign up to a Terms of Service if they have any reservations or questions about the Terms. If they have any concerns, they should be advised to approach the teacher for clarification before they make their decision about whether or not to sign up.

If it all goes wrong ... (risk response):

- Consider alternative assessment arrangements for students who do not want to assign their IP under an unnecessarily broad licence.
- Strip or neutralise relevant content from the site.

> **Student copyright and IP bottom line**: Students are not normally required to give over any of their copyright or intellectual property to an institution they are enrolled in. Whether students are prepared to give a licence to their IP to a service provider is a matter for them and their parents.

Third-party copyright and IP

In today's 'mashup' and sharing culture there are continual breaches of third-party copyright. If, on your social media site, you want to include materials that a third party owns copyright in, then you are likely to be bound by copyright legislation in your jurisdiction regarding how you can use that material. This means obtaining permission from the copyright owner to use the material on your site in a particular way, as you would ordinarily do for use of that material anywhere else.

The copyright obligations you have will depend on a number of things, including how much of the material is being posted, what conditions apply for 'educational use' (or similar exceptions), the type of material that is being posted, and who can access the material and under what conditions (for example, is the material hosted on a learning management system run by your education authority and to which only authorised users have access, or is it being posted on a site that is visible and open to the world?). This is a really tricky area, so if you are unsure about whether or not you should be posting material owned by a third party, you should contact your education authority's legal office or similar.

Points for consideration:

- Are you posting material over which you do not hold copyright? Unless you are sure that your use of copyright material is legal, you should not.
- Are you only using what you need? Is this covered by educational use or other exceptions?
- If you need to give students access to copyrighted material, can you instead link out to non-infringing material? Try to find legitimate copies of the relevant material elsewhere on the web and link out to them.

- Have you bypassed any protections to get this material? If you have illegally downloaded a video, or hacked into a site, then you could be in trouble. Similarly, do not download an object (video, image, whatever) and then upload it to your own site.
- Have you labelled all materials and their sources correctly?

If it all goes wrong ... (risk response):

- Immediately strip all infringing material from the site.

What if I am found to be in breach of copyright?

In most cases of copyright violation you are asked to remove the infringing material immediately and to destroy any remaining copies of the material you have. If you do not comply with such requests you open yourself up to potential legal action.

Third-party copyright bottom line: Do not post infringing material on your site.

Privacy and confidentiality

Most developed countries have serious penalties for breaches of privacy and confidentiality. If you violate privacy laws in your jurisdiction you may be exposing not only yourself but also your institution to prosecution, because even though your institution is not itself entering into a contract with a service provider, it might nevertheless be claimed that you are using these sites and services as part of your authorised employment duties. Privacy Impact Statements (or Privacy Impact Assessments) can help you determine the privacy risks as they apply to the Privacy Policy of the site or service you are signing up for.

Points for consideration:

- Will the service disclose your private information to another party? If so, to whom? Trustworthy services will only disclose your private information to those with legitimate reasons for accessing it, such as contractors or technicians who work on the service to make improvements or to carry out repairs.
- What guarantees do you have about the service's privacy policy?
- Does the service meet the legislative requirements of your jurisdiction, especially those covered by privacy acts, freedom of information acts, disability discrimination acts, and the like?
- Do you need to find alternative assessment tasks for students who do not want to sign up for such a service?

If it all goes wrong … (risk response):

- Find alternative assessment tasks for students who do not want to sign up for a service.
- Advise students/parents on how to strip or neutralise the relevant content from the site.
- Advise students/parents that they might have some redress under the service's Privacy Policy, or Terms of Service.

Privacy and confidentiality bottom line: Make sure you know how your private data are handled by the social media companies you are signed up with.

Use of your institution's name, branding, and logo

If you are going to use the site to represent your institution then you may have to obtain institutional approval to do so, especially if you are posting content that includes things such as names, logos, and trademarks. When you sign up to a Terms of Service you might be giving the service provider permission to use any content posted to the site – which means also giving them permission to use your institution's brand. Whether or not this is actually the case will depend on the details of the Terms of Service for the site (for example, names, logos, and trademarks might not be included in the definition of 'content' posted to the site), so you should check carefully before signing up.

Points for consideration:

- Have you in any way branded the site using your institution's logo, name, or other brand identifiers? Unless you have express permission to do so, do not post school logos, use your school's name in the site URL, or otherwise include content that could identify your organisation.
- In posting branded material to the site or service, are you also giving the service provider permission to use your brand? If you do have permission to use institutional branding, then it is essential that both you and your institution understand what kinds of licences you are posting branded material under and that you are happy with these conditions.

If it all goes wrong … (risk response):

- Remove all institutional branding and/or identification.

> **Institution's name, branding, and logo bottom line**: Do not use your institution's name and/or logo, or anything else that identifies the institution, on any external site that you use unless this has been cleared by your legal department.

Jurisdictional issues

'Jurisdiction' in this sense refers to the country or state whose laws you are working under. Laws may be quite similar between countries or they may be wildly different. When you sign up for a site or service, then it is likely that the Terms of Service that you agree to will be governed by the laws of the country in which the service provider is located and out of which it legally operates. So, if you are using a US-based service, then the chances are that US courts will have jurisdiction over any disputes arising from the use of the service and that any court hearings would be subject to US law and be held in the USA. Problems can arise when, for example, a breach of privacy in the UK under UK laws cannot be prosecuted in the jurisdiction of the service provider because the rights and obligations in that jurisdiction are different from those that apply in the UK. What is legal in one jurisdiction may not be legal in another.

Points for consideration:

- Where is the service you are signing up for located? What jurisdiction is it operating within? This information should be available on the service's 'about' or similar information pages.
- Is the service located in a country with sound and rigorous privacy, access, copyright, IP, and similar laws that protect users, consumers, citizens, and creators?
- If you are using a service that is located outside your jurisdiction, are you confident that you can comply with the laws of that jurisdiction? If you cannot, you may find yourself facing legal action for breaches of that country's laws.

If it all goes wrong ... (risk response):

- Seek legal advice.

> **Jurisdiction bottom line**: What is legal in your country may not be legal in another.

Accessibility

There are laws preventing discrimination against people with disabilities in most developed countries. Your use of social media sites must comply with these laws so that, for example, vision- or hearing-impaired students are not disadvantaged by your class activities.

If a website is poorly designed, it limits access to some users. Particular problems are caused by hyperlinks that state only 'click <u>here</u>' (hyperlinks should be embedded in prose so that users know where they'll end up when they follow the link), the automatic loading of audio and video, alternative text/metadata (too much or too little), links opening in new windows, and consecutive one-word links. All of this can make it difficult for some people with disabilities to navigate the web.

Points for consideration:

- Is the service you are using accessible to people with disabilities? W3C's Web Accessibility Initiative describes web design principles that meet accessibility standards (search 'W3C Web Accessibility Initiative') and you can use a web accessibility checker or evaluator to find out whether or not a site or service that you are using is accessible (search 'Web accessibility checker' or 'Web accessibility evaluation tool').

If it all goes wrong … (risk response):

- Address accessibility issues yourself, where possible.
- If the problems are endemic to the service you are using, switch to a web-accessible service.

Accessibility bottom line: Any social media services you use in class must be accessible to students with disabilities.

Considerations under the Terms of Service

When you sign up for a Terms of Service (also called a 'Terms of Use') you are essentially entering into a contract with a service provider. The considerations you have under the Terms will often be slightly different from your legal and institutional obligations, although many overlap.

Copyright and the Terms of Service

Your copyright
Any web-based service provider should allow you to retain copyright over any material in which you legally hold copyright. At the same time, when signing up for such a service, you will likely be confirming to that provider that you

hold the copyright to content that you post to the service. As we saw earlier, this may or may not be the case, depending on the conditions of your employment (student copyright is covered above). You need to check your contract to see whether or not you would be in breach of your agreement with your employer by posting certain material to an external service provider.

If you feel that your own copyright has been violated, a reputable service provider will respond to notices of alleged copyright infringement, investigate your claims, and then act as appropriate.

Points for consideration:

- Does the service allow you to retain copyright over any material in which you legally hold copyright and which you post to the site? Or in signing up are you giving away your copyright to the service? Reputable services will acknowledge your copyright, but you need to check exactly what you hold on to and what you give away.
- How will the service deal with breaches of your copyright? Choose a service that is bound, either under its own Terms of Service, or by legislation, to investigate any notices you provide of copyright infringement.

If it all goes wrong ... (risk response):

- Lodge a notice of copyright infringement with the service provider.
- You may wish to explore avenues for legal redress, but this may depend on the jurisdiction in which the infringement occurred.

Your copyright bottom line: You should keep your copyright, but be sure to know what copyright you actually own.

Others' copyright

You will be in breach of a whole load of regulations (including, potentially, the copyright act in your country, institutional policies and regulations, and/or your employment contract) if you post other people's copyrighted work to a social media service. This means that you should not, for example, upload images of artworks or images that you otherwise do not own yourself; you should not upload video or audio content that you do not own; and you should not upload electronic copies of journal articles to your site. It is especially important to note that you should not rely on any 'educational use' clauses in your country's copyright act – they may not cover you in this situation. Similarly, you should also understand that what may be legal in your country may not be legal in other jurisdictions.

The safest way to deal with this issue is to link out to legitimate and non-infringing material, but bear in mind that copyright issues on the internet are a long way from being solved.

Points for consideration:

- Have you posted infringing material on your site? This may be the case if you have uploaded electronic copies of journal articles to your site, added images of artworks or images that you otherwise do not own yourself, or included video or audio content that you do not own.
- Are students clear about what they can and cannot post in terms of copyright? Advise or remind them that they have signed/will sign a Terms of Service that states that they will not post others' copyrighted material to the service.
- How familiar are you with copyright issues as they relate to you? You may need to improve your knowledge in this area.

If it all goes wrong … (risk response):

- Remove infringing material from your site.

> **Others' copyright bottom line**: Do not post others' copyrighted work.

Content distribution, including Creative Commons

Signing up for a Terms of Service automatically implies that you will have to grant the service provider some control over the distribution of your content. You need to know the degree of that control and under what conditions your content is being distributed.

A standard Terms of Service from a reputable company will state that you grant the service a non-exclusive, royalty-free licence to reproduce, modify, adapt, publish, and so on, your work for the sole purpose of displaying, distributing, or promoting the service. This is standard because the service doesn't want to be sued by you for breach of your copyright when they display your material. If the service does not specify that it will only use your work for the sole purpose of displaying, distributing, or promoting the service, then find another service.

Of course, this also assumes that you hold copyright in the material you post to the service; if you do not hold copyright in the material that you post, you may be in breach of the copyright act in your country, institutional policies and regulations, and/or your employment contract (see above).

Some Terms of Service state that your work will also be automatically distributed under a Creative Commons (CC) licence. Creative Commons is a new way of dealing with copyright. Whereas copyright is 'all rights reserved', Creative Commons allows you to release and license your work with 'some rights reserved'. With a Creative Commons licence, you choose how you want your work to be used and distributed; for example, you might choose a CC licence that allows people to reuse and remix your work as long as they give you attribution and use your work only for non-commercial purposes. Creative Commons licences are a popular way to distribute content on the internet because they begin to get around some of the restrictions of copyright that make content distribution on the web so difficult.

Students and/or their parents may be happy to sign up to a Terms of Service that allows them to retain their full copyright, but they may not be so happy to have their copyright automatically distributed under a Creative Commons licence. You need to make sure that users understand the implications of Creative Commons if such a licence is a requirement of signing up for a service.

Points for consideration:

- How is your content distributed and for what purposes?
- Is your work automatically licensed or sub-licensed under a Creative Commons licence? If so, what sort of CC licence is it? Both you and your students need to understand the implications of Creative Commons for the distribution of content.

If it all goes wrong … (risk response):

- Advise users on how to strip or neutralise the infringing content or data from the site.
- Advise users that they might have some redress under the service's Privacy Policy, or Terms of Service, but that the jurisdiction in which they can seek such redress may be outside their own.

Content distribution, including Creative Commons, bottom line: Understand how your content is being distributed by the service provider, especially if that involves automatic distribution under a Creative Commons licence.

Data control and security

You need to know how social media service uses your data. For example, you need to know whether or not the service will sell the data you supply (including personal information) to a third party, thus exposing you to unwanted use of your information. Reputable services will limit who can access your personal information.

Generally speaking, employees of the service, contractors, and agents are the only people who should have access to your data, and those people should only need that access in order to operate, develop, repair, or improve the service. These individuals should be bound by confidentiality obligations and 'subject to discipline, including termination and criminal prosecution' (a common phrasing under a Terms of Service), if they fail to meet those obligations.

Finally, you need control over your data format. You should choose a service that works in a recognised and widely used format (such as html, opml, xml, or similar) so that if you choose to take your data elsewhere you can.

Points for consideration:

- Does the service have arrangements for protecting your data from deletion or unauthorised access? Check the Terms of Service and the Privacy Policy to see exactly how data is handled by the provider, and make sure you can backup your work in some way.
- How much control do you have over what can be done with your or your students' data? You should only sign up for a service that limits access to your data, as described above.
- Do you need to consider backup options? If so, you should choose a service that can be backed up or copied, either through (a) an explicit export function on the site, (b) through the use of a website backup software, or (c) by saving pages as html.
- Will your data be 'locked in' to a service because it uses a unique data format? Choose services that only deal in recognised formats such as html, xml, and opml.

If it all goes wrong ... (risk response):

- Advise affected users on how to strip or neutralise the affected content from the site.
- Advise affected users that they might have some redress under the service's Privacy Policy, Terms of Service.
- Open your backup copy and transfer your data to another service.

Data control and security bottom line: Know who has access to your data and under what conditions.

Ability to delete information

It is important that you can delete the material that you or your students post to a site. In extreme cases, you may need to quickly delete offensive or hateful material, or material that breaches copyright or privacy legislation.
   Points for consideration:

- Can you take down or delete information on the service? Or do you want the information to be available to future classes? Choose a service that lets you control when and if information can be removed, and be sure to test how easy it is to remove, delete, and restore content from the site.
- Can you take down information quickly and easily if defamation or a breach of copyright, privacy, or legislation has occurred? Choose a service that gives you control over posts, comments, and discussions.
- If you haven't accessed your site for a while, will the service delete your information? This may not be a problem if you want to delete the site after an interval, but your institution may have regulations about the length of time that information should be stored.

If it all goes wrong … (risk response):

- Remove defamatory and similar material immediately or shut down your site.
- Make sure you keep your account 'active', to avoid deletion of idle data.

> **Deleting information bottom line**: You must be able to delete information from a service.

Providing information about others to the service provider

If you are thinking about uploading database files containing people's names, addresses, or other details, then don't: you may be in breach of any number of laws and regulations, apart from which it is simply not your information to give away. Students should also be made aware of this issue.

Points for consideration:

- Does the service provider ask you to provide information about other users in order to sign up? If so, choose a different provider.
- Can you delete information, just in case a breach occurs? Test procedures for this before using a service with your class.

If it all goes wrong ... (risk response):

- If a breach occurs, delete or neutralise the infringing content or data.
- Advise users on how to strip or neutralise the infringing content or data from the site.
- Advise users that they might have some redress under the service's Privacy Policy, or Terms of Service, but that the jurisdiction in which they can seek such redress may be outside of your own.

> **Providing information about others to the service provider bottom line**: Don't. It is not your information to give away.

Communication from the service provider

Services may send users notifications of changes that have been made to the user's site, for example, 'A page has been updated' or 'You have a new message in your inbox'. You should choose a service that allows users to control the amount and type of communications they receive from the service.
Points for consideration:

- Is it straightforward to unsubscribe from communications that users receive from the service provider? Users should be able to do this easily under their individual profile settings or preferences.

If it all goes wrong ... (risk response)

- Show users how to turn off communications and notifications.

> **Communication from the service provider bottom line**: You should be able to turn off notifications and similar messages from the service provider.

Changes to the Terms of Service

Most web services reserve the right to change their Terms of Service at any time without notifying you of those changes. Continued use of, or access to, the service after any changes to the Terms of Service normally constitutes acceptance of those changes. When you sign up for a service, it is your responsibility to check the Terms periodically for any changes.

Points for consideration:

- What if the Terms of Service that you signed up for are changed? Will it affect how you and your students use the service? What if you don't agree with the changes that have been made? Monitor the Terms of Service periodically for such modifications and adjust your approach accordingly. Be sure to read carefully any emails you receive from the service that outline any changes.
- If the service is taken over by another company, will this result in changes to the Terms of Service? Check social media news sites such as Mashable.com, Cnet.com, and TechCrunch.com for any news about the service you are using. Choose a service that has a large, stable, ongoing community of users – it's normally a good sign that the Terms of Service are considered reasonable by most people.

If it all goes wrong … (risk response):

- Cease use of the service and find an alternative service with more reasonable and acceptable Terms.
- Export your content and import it into another service with more reasonable and acceptable Terms.
- Cease use of the service and ask students to complete the assignment in a different format. Assure students that they will not be penalised in their grades.
- If students have been affected, consider extending the due date for the assignment.
- Consult with students to see what they would like to do about the situation.

> **Changes to the Terms of Service bottom line**: A service provider can change its Terms of Service at any time. Keep up to date with the latest version of the Terms.

Changes to pricing

Many social media services are provided for free or provide their basic services for free and then charge for 'premium' or extended products. This is how they make their money (that, and advertising). Just as a service may change its Terms of Service at any time so, too, may it change its pricing structures; however, reputable services will provide you with written notice of any changes.

Points for consideration:

- Do you need the 'premium' services offered by a provider in order for your online class activities to work? If so, you might consider changing the design of your activities so that you don't run the risk of getting 'locked in' to a service that might change its pricing structures. Choose a service whose baseline, free services meet your needs.
- What if a service changes its pricing structures? What would be your financial obligation if this happened? It's best to choose a service whose free services provide you with all the functionality that you need.

If it all goes wrong ... (risk response)

- Cease use of the service and find an alternative service with a more reasonable and acceptable pricing structure, or a service that does not charge a fee at all.
- Export your content and import it into another service.
- Cease use of the service and ask students to complete the assignment in a different format. Assure students that they will not be penalised in their grades.
- If students have been affected, consider extending the due date for the assignment.
- Consult with students to see what they would like to do about the situation.

> **Changes to pricing bottom line**: Choose services that provide the basic functionality you need for free.

Considerations regarding the service itself

Business robustness and longevity

Social media services are usually provided by regular businesses and companies out to make a profit (as are businesses such as Blackboard, WebCT, Desire2Learn, and many others that sell learning management systems to educational institutions). These businesses are subject to the same market forces as any other company. Many social media services are provided for free, but not all businesses can sustain this kind of commercial model. You need to find a company that has a proven and enduring business model.

Points for consideration:

- How robust is the service? Choose a large, proven business with a solid reputation that provides a generally reliable, stable, available service. Use the service regularly for at least six months before applying it in class.
- Have your backup or export plans in place, just in case you need to 'jump ship'. You might also consider checking any discussion forums, mailing list archives, or industry blogs (such as TechCrunch, Mashable, and Cnet) for evidence of difficulties.

If it all goes wrong … (risk response):

- Open your site backup or copy and move to another service.

> **Business robustness and longevity bottom line:** Choose a service that has a proven and enduring business model.

Reliability

A major consideration when using any online tool (whether it is hosted by your school or by an external provider) is how reliable it is. All online electronic communication tools are subject to network breakdowns (including those provided by your school), whether the breakdown be at the provider or user end. However, some businesses are more reliable than others and you need to know about the ongoing dependability of the social media service you want to use in class.

Points for consideration:

- Is the service reliable or is it regularly unavailable? If you try to log on but the service frequently cannot be contacted or accessed due to technical failures, then you should be looking elsewhere.
- Does the service regularly undergo maintenance? Every service will have to undergo maintenance now and then, and the better providers will frequently update and improve their services. This means that inevitably a service will be unavailable periodically whilst updates are made. However, you need to consider how often (and when) such updates occur and how much an effect this would have on students' (and your) access to the service. If so, how much of an effect would this have on students' (and your) access to the service?

If it all goes wrong … (risk response):

- Cease use of the service and find an alternative, more reliable, service.
- Cease use of the service and ask students to complete the assignment in a different format. Assure students that they will not be penalised in their grades.
- Consider extending the due date for the assignment.
- Consult with students to see what they think is a fair thing to do in the situation.

> **Reliability bottom line**: The social media services you use in the classroom need to be available and reliable.

Software version control

Much of the software provided online by social media services is said to be in 'perpetual beta', meaning that improvements and changes are continually being made to the underlying code and then uploaded to the site. This means that the interface you are looking at one day may be different the next. You need to be confident in both your own and your students' abilities to absorb any changes made to the software.

It's a good idea to use a service for a period of time so that you get to know its systems and procedures and whether or not they are likely to affect your ability to use the service. You want a service that cares enough about its product that it makes continuous improvements, but you don't want those improvements to be unstructured or random.

Points for consideration:

- Will it be a problem if the service provider updates their software? Choose a service that makes continuous, structured, logical improvements to its product.
- Are you confident enough in your own and your students' abilities to absorb any changes in the software? You and your students need to be aware that things might change, even slightly, and you need to be relaxed about such changes.
- Do you know the service well enough to make a judgement about how likely changes to its systems and procedures will affect your ability to use the service? Give the service a trial run for a few months so that you can monitor its routines.

If it all goes wrong … (risk response):

- Cease use of the service and find an alternative, more reliable, service.
- Give special assistance to any students who are struggling to use the software.

> **Software version control bottom line:** Both you and your students need to be able to absorb any changes made to the software.

Advertising

To subsidise their free services, many social media services will display advertising on a site you create. This advertising will more than likely be 'targeted' at your audience based on the content of your site. Removal of advertising may involve the payment of a fee.

You should choose a service that allows you to switch off advertising for free, or that does not display advertising in the first place. The next best alternative is to choose a service that will allow you to switch off advertising as part of its premium services *for a reasonable price*. How you receive reimbursement for fees paid will be up to you: your school, department, or area might help you out, here, or you might be able to claim things back on tax.

Points for consideration:

- Is advertising displayed on your site? If so, can you turn it off? You should choose a service that allows you to switch off advertising for free, or that does not display advertising in the first place.

If it all goes wrong … (risk response):

- Cease use of the service and find a service that does not display or that allows you to switch off advertising
- Cease use of the service and ask students to complete the assignment in a different format.

> **Advertising bottom line:** Choose a service that allows you to switch off advertising, or that does not display advertising in the first place.

Activity. Write a risk analysis

It is highly advisable that you conduct a risk analysis before you use any social media tool or service in your classroom. Without a risk analysis, we tend to assume that everything will go according to plan; in other words, we base our assumptions on an ideal situation. A risk analysis deals with 'real-world' practicalities and can give you an idea of how much risk you are exposing your own, your students', and your institution's reputation to.

For this activity, think of a project for which you want to use social media with your class. Write a risk analysis for your project.

Step 1. Find a website that describes the various elements of risk management. The site should cover topics such as:

- Definitions of risk and risk management.
- Risk management principles.
- How to identify, assess, respond to, monitor, and control risk.
- How to write a risk management plan.

JISCInfoNet.ac.uk is an excellent place to start (search: 'JISC risk').

Step 2. Create a risk log for each item of risk. A risk log helps you document the factors relating to each risk, such as:

- *Description*. Phrased as 'There is a risk that X could occur, caused by Y, resulting in Z'. An example from one of my own risk analyses is, 'There is a risk that the University is sued under the *Privacy Act (1988)*, due to inappropriate disclosure of personal information, resulting in damage to reputation and financial loss'.
- *Probability*. The chances of the risk occurring.
- *Impact*. The effects on you, other staff, students, and/or the organisation if the risk were to be realised.
- *Mitigation strategies*. Pre-emptive plans and actions that you have in place *right now* to prevent the risk occurring. Many such strategies are covered under 'points for consideration' in the sections above.
- *Risk response*. What you will do if the risk is realised. See 'If it all goes wrong ...' above for some ideas about what you might do in the event of a risk eventuating.

Step 3. Run your risk management plan past a colleague, or, even better, past a risk management specialist who works for your education authority. Keep your plan up to date and amend it to account for changes that may have occurred since you first wrote it.

Summary

- You cannot abolish risk, only control it. Your use of social media in the classroom must be informed by an understanding of privacy and copyright laws, Terms of Service, and how businesses operate in the social media environment.
- If you feel uncomfortable in any way when using a social media service with your students, or if a breach occurs, cease use of the service immediately and take stock of your situation. Do not 'go rogue' and use social media with your students thinking that 'it'll all be OK': problems do arise, most of them small, but there is always the possibility of inviting legal proceedings against yourself, your students, and your institution.
- If it all goes wrong, ask students and parents about what they think should be done. Involve students and parents as much as possible in the processes. Keep them informed and normalise social media as something that is part of our everyday lives.

Resources

Online resources

- Copyright. Search for the copyright council or authority in your jurisdiction. Education authorities and university libraries also often have good copyright pages.
- The CreativeCommons.org website will help you understand how Creative Commons works and will direct you to the CC website in your jurisdiction.
- W3C's Web Accessibility Initiative describes web design principles that meet accessibility standards (search, 'W3C Web Accessibility Initiative'). Web accessibility checkers are also useful (search 'Web accessibility checker' or 'Web accessibility evaluation tool').
- Industry blogs such as Mashable.com, Cnet.com, and TechCrunch.com can give you the latest news on many social media companies.

- Visit the *Using Social Media in the Classroom* companion website for links, risk management templates, discussions, and other materials relating to understanding online risk. You can find this at www.sagepub.co.uk/poore

Further reading

- De Zwart, M., Lindsay, D., Henderson, M., and Phillips. M. (2011) *Teenagers, legal risks and social networking sites*. Faculty of Education, Monash University, Melbourne. Available at http://newmediaresearch.educ.monash.edu.au/moodle/course/view.php?id=37. Accessed 13 October 2011.
- Education Review (2011) Pirates in the playground, *Education Review*, 8 February 2011. Available at http://www.educationreview.com.au/pages/section/article.php?s=Technology& idArticle=19841. Accessed 24 October 2011.

- Electronic Frontier Foundation (n.d.) Legal guide for bloggers. Available at https://www.eff.org/issues/bloggers/legal. Accessed 26 October 2011.
- JISC infoNet. (2011) Infokit: Risk management. Available at http://www.jiscinfonet.ac.uk/InfoKits/risk-management/index_html. Accessed 26 October 2011.
- University of Edinburgh. (2007) Guidelines for using external Web 2.0 services. Available at https://www.wiki.ed.ac.uk/display/Web2wiki/Web+2.0+Guidelines. Accessed 26 October 2011.

CHAPTER 17

PRACTICAL AND IN-CLASS CONSIDERATIONS

Overview

This final chapter points to some of the general practical and in-class considerations you face when using social media with your students. We will cover private versus public sites, making backups, turning on or off cookies and monitoring, bandwidth quotas, students' home access, student usernames, and more. The main thing to take away from the information provided here is that you need to design any social media activities carefully, and with an eye to some of the more mundane elements of everyday teaching and learning practice.

Practical and in-class considerations

Private vs public sites

Each service will have different levels of privacy available to site or content creators. Some services allow you to set your site to private so that only invited members can join. Others may not offer this functionality at all, or only offer it as part of an 'upgrade' package that you have to pay for. Still others offer you very fine gradations of privacy, for example allowing you to block search engines but otherwise allow regular visitors (that is, people with a direct link).

You need to consider the risks and benefits of making a site public (that is, potentially viewable by anyone on the internet) or private (that is, accessible to only those people you invite). In some cases, an entirely private class site will be most appropriate for your purposes – maybe you are discussing sensitive issues – whilst in others you may be deliberately seeking input from the broader community and thus wanting people to find you. Whatever settings you choose (public or private) you need to inform students and parents about how your site is set up and why. Or, even better, bring them into the conversation and get their input before you begin.

Backups

Unlike most institution-supplied online services where data is backed up every 24 hours, there is no guarantee that a social media service will backup your data. Even if the service were to backup your data (and most reputable services will, indeed, do so regularly – and frequently more often than every 24 hours), there is no certainty that you will be able to retrieve lost data. Therefore, backup solutions must be found that work independently of any backup procedures that a social media provider might already have in place. Here are some issues you will need to consider:

- *Does the service allow users to backup or export their work to their desktops?* Avoid services that do not support this function.
- *What if the service I am using does not have an in-built backup function?* There are alternatives. Conduct a websearch for 'website backup software' and see what you come up with. This software will normally 'suck down' an entire site in html format – but you should only use it to take a copy of sites that you own. You will have to pay for some backup software, but HTTrack for PC and SiteSucker for Mac are free. You can also do a search for a specific backup tool; for example, there is a specific backup tool for the Tumblr blogging service, which has been developed by a Tumblr user. Simply search 'Tumblr backup tool' (or whatever service you want to back up) and you will likely find something suitable to your purposes.
- *What is an acceptable file format for backups?* Choose a format that is transferable (for example, html, xml, opml), and that isn't specific to this provider, that is, it can be easily imported into another system. Xml, html, and opml formats are generally portable, depending on the type of service you are using. Before you use a service in class, test the backup function

that a website offers by exporting your content to your desktop and then importing it into another service to see if it works.

- *If necessary, will you be able to read the backup file easily?* For example, html can be easily read in an internet browser, but xml will require you to convert the file so that it *is* human-readable.
- *What responsibility do students have for backing up their work?* Teach students how to backup their work and make them responsible for doing so regularly. Advise them to make a backup each time they have made a significant change to their site, and to make a backup of the final submitted version of their work. Just as we should expect students to have an extra copy of any assignment at home (to avoid 'the dog ate it' excuses), we should expect them to have a backup of work they have created online. This will help mitigate the situation where a student claims that their work has disappeared from a website.
- *What should my backup plans look like?* Teachers should backup their entire site at least weekly – more often if you are making significant additions or changes. You should plan and test a migration and restore procedure for course data and you should advise students in class on how to keep an html copy of their work by saving the page their work appears on as soon as they publish it. Inform students that they may be asked to re-submit their work if they cannot provide an html copy to the lecturer.

Student back-ups

It is essential that students backup their own online work and that you get them into the habit of doing so, no matter what level or age they are at. Students should be keeping backups of any work they produce (both during the drafting stages and at the point of final submission) just in case their computer crashes. The same applies online: students should be advised to backup their site on a regular basis, whenever they make significant additions or alterations to the site, and at the point where they submit the work for assessment. Similarly, each time students publish something new on the class site, they should make a copy of it. If a student claims that their work has disappeared, then they should be expected to provide their html copy to you for assessment. If they cannot provide an html copy of their work, you may have to ask them to submit the work again.

Finally, students should not save their work as a Word document, as the date stamp on Word documents can easily be manipulated. Saving as html, rather than as a Word doc, goes some way (as even this procedure can be manipulated) to proving to you that the student published their work when they said they did and that they didn't put everything together after the due date. Methods for creating backups are covered in Chapter 3.

Use of cookies and monitoring

Most internet browsers collect 'cookies', that is small packets of data that are used again when you login to a website. Cookies are what enable a browser to monitor or track your user details so that your preferences are remembered on a website, meaning that you don't have to enter the same information over and over again. Cookies are not viruses or worms, do not generate spam or popups, and are not used for advertising. However, some internet users would prefer it if a 'cookie trail' weren't left behind every time they visit a website, so most internet browsers let you turn off cookies (under 'settings' or 'preferences' or similar) so that such a trail is not laid down. You need to advise students how to do this via their internet browser. If you need more information about cookies, visit the Wikipedia entry on 'HTTP cookies'.

Help and support available via social media services

Most social media services provide their services for free. That means they are unlikely to provide you with a helpdesk phone number that you can call toll free, 24 hours a day. However, to expect such helpdesk access is to assume a model of support that is unnecessary when you are using a well designed online software service, as the software itself will give you all the instructions you need on the screen, at the appropriate time (see Chapter 3 for more information).

Having said all that, however, if something does go wrong, and you can find no solution to your problem, you could be on your own. It is prudent, therefore, to choose a service that has a solid community of users around it, including a robust discussion forum and comprehensive FAQs. It is also helpful if there is an email or telephone contact or an online form supplied so that you can get in touch if you don't find an answer via the forums, Google, or the FAQs – but there can be no guarantee that you will get a timely answer to your message (or even an answer at all). You also need to consider time-zone differences. What if you *can* send an email or make a telephone call but your problem occurs in the middle of the night in the country where the service is hosted on the other side of the world?

You need to get skilled up in problem-solving online. Ask yourself, 'Do I have the skills to work through problems myself? Do I have enough social media vocabulary to (1) identify my problem, (2) to search for a solution, and (3) to implement the solution? You should have good online problem-solving skills before you embark on a teaching and learning project that uses an external social media service.

Help and support available at school

Because your school has not supplied the service you are using as part of its enterprise systems, you cannot expect school to help you out if things go wrong: you – and your students – could be on your own. Nevertheless, there are likely to be some people around who would be willing (but not always able) to assist.

You also have to consider the needs of your students: you must be prepared to provide a reasonable amount of assistance for students who find themselves in difficulty. Students may have trouble with technical aspects of the service (for example, it may not be available at certain times), or they may not have the skills to quickly learn the way the software operates. In these instances, you will be the one they will call upon for help. Do you have the expertise and time to provide students with the technical and skills assistance they might need? You may have to provide a workshop for your class on how to use the online software, and you may have to act as a 'helpdesk' for individual problems and enquiries, so get to know the software and the service well enough to provide a good level of support for students, if required.

Cross-platform and cross-browser functionality/usability

Any service you ask students to use must work at least on both Mac and PC, and in any versions of Firefox and Internet Explorer that your institution supports. You need to test the service in all environments to make sure that it works before you ask students to use it.

School bandwidth quotas

Students are sometimes given access only to a certain amount of free bandwidth per day on school computers or on student laboratory computers. You need to consider how quickly your use of an externally hosted site will chew through their quota. If the quota is inadequate for your purposes (for example, you are using lots of rich media such as video), you may need to lobby your technical services people to increase your students' bandwidth quotas, especially if lack of bandwidth becomes an impediment to students' successful completion of an assignment.

You should also monitor students' bandwidth usage and ask them to inform you if lack of bandwidth is becoming an issue for them.

Students' home internet access

Even though students might have broadband internet at home, it doesn't mean that they necessarily can access that internet easily: maybe other family or household members have priority (see Chapter 14). Make sure you set assignments well in advance to help counter this situation and get to know something of your students' effective access to the internet.

Requiring students to register

Quite simply, *do not make it mandatory that students sign up for any social media service in order to complete their school work.* You may have to find other ways for students to undertake their studies if they or their parents do not wish to sign up. If students or their parents do not wish to sign up for a social media service, that is their own business.

Choice of service

Students may already be signed up with a different service provider – one that suits their individual needs better. In such cases, you may choose to be flexible and allow them to continue to use their current site providing that it meets your minimum requirements, for example, that the site can be backed up in a readable format, that the Terms of Service grant copyright and intellectual property rights to the student, that you can become an administrator for the site, that the student can prove that the service is stable, reliable, accessible, and so on.

Alternatively, you may wish to provide students with some suggested or recommended services to use, but also allow them to find their own service if they prefer to do so – but again so long as it meets your minimum requirements.

Student identification and usernames

Keeping track of who has posted or contributed what material to a group site can be a problem. Think about how your students will identify themselves as the true author of a post or comment yet still maintain a certain degree of anonymity (if that is necessary – and it probably will be if you have a duty of care to minors). Here are some ideas:

- Ask students to use a public name that consists of their first name and last initial, for example, Chris S. (Make sure you have chosen a service that allows users to generate a public name that is different from their username.)
- Get students to generate an avatar of themselves using an online avatar generator such as Gravatar, Build Your Wild Self, Unique, or Meez. Tell them to use it as their profile photo. That way, you'll know that 'Chris S.' is a member of your class and not some other person.

Students' responsibility for work done under their own login details

Students must be clear that they are responsible for any work that appears under their username/login. If, for example, Alice and Rachel are working together, but Rachel is doing all the work under Alice's login, then Alice will get the credit for the work. Students need to keep track of which work is done under whose login and when.

Visibility of students' work to each other

In some cases, you will want students to view and comment upon others' work. In other cases, you will not. If students are working in small groups you may want each group to be able to see what the others are producing. Or you might not, in which case you need a service that allows you to keep each group's work private until a final class presentation or similar. In other instances, you might only want students' work to be viewable to yourself as teacher, especially if students are working on more personal projects. Much will depend on the educational design of the task or assignment you are setting (see Chapter 2).

Preventing changes being made to the site after the due date

If you are the owner or administrator of a site, then you have control over the site's date- and timestamp. If students are working on the site and they submit work after the due date and time, you will know about it. If, however, students are the owners and administrators of their own sites, then there is the chance that they may submit their work late and then 'backdate' their site's time settings so that it appears that the work was submitted on time. There are a number of ways to manage this situation:

- Tell students not to make any changes to the site after the due date. Tell them you will be checking the datestamp on the latest material so that you will know if any alterations have been made. Of course, this does not prevent students from changing the clock settings on their computers or in their account settings and 'tricking' the system into thinking it is another date. Many services allow you to set a time zone for your account that is based on the service's own clock – again, this doesn't prevent students from changing the settings to as far behind your time zone as possible, but it at least restricts things to a 24-hour time period.
- Ask students to each provide you (via email or via upload to a central repository) with an electronic backup file of their site *on the due date*. You can assess the site as it stands on the internet, but if you suspect that they

have made changes after the due date, you can easily check the online site against the backup file.

The point here is to avoid accusations of your marking one piece of work that later gets changed (and possibly improved) by the student who then claims that you have given them too low a grade for their assignment. Although we might not like having to second-guess our students in this way, it is, regrettably, sometimes necessary.

Posting of offensive material

There is always the chance that students or uninvited others will post offensive (that is, hateful, racist, sexist, pornographic, and so on) material on your site. Posting such material usually constitutes a breach of the Terms of Service and will probably also be counted as a criminal act in your country (most developed countries have laws against hate speech, racism, harrassment, and so on). Students need to be aware that posting such material might not only cause hurt, but may also be illegal and subject to prosecution. You need to remind students that they must not post or upload material that brings either themselves or their institution into disrepute, that causes offence, or that breaks the law. Here is some advice for dealing with this issue:

- Ensure that you have administration privileges for the class site.
- Choose a service that allows administrators to remove content.
- Choose a service that allows administrators to ban members from the site.
- Monitor student-created content for offensive or potentially damaging material.
- Inform students that they must notify you immediately they notice that any offensive or potentially damaging material appears on the site.

Student user roles

You need to think carefully about the degree of control students have over any site you may set up for them. Most services allow you, as the creator, to assign different 'roles' to your users. Some basic roles include:

- Administrator: full control over the whole site, including the ability to delete content, ban users, and to change site settings and themes.
- Editor: ability to delete others' content, plus some management capacity.
- Author or writer: control over their own content only – they can edit, delete, publish their own work, but not that of others.
- Registered user: can visit the site and add to discussions or make comments, but that's about all.

You need to consider what happens to your site if you are the only administrator and your account cannot be accessed for some reason. You should appoint at least one other administrator to your site (preferably a teacher colleague), just in case something goes wrong. In general, only give your students user roles that allow them control over their own, individual content.

Student administrators of class sites

It can be tempting to want to give students administration privileges over a class site as a way of encouraging them to take responsibility for the site, or to reward the enthusiastic, or to teach them about site moderation, and so forth. However, doing so could place student administrators in a difficult position: What if they accidentally delete the entire content of the site? What if their best efforts at moderation are lampooned by classmates? You may decide that in the end you have a risk management plan that accounts for these possibilities, but in general you should not expect such a large responsibility to be accepted by students. For my own, I *never* ask students, even my adult university students, to take on this responsibility. No matter how trustworthy, dependable or keen students are, accidents can always happen.

Assessment

The decision to use an externally hosted web service provider as part of your assessment regime is a significant one and you need to make sure that you have thought through all the potential risk areas and trouble spots carefully. You will need to consider everything from how the service provider handles your data and how that relates to your institution's policy on data retention (if it has one), to backup options, to circumventing student 'trickiness' such as manipulating datestamps or claiming that their work disappeared and they don't know where it went. Here are some issues you will need to consider if using a social media service as part of an assessment regime:

- *Does use of the service comply with your institution's policies and regulations on assessment?* Check this closely. For example, you may choose a service that deletes your information if you haven't accessed your account for a set period of time, but your institution requires that data be kept for two years.
- *How visible is a student's work to other students?* Is this appropriate? Choose a service that lets you or your students control who can view their work: the whole world, just classmates, or just the teacher?
- *If you are asking students to work on a group task, can you track who has contributed what to the assignment?* You need a service that allows users to be identified when they make a post, comment, or other contribution.

- *What will you do if a site is unavailable?* You may need to have a backup plan where you can ask students to complete the assignment in a different format. However, if you have insisted that students have backed up their work in an appropriate file format, then you should be covered.
- *What will you do if a student says that they have done the work but that it has disappeared from the site?* Again, you should have a backup plan for this situation. If students are the administrators of their own sites, then it should be their responsibility to backup their work every time they make significant changes, and at the time when they submit the assignment.
- *What if a student claims that they are the true author of a work, but that it was done under someone else's login details?*
- *How will you prevent students from making changes after the due date?* Choosing a service that will allow students to give you 'super admin' privileges may give you the right to lock a site or page from further changes. This may mean temporarily demoting students' current privileges from 'editor' to 'registered user' only.
- *How will you know if changes have been made to the site after the due date?* The service you sign up for should give a datestamp for each entry that is made to the site. This is one way of telling when changes are made, but students might 'backdate' their own computer's clock to get around this. Similar to the point above, choosing a service that gives you the capacity to lock pages might be your best solution.
- *How long will you need to keep the assessment item? Will the service still be around by then?* This links in with your institution's assessment guidelines, policies, and procedures. You need to be clear about what is required of you in this regard, and you need to have a fair amount of faith in the service's longevity. You should at least have electronic backups of all work handed in for assessment. See the points under 'Backups,' above.

Including parents

Regardless of the extent of social media use in your classroom, you should try to include parents in your decision-making for your social media project. Send a note home, post announcements on your website, hold information sessions – do everything you can to keep them up to date with your plans and to involve them in the project once things are under way. You may even consider conducting a structured series of workshops that takes parents through some of the social media basics described in this book, and particularly some of the issues described in Part 4.

In any case, it is vital that you have parental and school endorsement for your work in this area, and that means being open about the risks involved and how you are accounting for them, but also illuminating for others your sound educational and pedagogical reasons for designing tasks using social media.

Demonstrate that you have been diligent in your considerations and that you have thought things through carefully and you will gain their respect, support, and encouragement.

  Summary

- Practical and in-class considerations must not be overlooked when using social media in the classroom. Everything from privacy options to backups to bandwidth quotas needs to be considered in the design of your social media use.
- You should be particularly careful if using social media for assessment, as there is a lot riding on the outcome, both for you and for students. Make sure you have carefully assessed the tool or service, and have backup options and risk management plans firmly in place.
- Be sure to include parents in any plans you have for using social media in the classroom. Inform them about the risks involved and how you intend to manage and/or mitigate them, and be sure to gain their support for your project.

Resources

Online resources

- Industry blogs such as Mashable.com, Cnet.com, and TechCrunch.com can give you the latest news on many social media companies.
- HTTrack for PC and SiteSucker for Mac will backup an entire site that you own.
- Check the University of Edinburgh's Guidelines for using external Web 2.0 services (search 'University of Edinburgh web 2.0 Guidelines').

- Visit the *Using Social Media in the Classroom* companion website for links, materials, and discussions relating to practical considerations when using social networks for teaching and learning. You can find this at www.sagepub.co.uk/poore

AFTERWORD

Having made your way to this afterword, you should now be in a good position to safely, sensibly – and, above all, creatively – use social media in your classroom.

This book has taken you through the basics of theory, pedagogy, and practice as they relate to teaching and learning with digital technologies. But more than this, it has explored the important social, legal, and policy contexts that make this area of study and practice such a complex one, and one that is subject to the dynamic cultural landscape that constitutes education in and for the twenty-first century. We are at a point in our history where we must acknowledge the roles that social media play in our everyday communications – and inasmuch as education is itself a communicative act, then so must we find ways of harnessing these forms to the service of our profession. With care and imagination – those hallmarks of good teaching – we can find ways of making them work.

Hopefully this book has shown you the myriad possibilities that exist for integrating digital technologies into your everyday teaching practice. But, even more, I hope you have found some inspiration: if you were doubtful about the value of social media in education, I hope you can now see the tremendous benefits for both you and your students; if you were timid, I hope you have gained some nerve to try new things; if you were keen – but unsure about how to do things – I hope you now have a place to start; if you had a tendency towards incaution, I hope you can see the value of prudence.

In any case, I hope I have galvanised your curiosity and set you on your way to make your own discoveries and to share those discoveries with students, colleagues, and parents. I hope you feel energised and excited, but also informed and confident, about the possibilities of teaching and learning with digital technologies.

Using social media in the classroom rewards both courage and enterprise. Be intrepid: get out there and try new and different things ... but always within the limits of safety.

REFERENCES

ACDE (2001) New learning. A charter for Australian education. Australian Council of Deans of Education. Melbourne: ACDE.

ACMA (2010) Trends in media use by children and young people: Insights from the Kaiser Family Foundation's Generation M2 2009 (USA), and results from the ACMA's Media and communications in Australian families 2007. Australian Communications and Media Authority. Report. Available at http://www.acma.gov.au/WEB/STANDARD/pc=PC_312210. Accessed 10 October 2011.

Anderson, P. (2007) What is Web 2.0? Ideas, technologies and implications for education. JISC Technology and Standards Watch, February 2007. Available at http://www.jisc.ac.uk/publications/reports/2007/twweb2.aspx. Accessed 1 November 2011.

Andes, L. and Claggett, E. (2011) Wiki writers: students and teachers making connections across communities, *The Reading Teacher,* 64(5), 345–50.

Armstrong, L., Berry, M. and Lamshed, R. (2004) Blogs as electronic learning journals, *e-Journal of Instructional Science and Technology (e-JIST),* 7(1). Available at http://www.ascilite.org.au/ajet/e-jist/docs/Vol7_No1/CurrentPractice/Blogs.htm. Accessed 13 October 2011.

Attwell, G. (2007) Web 2.0 and the changing ways we are using computers for learning: what are the implications for pedagogy and curriculum? Available at http://www.elearningeuropa.info/en/article/Web-2.0-and-the-changing-ways-we-are-using-computers-for-learning%3A-what-are-the-implications-for-pedagogy-and-curriculum. Accessed 13 October 2011.

Beach, R. and Doerr-Stevens, C. (2011) Using social networking for online role-plays to develop students' argumentative strategies, *Journal of Educational Computing Research,* 45(2), 165–81.

Bell, A. (2009) *Exploring Web 2.0: Second Generation Interactive Tools – Blogs, Podcasts, Wikis, Networking, Virtual Worlds, and More*. Georgetown, TX: Katy Crossing Press.

Benz, A. (2010) Writing a book with students, using Google Docs as shared learning environment: an experience, *International Journal of Innovation in Education,* 1(2), 139–47.

Blau, I. and Caspi, A. (2009) What type of collaboration helps? Psychological ownership, perceived learning and outcome quality of collaboration using Google Docs, in Y. Eshet-Alkalai, A. Caspi, S. Eden, N. Geri and Y. Yair (eds), *Proceedings of the Chais Conference on Instructional Technologies Research 2009: Learning in the Technological Era*. Raanana:

The Open University of Israel. Available at http://telem-pub.openu.ac.il/users/chais/2009/noon/1_1.pdf. Accessed 13 October 2011.

Bostrom, N. (2007) Technological revolutions: ethics and policy in the dark, in N. M. de S. Cameron and M. E. Mitchell (eds), *Nanoscale: Issues and Perspectives for the Nano Century*. Hoboken, NJ: John Wiley. pp. 129–52.

Bowman, L. L., Levine, L. E., Waite, B. M. and Gendron, M. (2010) Can students really multitask? An experimental study of instant messaging while reading, *Computers & Education,* 54(4), 927–31.

boyd, d. (2011) Social network sites as networked publics: affordances, dynamics, and implications', in Z. Papacharissi (ed.), *Networked Self: Identity, Community, and Culture on Social Network Sites*. New York: Routledge. pp. 39–58.

Bruns, A. (2008) *Blogs, Wikipedia, Second Life, and Beyond. From Production to Produsage*. New York: Peter Lang.

Buckingham, D. (2006) Defining digital literacy – What do young people need to know about digital media? *Nordic Journal of Digital Literacy,* 1(4), 263–76.

Buckmaster, L. and Thomas, M. (2009) *Social inclusion and social citizenship – towards a truly inclusive society*. Research Paper, 23 October 2009, no. 8, 2009–10. Parliamentary Library, Parliament of Australia. Available at http://www.aph.gov.au/library/pubs/rp/2009-10/10rp08.htm. Accessed 13 October 2011.

Burton, R., Barlow, N. and Barker, C. (2010) Using visual tools for analysis and learning. University of Huddersfield. Available at http://eprints.hud.ac.uk/7843/. Accessed 1 September 2011.

Byington, T. A. (2011) Communities of practice: using blogs to increase collaboration, *Intervention in School and Clinic,* 46(5), 280–91.

Byron, T. (2008). *Safer children in a digital world*. The report of the Byron Review. Available at http://www.education.gov.uk/ukccis/about/a0076277/the-byron-reviews. Accessed 1 November 2011.

Carr, N. (2010) *The Shallows. How the Internet is Changing the Way We Think, Read and Remember*. London: Atlantic Books.

Carrington, V. and Robinson, M. (2009) *Digital Literacies. Social Learning and Classroom Practices*. Los Angeles, CA: UKLA and Sage.

Chiong, C. and Shuler, C. (2010) *Learning: is there an app for that? Investigations of young children's usage and learning with mobile devices and apps*. New York: The Joan Ganz Cooney Center at Sesame Workshop. Available at http://www.joanganzcooneycenter.org/Reports-27.html. Accessed 13 October 2011.

Christudason, A. (2003) Peer learning. Available at http://www.cdtl.nus.edu.sg/success/sl37.htm. Accessed 13 October 2011.

Churches, A. (n.d.) 21st century learning spaces. Available at http://edorigami.wikispaces.com/21st+Century+Learning+Spaces. Accessed 23 July 2009.

CIBER (2008) Information behaviour of the researcher of the future. Centre for Information Behaviour and the Evaluation of Research. Available at http://www.ucl.ac.uk/infostudies/research/ciber/downloads/. Accessed 13 October 2011.

Collin, P., Rahilly, K., Richardson, I. and Third, A. (2011) Benefits of social networking services. Cooperative Research Centre for Young People, Technology and Wellbeing, Melbourne. Available at http://www.inspire.org.au/wp-content/uploads/2011/03/FINAL_The_Benefits_of_Social_Networking_Services_Lit_Review.pdf. Accessed 13 October 2011.

Connolly, S. (2011) The New Addington primary schools animation project: using animation to build community relationships between schools, *Journal of Assistive Technologies,* 5(1), 37–9.

Conole, G. (2008) New schemas for mapping pedagogies and technologies, *Ariadne,* 56, July. Available at http://www.ariadne.ac.uk/issue56/conole/. Accessed 13 October 2011.

Davies, J. (2004) Wiki brainstorming and problems with wiki. MSc Project submitted September 2004. Available at http://www.jonathan-davies.co.uk/portfolio/wiki.php. Accessed 13 October 2011.

Davies, J. (2007) Display, identity and the everyday: self-presentation through online image sharing, *Studies in the Cultural Politics of Education*, 28(4), 549–64.

Davies, J. (2009) A space for play: crossing boundaries and learning online, in V. Carrington and M. Robinson (eds), *Digital Literacies. Social Learning and Classroom Practices*. Los Angeles, CA: UKLA and Sage.

Davies, J. and Merchant, G. (2009) *Web 2.0 for Schools. Learning and Social Participation*. New York: Peter Lang.

De Zwart, M., Lindsay, D., Henderson, M. and Phillips, M. (2011) Teenagers, legal risks and social networking sites. Faculty of Education, Monash University, Melbourne. Available at http://newmediaresearch.educ.monash.edu.au/moodle/course/view.php?id=37. Accessed 13 October 2011.

DEECD (2011). In their hands. Getting started. Classroom ideas for learning with the iPad resource booklet for schools. Department of Education and Early Childhood Development, State of Victoria. Available at http://www.ipadsforeducation.vic.edu.au/userfiles/files/ipads_for_learning_21Steps.pdf. Accessed 13 October 2011.

Dewey, J. (2004 [1916]) *Democracy and Education*. Mineola, NY: Dover.

Downes, T., Fluck, A., Gibbons, P., Leonard, R., Matthews, C., Oliver, R., Vickers, M. and Williams, M. (2001) Making better connections. Models of teacher professional development for the integration of information and communication technology into classroom practice. Australian Curriculum Studies Association, Australian Council for Computers in Education, Technology Education Federation of Australia, University of Western Sydney. Available at http://www.dest.gov.au/sectors/school_education/publications_resources/profiles/making_better_connections.htm. Accessed 3 November 2011.

Eaton, S. E. (2010) Using Skype in the second and foreign language classroom. Paper presented at the Social Media Workshop 'Get Your ACT(FL) Together Online: Standards Based Language Instruction via Social Media', San Diego, CA, 4 August 2010. Available at http://eric.ed.gov/ERICWebPortal/search/detailmini.jsp?_nfpb=true&_&ERICExtSearch_SearchValue_0=ED511316&ERICExtSearch_SearchType_0=no&accno=ED511316. Accessed 1 November 2011.

Education Review (2011) Pirates in the playground, *Education Review*, 8 February 2011. Available at http://www.educationreview.com.au/pages/section/article.php?s=Technology&idArticle=19841. Accessed 24 October 2011.

Edwards, G. and Mosley, B. F. (2011) Technology integration can be delicious: social bookmarking as a technology integration tool, in C. Wankel (ed.), *Educating Educators with Social Media* (Cutting-edge Technologies in Higher Education, Vol. 1), Bradford: Emerald Group Publishing Limited. pp. 207–25.

Electronic Frontier Foundation (n.d.) Legal guide for bloggers. Available at https://www.eff.org/issues/bloggers/legal. Accessed 26 October 2011.

Fitzgerald, R. and Steele, J. (2008) Digital Learning Communities (DLC): investigating the application of social software to support networked learning. Report. Available at http://eprints.qut.edu.au/18476/. Accessed 13 October 2011.

Glassman, M. and Kan, M. J. (2011). The logic of wikis: the possibilities of the Web 2.0 classroom, *Computer-Supported Collaborative Learning*, 6(1), 93–112.

Grant, L. (2007) Learning to be part of the knowledge economy: digital divides and media literacy. Available at http://www2.futurelab.org.uk/resources/publications-reports-articles/discussion-papers/Discussion-Paper816. Accessed 13 October 2011.

Grant, L. (2010). Connecting digital literacy between home and school. Futurelab. Available at http://www.futurelab.org.uk/resources/connecting-digital-literacy-between-home-and-school. Accessed 13 October 2011.

Green, H. and Hannon, C. (2007) Their space. Education for a digital generation. Available at http://www.demos.co.uk/publications/theirspace. Accessed 21 October 2008.

Habgood, M. P. J. and Ainsworth, S. E. (2011) Motivating children to learn effectively: exploring the value of intrinsic integration in educational games, *Journal of the Learning Sciences,* 20(2), pp. 169–206.

Hague, C. (2010) 'It's not chalk and talk anymore'. School approaches to developing students' digital literacy. Futurelab report. Available at http://www.futurelab.org.uk/resources/%E2%80%9Cit%E2%80%99s-not-chalk-and-talk-anymore%E2%80%9D-school-approaches-developing-students%E2%80%99-digital-literacy. Accessed 13 October 2011.

Hague, C. and Payton, S. (2010) Digital literacy across the curriculum. A Futurelab handbook. Available at http://archive.futurelab.org.uk/resources/publications-reports-articles/handbooks/Handbook1706. Accessed 13 October 2011.

Hague, C. and Williamson, B. (2009) Digital participation, digital literacy, and school subjects. A review of the policies, literature and evidence. Available at http://archive.futurelab.org.uk/projects/digital-participation. Accessed 13 October 2011.

Harrison, C. (2011) Literacy, technology and the internet: what are the challenges and opportunities for learners with reading difficulties, and how do we support them in meeting those challenges and grasping those opportunities? in C. Wyatt-Smith, J. Elkins and S. Gunn (eds), *Multiple Perspectives on Difficulties in Learning Literacy and Numeracy*. Dordrecht: Springer Netherlands. pp. 111–31.

Hennis, T. and Ubacht, J. (n.d.) Wiki in classroom. [*sic*] Experiences and tips. Available at http://www.scribd.com/doc/2227102/Wiki-in-classroom-Experiences-and-tips. Accessed 12 January 2011.

Hew, K. F. and Cheung, W. S. (2010) Use of three-dimensional (3-D) immersive virtual worlds in K-12 and higher education settings: a review of the research, *British Journal of Educational Technology,* 41(1), 33–55.

Hinduja, S. and Patchin, J. (2010) Cyberbullying prevention, and response. Cyberbullying Research Centre. Available at http://www.cyberbullying.us/resources.php. Accessed 18 October 2011.

Hoover, E. (2009) The Millennial muddle: how stereotyping students became a thriving industry and a bundle of contradictions, *The Chronicle of Higher Education*, 11 October 2009. Available at http://chronicle.com/article/The-Millennial-Muddle-How/48772/. Accessed 25 January 2010.

Huvila, I. (2010) Where does the information come from? Information source use patterns in Wikipedia. *Information Research,* 15(3). Available at http://informationr.net/ir/15-3/paper433.html. Accessed 3 November 2011.

Jenkins, H. (2006) Confronting the challenges of participatory culture. Media education for the 21st century. Available at http://www.nwp.org/cs/public/print/resource/2713. Accessed 13 October 2011.

JISC (2007) Student expectations study: findings from preliminary research. Joint Information Systems Committee. http://www.jisc.ac.uk/publications/publications/studentexpectationsbp.aspx. Accessed 12 February 2008.

JISC (2008) Great expectations of ICT: how higher education institutions are measuring up. Joint Information Systems Committee. Available at http://www.jisc.ac.uk/publications/publications/greatexpectations. Accessed 7 Feb 2009.

JISC infoNet. (2011) Infokit: risk management. Joint Information Systems Committee. Available at http://www.jiscinfonet.ac.uk/InfoKits/risk-management/index_html. Accessed 26 October 2011.

Johnson, S. (2006 [2005]) *Everything Bad is Good For You. Why Popular Culture is Making us Smarter*. London: Penguin.

Juvonen, J. and Gross, E. F. (2008) Extending the school grounds? Bullying experiences in cyber-space, *The Journal of School Health*, 78 (9), 496–505.

Kaimuloa Bates, B. (2011) Using Google Apps in professional learning communities. PowerPoint presented at the Technology, Colleges and Community Worldwide Online Conference, 14 April 2011. Available at http://scholarspace.manoa.hawaii.edu/bitstream/handle/10125/19960/etec_kaimuloabates.pdf?sequence=1. Accessed 13 October 2011.

Kennedy, G., Krause, K. L., Gray, K., Judd, T. and Bennett, S. (2006) Questioning the net generation: a collaborative project in Australian higher education. Who's learning, 2006 Proceedings of the 23rd annual ascilite conference: Who's learning? Whose technology? Sydney: Sydney University Press.

Laia, H. and Chenc, C. (2011) Factors influencing secondary school teachers' adoption of teaching blogs, *Computers & Education,* 56(4), 948–60.

Lankshear, C. and Knobel, M. (2006). Blogging as participation: The active sociality of a new literacy. Paper presented to the American Educational Research Association, San Francisco, USA. 11 April 2006. Available at http://citeseerx.ist.psu.edu/viewdoc/summary?doi=10.1.1.135.3944. Accessed 13 October 2011.

Lave, J. and Wenger, E. (2009 [1991]) *Situated Learning. Legitimate Peripheral Participation*. Cambridge: Cambridge University Press.

Leshed, G. and Sengers, P. (2011) 'I lie to myself that i have freedom in my own schedule': productivity tools and experiences of busyness, in *Proceedings of the 2011 Annual Conference on Human Factors in Computing Systems*. Available at http://leshed.comm.cornell.edu/pubs/p905-leshed.pdf. Accessed 13 October 2011.

Levin, S. (2010) Student created videos. Teaching copyright and media literacy through student-produced documentaries, *Knowledge Quest,* 38(4), 52–5.

LifeSkills4Kids (2009) How to spot and stop cyberbullying. Available at http://lifeskills4kids.com/kb/2009/03/cyber-bullying/. Accessed 5 November 2011.

Lindgren, S. (2011) YouTube gunmen? Mapping participatory media discourse on school shooting videos, *Media, Culture & Society,* 33(1), 123–36.

Loader, D. (2007) *Jousting for the New Generation. Challenges to Contemporary Schooling*. Camberwell: ACER Press.

Mallan, K. M., Foth, M., Greenaway, R. and Young, G. T. (2010) Serious playground: using Second Life to engage high school students in urban planning, *Journal of Learning, Media and Technology*, 35(2), 203–25.

Mathison, C. and Billings, E. (2010) The effect of primary language podcasts on third grade English language learners' performance in English-only science education contexts, *Electronic Journal of Literacy Through Science,* 9, 1–30.

McCarty, C., Prawitz, A. D., Derscheid, L. E. and Montgomery, B. (2011) Perceived safety and teen risk taking in online chat sites, *Cyberpsychology, Behavior, and Social Networking,* 14(3), 169–74.

MCEECDYA (2010) National Assessment Program – ICT Literacy Years 6 & 10. Ministerial Council for Education, Early Childhood Development and Youth Affairs. Report 2008. Available at http://www.mceecdya.edu.au/verve/_resources/NAP-ICTL_2008_report.pdf. Accessed 2 June 2010.

MCEETYA (2007) National Assessment Program – ICT Literacy Years 6 & 10. Ministerial Council on Education, Employment, Training and Youth Affairs. Report 2005. Available at http://www.mceetya.edu.au/verve/_resources/NAP_ICTL_2005_Years_6_and_10_Report.pdf. Accessed 2 June 2010.

McGrail, E. and Davis, A. (2011) The influence of classroom blogging on elementary student writing, *Journal of Research in Childhood Education,* 25(4), 415–37.

Moayeri, M. (2010) Classroom uses of social network sites: traditional practices or new literacies? *Digital Culture & Education,* 2(1), 25–43. Available at http://www.digitalcultureandeducation.com/uncategorized/dce1029_moayeri_refs_2010/. Accessed 2 September 2011.

Mullen, R. and Wedwick, L. (2008) Avoiding the digital abyss: getting started in the classroom with YouTube, digital stories, and blogs, *Clearing House: A Journal of Educational Strategies, Issues and Ideas,* 82(2), 66–9.

Murthy, D. (2011) Twitter: microphone for the masses? *Media, Culture & Society,* 33(5), 779–89.

Nov, O., Naaman, M. and Ye, C. (2010) Analysis of participation in an online photo-sharing community: a multidimensional perspective, *Journal of the American Society for Information Science and Technology,* 61(3), 555–66.

O'Reilly, T. (2005) What is Web 2.0. Design patterns and business models for the next generation of software. Available at http://oreilly.com/web2/archive/what-is-web-20.html. Accessed 1 November 2011.

Oblinger, D. G. and Hawkins, B. L. (2006) The myth about student competency: our students are technically competent, *EDUCAUSE Review,* 41(2), 12–13. Available at http://connect.educause.edu/Library/EDUCAUSE+Review/TheMythAboutStudentCompet/40622. Accessed 7 February 2009.

Ofcom (2011) UK children's media literacy. Research document. Office of Communications. Available at http://stakeholders.ofcom.org.uk/market-data-research/media-literacy/medlit-pub/medlitpubrss/ukchildrensml11/. Accessed 13 October 2011.

Oliver, M. (2011) Technological determinism in educational technology research: some alternative ways of thinking about the relationship between learning and technology, *Journal of Computer Assisted Learning,* 27(5), 373–84.

Oradini, O. and Saunders, G. (2007) Introducing e-portfolios across a paper dominated university, *Association for Learning Technology Online Newletter,* 10. Available at http://news-weaver.co.uk/alt/e_article000925026.cfm. Accessed 13 October 2011.

Payton, S. and Hague, C. (2010) Digital literacy professional development resource. Futurelab. Available at http://www.futurelab.org.uk/resources/digital-literacy-professional-development-resource. Accessed 13 October 2011.

Prensky, M. (2001a) Digital natives, digital immigrants. A new way to look at ourselves and our kids, *On the Horizon,* 9(5), 1–6. Available at http://www.marcprensky.com/writing/. Accessed 4 November 2011.

Prensky, M. (2001b) Digital natives, digital immigrants, Part II: do they really think differently? *On the Horizon,* 9(6), 1–9. Available at http://www.marcprensky.com/writing/. Accessed 4 November 2011.

Richardson, W. (2006) *Blogs, Wikis, Podcasts, and Other Powerful Web Tools for Classrooms.* Thousand Oaks, CA: Corwin Press.

Rideout, V., Foehr, U. and Roberts, D. (2010) Generation M2. Media in the lives of 8- to 18-year-olds. A Kaiser Family Foundation Study. Available at http://www.kff.org/entmedia/mh012010pkg.cfm. Accessed 13 October 2011.

Rule, L. (2010) Digital storytelling: never has storytelling been so easy or so powerful, *Knowledge Quest,* 38(4), 56–7.

Salaway, G., Caruso, J. B. and Nelson, M. R. (2009) The ECAR Study of Undergraduate Students and Information Technology, 2008 (Research Study, Vol. 8). Boulder, CO: EDUCAUSE Center for Applied Research. Available at http://www.educause.edu/ECAR/TheECARStudyofUndergraduateStu/163283. Accessed 9 July 2009.

Sawmiller, A. (2010) Classroom blogging: What is the role in science learning? *The Clearing House,* 83, 44–8.

Schillinger, T. (2011) Blurring boundaries: two groups of girls collaborate on a wiki, *Journal of Adolescent and Adult Literacy,* 54(6), 403–13.

Schwarz, O. (2011) Who moved my conversation? Instant messaging, intertextuality and new regimes of intimacy and truth, *Media, Culture & Society,* 33(1), 71–87.

Shamburg, C. (2009) *Student-Powered Podcasting. Teaching for 21st Century Literacy.* Washington, DC: International Society for Technology in Education (ISTE).

Shariff, S. (2008) *Cyber-bullying. Issues and Solutions for the School, the Classroom and the Home*. London: Routledge.

Sieber, D. E. (2010) Teaching with social networks: establishing a social contract. ECAR Research Bulletin 10. Boulder, CO: EDUCAUSE Center for Applied Research. Available at http://www. educause.edu/ecar. Accessed 2 September 2011.

Smythe, S. and Neufeld, P. (2010) 'Podcast Time': negotiating digital literacies and communities of learning in a middle years ELL classroom, *Journal of Adolescent & Adult Literacy*, 53(6), 488–96.

Solomon, G. and Schrum, L. (2010) *Web 2.0. How-to for Educators*. Eugene, OR: International Society for Technology in Education.

Ulicsak, M. and Williamson, B. (2010) Computer games and learning. A Futurelab handbook. Available at http://www.futurelab.org.uk/resources/computer-games-and-learning-handbook. Accessed 1 November 2011.

University of Edinburgh (2007) Guidelines for using external Web 2.0 services. Available at https:// www.wiki.ed.ac.uk/display/Web2wiki/Web+2.0+Guidelines. Accessed 26 October 2011.

Varnhagen, C. K., McFall, G. P., Pugh, N., Routledge, L., Sumida-MacDonald, H. and Kwong, T. E. (2010) lol: new language and spelling in instant messaging, *Reading and Writing*, 23(6), 719–33.

Vass, D. (2011) To iPad or not to iPad. Available at http://cityexperience.mlcsyd.nsw.edu.au/blog/ to-ipad-or-not-to-ipad. Accessed 26 October 2011.

Waddington, J. (2011). Social networking: the unharnessed educational tool, *Undergraduate Research Journal at UCCS*, 4(1). May 2011. Available at http://ojs.uccs.edu/index.php/urj/ article/viewArticle/113. Accessed 2 September 2011.

Walker, L., and Logan, A. (2009) Using digital technologies to promote inclusive practices in education. Futurelab handbook. Available at http://archive.futurelab.org.uk/resources/publications-reports-articles/handbooks/Handbook1248. Accessed 13 October 2011.

Wang, W-C., Lee, C-C. and Chu, Y-C. (2010) A brief review on developing creative thinking in young children by mind mapping, *International Business Research*, 3(3), 233–8.

Weaver, A. (2010) Twitter for teachers, librarians and teacher librarians, *Access*, 24(2), 16–20.

Webster, C. (2004) Ghyslain Razaa. Available at http://www.cyberbullying.info/examples/star-wars.php. Accessed 21 October 2011.

Whitehead, A. N. (1967 [1929]) *The Aims of Education*. New York: The Free Press.

Williamson, B. and Payton, S. (2009) Curriculum and teaching innovation. Transforming classroom practice and personalisation. A Futurelab handbook. Available at http://www.futurelab. org.uk/resources/curriculum-and-teaching-innovation-handbook. Accessed 1 November 2011.

Woo, M., Chu, S., Ho, A. and Li, X . (2011) Using a wiki to scaffold primary-school students' collaborative writing, *Journal of Educational Technology & Society*, 14(1), 43–54.

Yelland, N. (2007) The millennials, in N. Yelland, *Shift to the Future. Rethinking Learning with New Technologies in Education*. New York: Routledge. Ch. 1.

Zammit, K. (2010) Working with wikis: collaborative writing in the 21st century. Key competencies in the knowledge society, in N. Reynolds and M. Turcsányi-Szabó (eds), *Advances in Information and Communication Technology*, held as part of WCC 2010, Brisbane, Australia, 20–23 September 2010. Proceedings, vol. 324, pp. 447–55.

INDEX

Added to a page number 'f' denotes a figure and 't' denotes a table.

WRITING FOR ACADEMIC SUCCESS

Second Edition

Gail Craswell *Australian National University, Canberra* and **Megan Poore** *University of Canberra*

Writing for Academic Success is a vital practical guide for any postgraduate student. If you seek to manage your writing effectively, reduce stress, and improve your confidence and efficiency, this book is for you. The authors show you how to acquire communicative rigor in research essays, reports, book and article reviews, exam papers, research proposals, and literature reviews, through to thesis writing, posters and papers for presentation and publication.

This second edition has been fully revised to reflect the online learning explosion. The authors provide insightful new material about how to work productively in different online contexts such as with blogs and wikis, setting up an e-portfolio, and raising an online profile. They also set out a focused guide to issues unique to digital communication, and working with and across different media and technologies. The book includes advice on common writing concerns, cross-cultural and inter-disciplinary practices, a list of helpful words and phrases, and subject-specific examples of writing ranging from economics to philosophy to medicine.

Visit **www.sagepub.co.uk//studyskills.sp**

for free downloads, special offers and more!

READERSHIP

Essential reading for undergraduate and graduate students seeking the best advice on successful academic writing.

SAGE STUDY SKILLS SERIES

 2011 • 264 pages
Cloth (978-0-85702-927-0) • £65.00
Paper (978-0-85702-928-7) • £22.99

ALSO FROM SAGE

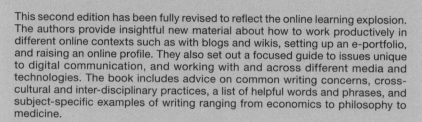

E-LEARNING THEORY AND PRACTICE

Caroline Haythornthwaite *University of Illinois at Urbana-Champaign* and **Richard Andrews** *Institute of Education University of London*

In E-learning Theory and Practice the authors set out different perspectives on e-learning. The book deals with the social implications of e-learning, its transformative effects, and the social and technical interplay that supports and directs e-learning. The authors present new perspectives on the subject by:

- exploring the way teaching and learning are changing with the presence of the Internet and participatory media
- providing a theoretical grounding in new learning practices from education, communication and information science
- addressing e-learning in terms of existing learning theories, emerging online learning theories, new literacies, social networks, social worlds, community and virtual communities, and online resources
- emphasising the impact of everyday electronic practices on learning, literacy and the classroom, locally and globally.

This book is for everyone involved in e-learning. Teachers and educators will gain an understanding of new learning practices, and learners will gain a sense of their new role as active participants in classroom and lifelong learning. Graduate students and researchers will gain insight into the direction of research in this new and exciting area of education and the Internet.

READERSHIP
Graduate students and researchers wanting to gain an insight into the direction of research in e-learning and education and the Internet

2011 • 272 pages
Cloth (978-1-84920-470-5) • £70.00
Paper (978-1-84920-471-2) • £23.99

ALSO FROM SAGE

TRAINING TO TEACH

A Guide for Students

Second Edition

Edited by **Neil M Denby** *University of Huddersfield*

Teaching is a tough and challenging job and society demands more from its teachers than ever before. This new edition is an essential companion for those training to teach providing an overview of important professional issues that all future teachers need to engage with in order to succeed in the classroom.

Previously known as **How to Achieve your QTS**, this second edition is equally valuable to those training to teach in both primary and secondary education and aims to give students the confident start they need in the classroom. Features new to this edition include more balanced primary education coverage, and four new chapters on: child protection issues, teaching pupils with English as an Additional Language, cross-curricular teaching issues and your first teaching post: applications, interviews and induction.

The accompanying website (www.sagepub.co.uk//denby), has been updated to include additional material expanding on and complementing the contents of the book.

This book is essential reading for professional studies modules on both primary and secondary initial teacher education courses at both udergraduate and postgraduate level, and on university-based and school-based training courses.

READERSHIP

Students on initial teacher training courses in primary and secondary education

January 2012 • 352 pages
Cloth (978-0-85702-761-0) • £65.00
Paper (978-0-85702-762-7) • £21.99

ALSO FROM SAGE

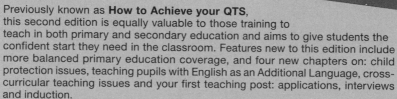